Road to Manzikert:

Byzantine and Islamic Warfare, 527–1071

Road to Manzikert:

Byzantine and Islamic Warfare, 527–1071

Brian Todd Carey

Joshua B. Allfree
Tactical and Strategic Map Illustrator

John Cairns
Regional Map Illustrator

Pen & Sword

First published in Great Britain in 2012
and republished in this format in 2021 by
Pen & Sword Military
An imprint of
Pen & Sword Books Ltd
Yorkshire – Philadelphia

Text Copyright © Brian Todd Carey 2012, 2021
Map Copyright © Joshua B. Allfree and John Cairns 2012, 2021

ISBN 978 1 52679 664 6

Printed and bound in the UK by CPI Group (UK) Ltd,
Croydon, CR0 4YY.

Pen & Sword Books Limited incorporates the imprints of Atlas,
Archaeology, Aviation, Discovery, Family History, Fiction, History,
Maritime, Military, Military Classics, Politics, Select, Transport,
True Crime, Air World, Frontline Publishing, Leo Cooper,
Remember When, Seaforth Publishing, The Praetorian Press,
Wharncliffe Local History, Wharncliffe Transport, Wharncliffe
True Crime and White Owl.

For a complete list of Pen & Sword titles please contact

PEN & SWORD BOOKS LIMITED
47 Church Street, Barnsley, South Yorkshire, S70 2AS, England
E-mail: enquiries@pen-and-sword.co.uk
Website: www.pen-and-sword.co.uk

Or
PEN AND SWORD BOOKS
1950 Lawrence Rd, Havertown, PA 19083, USA
E-mail: Uspen-and-sword@casematepublishers.com
Website: www.penandswordbooks.com

Contents

Preface and Acknowledgements

The battle of Manzikert is often referenced as a 'turning point' when studying the clash of civilizations between Islam and Christian Europe in most college freshmen-level western and world civilization textbooks, a battle where a Seljuk victory over the Byzantine army led to the rapid Islamization of Anatolia and marked the decline of the Byzantine Empire. The battle is also often portrayed as the '*casus belli*' for the Levantine crusades that for ever altered the relationship between the Islamic Middle East and the West. In fact, the battle of Manzikert is frequently the only Byzantine military engagement identified by name from the sixth century wars of Justinian to the successful Catholic siege of Constantinople during the Fourth Crusade in 1204. Much of this is due to a western European focus when discussing the middle ages. However, a closer look at this dynamic period of Byzantine civilization reveals numerous important military engagements (Pliska, Anchialus, Dorostolon, to name a few) that marked the ebb and flow of Byzantine military fortunes and the usually sophisticated nature of the Byzantine approach to warfare.

Many of these same criticisms can be levelled at how Islamic warfare is treated in college textbooks. Muhammad's prowess as a general is implied but rarely discussed. Muslim Arab victories like Yarmuk River and al-Qadisiya the seventh century over Byzantine and Sassanian Persian forces respectively are rarely mention by name, although these battlefield successes are well known and widely celebrated in the Islamic world today as proof of a past golden age when Islamic civilization could match and defeat powerful regional powers. A resurgent modern Turkey has a similar relationship with the battle of Manzikert. This victory over Romanus IV Diogenes marks the beginning of the Turkification of the peninsula and is today celebrated as a perfect symbol for Turkish nationalism. This was evident forty years ago when the battle was treated as a national event on its nine-hundredth anniversary in 1971. Today, a statue of the victorious Seljuk commander, Alp Arslan, on a rearing warhorse, stands at the western entrance of the modern city of Malazgirt (medieval Manzikert), while each year, on the anniversary of the battle on 26 August, the engagement is re-enacted by Turkish Boy Scouts in costume in front of throngs of adoring Turkish citizens.

As the title of this book suggests, this study attempts to shine more light on the military histories of these two significant, but often neglected, regions and civilizations in the early medieval period – the Byzantine and Islamic east, intertwining military histories that culminated in the important battle of Manzikert. Once again I am joined by my excellent illustrators, Joshua B. Allfree and John Cairns, who illustrated our previous books, *Warfare in the Ancient World, Warfare in the Medieval World*, and *Hannibal's Last Battle: Zama and the Fall of Carthage*. These outstanding tactical, strategic and regional maps give this book its uniqueness and allow readers to easily visualize the military movements and strategic context of the battles covered in this book. Once again, we could not have completed this effort without the collaboration and support of a few notable people. First and foremost we would like to thank Pen and Sword Books for their dedication to this project. This is our second time working with Phil Sidnell and he has once again proved to be a wise editor, while the copy-editing of Ting Baker polished the narrative into its present form. Without their assistance this book would simply not have been possible. Special thanks are also extended to my superiors at the American Public University System, History and Military History Director Dr Brian Blodgett, Dean Linda Moynihan, and Provost Karan Powell, whose generous financial support through a research grant assisted me greatly in securing the materials needed to research and write my last two books. Finally, we would like to thank our family and friends whose unswerving support and sacrifice over the process of creating these past four books in the last six years has been instrumental to our success.

Brian Todd Carey
Loveland, Colorado

List of Maps

List of Illustrations

17 and 18. Statue of Alp Arslan located at the western entrance of the modern city of Malazgirt.
19. 'Gateway to Anatolia' monument erected on suspected battlesite of Manzikert outside of modern city of Malazgirt.
20. A 1959 postage stamp commemorating the 888th anniversary of the Seljuk victory over Byzantium at Manzikert.

Key to Maps

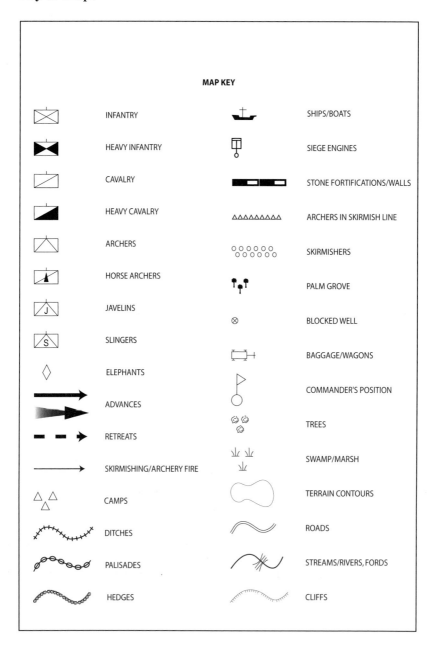

MAP KEY

INFANTRY		SHIPS/BOATS	
HEAVY INFANTRY		SIEGE ENGINES	
CAVALRY		STONE FORTIFICATIONS/WALLS	
HEAVY CAVALRY		ARCHERS IN SKIRMISH LINE	
ARCHERS		SKIRMISHERS	
HORSE ARCHERS		PALM GROVE	
JAVELINS		BLOCKED WELL	
SLINGERS		BAGGAGE/WAGONS	
ELEPHANTS		COMMANDER'S POSITION	
ADVANCES		TREES	
RETREATS		SWAMP/MARSH	
SKIRMISHING/ARCHERY FIRE		TERRAIN CONTOURS	
CAMPS		ROADS	
DITCHES		STREAMS/RIVERS, FORDS	
PALISADES		CLIFFS	
HEDGES			

Chronology of Byzantine and Islamic History from Justinian to the First Crusade

Byzantine Warfare from Justinian to Herakleios

527

Justinian becomes Byzantine emperor (r.527–565). Under his reign, the Eastern Roman Empire reaches its greatest territorial extent and expands into Italy and North Africa.

530

Justinian dispatches a Byzantine army under Belisarios that defeats the Sassanian Persians at the battle of Dara in Upper Mesopotamia.

532

Byzantines and Sassanians sign the Perpetual Peace to stabilize frontier zone. The treaty lasts less than a decade, and Byzantium and Persia continue to play strategic tug-of-war in the region until the early 630s when both empires face expansion of Islam out of the Arabian Peninsula.

533

Belisarios and his Byzantine army defeat the Vandals in North Africa at the battle of Tricameron, ending the Germanic kingdom and bringing this region into the empire.

535–554

A Byzantine army under Belisarios conquers the Ostrogothic kingdom in Italy in the Gothic War between 535 and 540. Goths and Germanic allies counterattack, forcing Justinian to send Narses to put down the resurgent Goths and Franks.

552

Narses defeats Ostrogothic king Totila at battle of Taginae. After the battle, Narses pursued the remaining Goths to Naples, killing their new king and continuing his campaign of extermination. A truce at Mons Lactarius in 553 allowed surviving Goths to leave Italy and settle north of the Po River.

554

Narses defeats a Frankish-Alemannic army at Casilinum near Naples in southern Italy. Eastern Roman rule would only last another fourteen years before the final wave of Germanic invaders, the Lombards, occupied the northern two-thirds of the peninsula, ending for ever Justinian's dream of imperial rule over Italy.

624–628

Byzantine Emperor Herakleios (r.610–641) personally leads three military expeditions against the Sassanians to recover territories lost in Anatolia, Mesopotamia and the Levant, re-establishing Byzantine rule after twenty-year absence.

Islamic Warfare from Muhammad to the Rashidun Caliphate

624

Muhammad (c.570–632) and his small Muslim army ambush and defeat the Meccans at the battle of Badr in Islam's first military victory.

625

Meccans counterattack and defeat the Muslim army outside of Medina at the battle of Uhud. Meccans do not follow up on their victory, allowing Muhammad to rebuild his forces.

627

A large Meccan army returns to the region around Medina, but is unsuccessful in defeating Muhammad who has prepared the battlefield to his advantage. The Muslims win the battle of the Ditch, opening the way for the conquest of Mecca.

632–661

After the death of Muhammad in 632, his successors Abu Bakr (r.632–634), Umar (r.634–644), Uthman (r.644–656), and Ali (r.656–661) begin the Rashidun Caliphate. Under the Rashidun caliphs, Islamic armies expanded into North Africa, the Levant and Persia at the expense of the Byzantine and Sassanian Persian Empires in the period between 632 and 661.

632–633

Muhammad's successor, Abu Bakr, initiates the short *Riddah* War to bring all of the Arabian Peninsula, both pagan and backsliders, into the Islamic faith. After consolidating his Muslim powerbase, Abu Bakr expands campaigning outside of the Arabian Peninsula.

636

Muslims defeat Byzantines at the battle of Yarmuk River and go on to conquer most of Syrian and Lebanon, greatly reducing Byzantine power in the Levant.

Muslim army defeats Sassanian Persians at battle of al-Qadisiya, press deeper into Mesopotamia and take Persian capital at Ctesiphon. Muslim campaigning continues into Persia and Sassanian Empire falls in 644. Caliph Umar declares Oxus River northeastern border of caliphate.

Byzantine Warfare in an Age of Crisis and Recovery

674–677

First Arab siege of Constantinople unsuccessful after Byzantines employ Greek Fire and destroy Muslim flotilla.

711

The Arab commander Tariq ibn Ziyad invades southern Spain with a Berber Muslim army. By 714 most of the Iberian Peninsula is under Muslim control. Within a year the Muslims begin raiding north of the Pyrenees, threatening Carolingian France.

717–718

Second Arab siege of Constantinople unsuccessful due to Byzantines using Greek Fire against Muslim navy and a Bulgar relief army attacking the Muslim siege lines.

811

Bulgar ruler Krum Khan (r.803–814) defeats Byzantine expeditionary force at the battle of Pliska, killing the Byzantine emperor Nikephoros I (r.802–811). After the battle, Bulgar raiding increased into Byzantine territory, with Constantinople sieged in 813. The new Byzantine emperor, Leo V (r.813–820), stabilized the Bulgarian frontier after Krum's death.

917

Bulgarian king Symeon (r.893–927) renews hostilities with Byzantium. Byzantine expedition deep into Bulgarian territory fails and Bulgarian victory at battle of Anchialus in 917 opens land up between Bulgaria and Constantinople to Bulgarian depredation. Frontier stabilized after Symeon's death in 927.

971

Emperor John I Tzimiskes (r.969–976) personally leads Byzantine army in victory over the Rus at Dorostolon, garrisoning the city and expanding imperial holdings in the Balkans. John next turns his attention to expanding Byzantine power in the Levant, but dies unexpectedly in 976.

987–988

The conversion of Kievan Grand Prince Vladimir I (r.980–1015) to Greek Orthodoxy establishes religious union with Constantinople. To strengthen political ties and secure a much needed ally Basil II offers his sister's hand to Vladimir in exchange for a force of 6,000 Varangian soldiers to assist the Greek emperor with the Anatolian rebellion and shore up his failing Bulgar frontier. Varangian Guard formed in 988.

1014

After years of annual campaigns into Bulgaria, Basil II defeats Czar Samuel (r.997–1014) at Kleidion, blinding 99 per cent of the 15,000 Bulgarian prisoners. Byzantine victory at Kleidion effectively ends large-scale organized resistance by Bulgarians. Northern frontier of Byzantine Empire once again set on Danube River.

Islamic Warfare from the Umayyads to the Coming of the Seljuk Turks

661–750

First major civil war within Islam ends with Sunni-Shia split and the rise of new Umayyad Caliphate (661–750) centred in Damascus. Wars of expansion continue into South Asia and Europe via North Africa.

664

Muslim generals begin raiding the Hindu-controlled Punjab region. Between 711 and 712 a large Arab expedition led by the brilliant young Arab general Muhammad bin Qasim, the son of a local Arab governor, brings the Sindh under Umayyad control, marking the beginning of the Muslim conquest of the Indian subcontinent

732

The Arab emir of Spain, Abdul Rahman al-Ghafiqi, crosses the Pyrenees and invades Aquitaine, then moves north and invests Orleans. Frankish major of the palace, Charles Martel (c.688–741), intercepts and defeats the Muslim raiding expedition at Tours.

750–1258

Muslim civil war ends Umayyad Caliphate with Abbasid victory at Zab River. New Abbasid Caliphate (750–1258) centred in Baghdad. Political fragmentation in Islamic world begins.

751

Provincial Islamic army defeats the Tang Chinese at battle of Talas River, stopping Chinese advances in Central Asia and opening the region to Islamization.

762

A new Muslim capital was established in Baghdad on the Tigris River, a move that continued the shift in Islam's political interests eastward while relieving some of the military pressure on Byzantium and Catholic Western Europe.

909–1171

Shia Fatimid Caliphate (909–1171) founded, centred first in Tunisia and then in Egypt. Cairo founded in 969. Fatimids control a vast empire stretching across the North Africa to the Atlantic Ocean, south into the Sudan and western Arabia, and north-east to the edge of Byzantine Syria and Abbasid domains in Mesopotamia.

945
Persian Buyids (932–1055) occupy Mesopotamia and push their way into Abbasid politics and confine the caliph to the palace. Fatimids support the Buyids in Baghdad, weakening the Abbasid Caliphate.

Eleventh Century Byzantine and Seljuk Campaigns in Anatolia and the Battle of Manzikert

1029–1063
Seljuk raiding begins in Armenia and eastern Anatolia in 1029, but intensifies after the Seljuk victory over the Ghaznavids at Dandanqan in 1040.

1048
Turkoman raiders destroy important regional trading centre of Arzen in south-eastern Anatolia, massacring and enslaving the Christian population.

1055
Seljuk sultan Toghril Beg (r.1055–1063) enters Baghdad in 1055 as champion of the Abbasid caliph, displacing the Buyids and assuming control of the Abbasid court. Toghril becomes first ruler of Great Seljuk Empire of Iran and de facto ruler of Islamic Persia and Mesopotamia. His new domain brushed up against the eastern frontiers of Byzantine-controlled Armenia and eastern Anatolia, retaken from the Arabs in the mid-tenth century.

1064
New sultan of the Great Seljuks of Iran, Alp Arslan (r.1063–1072), successfully sieges and takes ancient Armenian fortress city of Ani ('City of a Thousand-and-One Churches'), but does not allow his Turkoman allies to destroy the city.

1064–1068
Alp Arslan subdues kingdom of Georgia after four years of annual campaigns, taking the king's daughter as a wife to cement the alliance. Sultan continues to campaign in Upper Mesopotamia against Arab emirs to shore up frontier.

1067–1068
Prolonged and deep Turkoman raiding into Anatolia continues. Renegade Seljuk nobleman named Afsinios sacks Byzantine city of Caesarea and then wheels south to raid Cilicia and the region around Antioch in north-western Syria

1068–1070
Romanus IV Diogenes (r.1068–1071) becomes Byzantine co-emperor in 1068 and immediately campaigns in Syria to prop up and hopefully expand his possessions in the Levant. The emperor is forced to abandon 1069 campaign to Lake Van region when Greek rearguard is defeated by Seljuks. Romanus stays in Constantinople in 1070 to quell court intrigue and improve conditions of his army. The 1070 Byzantine

expedition sent to Lake Van region is annihilated near Sebastae in Anatolia. Turkoman raiding intensifies and Greek city of Chonae is destroyed.

1071

In March Romanus departs Constantinople at head of Manzikert expedition, arriving in Lake Van region in August. He divides army, sending over half to invest Chliat as he covers Manzikert. Alp Arslan abandons long-planned Fatimid campaign and surprises Romanus outside Manzikert. Byzantines lose battle because of desertion, defection and betrayal among the Byzantine troops and Romanus is captured and later released.

In April the city of Bari fell to the Norman adventurer Robert Guiscard. Bari had been the wealthiest and best defended city in Byzantine-held Apulia before succumbing to the Norman land and sea blockade, ending more than five centuries of Byzantine rule in Italy.

The Seljuk Invasion of Anatolia and the Origins of the Levantine Crusades

1071–1081

After the Byzantine loss at Manzikert, Turkoman raiding increases into Anatolia. Seljuk emirs settle in parts of the peninsula and assist Byzantine emperors and pretenders to the throne in this period of civil war, becoming power brokers in Byzantine affairs.

1072

Deposed after the loss at Manzikert, Romanus gathers a loyal army but is captured and blinded by his political rivals. He later dies in captivity. Alp Arslan is killed campaigning in his eastern provinces by a treasonous emir.

Malikshah (r.1072–1092) succeeds his father, Alp Arslan, as sultan of Great Seljuk Empire of Iran.

1077

In 1077, two Byzantine generals rebelled nearly simultaneously against the reign of Michael VII Doukas. Nikephoros III Botaneiates (r.1078–1081) wins power struggle with assistance of Seljuk troops. Nikephoros III marks the end of Byzantine Anatolia as the primary source of military manpower and horses.

Seljuk ruler Suleyman begins carving his own Seljuk Sultanate of Rum (1077–1243), named in honour of its location on hallowed Roman territory.

1081

The reign of Alexios I Komnenos (r.1081–1118) begins period of Byzantine military, economic and territorial recovery known as the 'Komnenian Restoration'.

1095

Alexios begins reconciliatory measures towards the papacy in order to secure western support for his wars against the Seljuk Turks, culminating in ambassadors appearing before Pope Urban II at the Council of Piacenza in northern Italy in early March.

1095

Urban II travels north to central France where he chairs Council of Clermont and calls into existence the First Crusade on 27 November 1095.

1096–1097

Enormous hosts of Roman Catholic soldiers and pilgrims begin gathering outside the walls of Constantinople between October 1096 and April 1097.

1097

With assistance from Alexios, the Catholic crusaders successfully cross Anatolia and defeat a Seljuk army led by Kilij Arslan (r.1092–1107) at the battle of Dorylaeum in the summer of 1097, clearing the way for further crusader conquests.

1097–1098

The Seljuk-held Antioch falls after a seven-and-a-half-month siege, followed by the Armenian Christian city of Edessa in early 1098.

1099

The Latin armies continue south to Jerusalem, capturing the Holy City after a five-week siege and infamously bloody storm in the summer of 1099. By the early twelfth century, the crusaders have carved out feudal possessions in the Levant consisting of the Kingdom of Jerusalem, the County of Tripoli in Lebanon, the Principality of Antioch, and the County of Edessa in Armenia. First Crusade ends.

Introduction: Byzantium, Islam and Catholic Europe – The Battle of Manzikert as Historical Nexus

The Battle of Manzikert in Modern History

The battle of Manzikert has long been considered a turning point in the history of the Byzantine civilization. In late August 1071 the Eastern Roman emperor Romanus IV Diogenes (r.1068–1071) formed his multi-national army outside of the walls of the fortress city of Manzikert near Lake Van on the empire's Armenian frontier. His adversary was the second sultan of the Great Seljuk Empire of Iran, Alp Arslan (r.1063–1072), ruler of the most powerful Muslim state in the Near East and champion of the Abbasid caliph in Baghdad. The battle that unfolded over the course of a few days would witness desertion, defection and betrayal among the Byzantine troops and the ultimate defeat and capture of Romanus. This event sent shockwaves across the Christian and Islamic worlds and opened the floodgates of Turkish invasion and migration into Anatolia, strategically the most important region to the Byzantine Empire. A decade of civil war and Seljuk depredations further weakened the Eastern Roman Empire, forcing Alexios I Komnenos (r.1081–1118) to ask for military assistance from Catholic Western Europe, and the First Crusade was born.

For more than two centuries historians have remarked on the magnitude of the Byzantine defeat at Manzikert and subsequent loss of Anatolia. The Enlightenment English historian Edward Gibbon wrote in his seminal work, *The Decline and Fall of the Roman Empire* (1789), that '[t]he Byzantine writers deplore the loss of an inestimable pearl: they forgot to mention that, in this fatal day, the Asiatic provinces of Rome were irretrievably sacrificed.'[1] Another Englishman, the military historian Charles Oman, echoed Gibbon when he wrote in 1898 that 'the empire had suffered other defeats as bloody as Manzikert, but none had such disastrous results.'[2] In volume three of his *History of the Art of War: Medieval Warfare* (1923), the German military historian Hans Delbruck challenged both Oman's assertion of the enormous size of the Byzantine and Seljuk armies and how the battle unfolded, but agreed with Oman that 'Alp Arslan destroyed most of the Byzantine army.'[3] A half century later, the esteemed crusade historian Steven Runciman reemphasized the importance of the engagement in volume one of his *History of the Crusades* (1951) when he boldly stated that '[the] battle of

Manzikert was the most decisive disaster in Byzantine history.'[4] About this same time, the eminent Russian-born Yugoslavian historian of Byzantium, George Ostrogorsky, commented that 'the numerically superior, but heterogeneous and undisciplined, Byzantine army was annihilated by the forces of Alp Arslan.'[5] In the decades that followed, other historians have added their voice to this chorus. More recently, John Norwich remarked in his *Byzantium: The Apogee* (2006) that 'the battle of Manzikert was the greatest disaster suffered by the Empire of Byzantium in the seven and a half centuries of its existence.'[6] All of these historians emphasized Manzikert as a decisive defeat and a pivotal engagement, after which Byzantine Anatolia was violently transformed into Muslim Asia Minor.

However, other historians have questioned the decisive nature and strategic significance of the battle of Manzikert and the fantastical troop strengths of the belligerents, prompting historians as early as Delbruck to comment that 'a study and review of the battle based on the sources would be desirable.'[7] This challenge was actually taken up in the early twentieth century when the French historian J. Laurent began to piece together the late eleventh century Manzikert campaign using Christian and Islamic sources. Detailed studies of Byzantine and Turkish Anatolia followed later in the late 1960s when the French historian Claude Cahen and American historian Speros Vryonis reconstructed the Islamization of Anatolia using Muslim and Byzantine primary sources and a growing body of archaeological evidence. Vryonis and the French scholar Jean-Claude Cheynet would write articles challenging old perceptions of Manzikert as a crippling military defeat and their findings would be reflected in the writings of many prominent contemporary and future historians writing on this subject, including Jonathan Riley-Smith, Warren Treadgold, and John Haldon, to name a few.[8]

The Battle of Manzikert Revisited

This work endeavours to follow the revisionist vein of scholarship concerning the battle of Manzikert and its place in military history. Although not the devastating loss described by contemporaries of the battle and repeated by some historians over the last two hundred years, Manzikert does represent a significant historical nexus with a cast of players from many of the major civilizations shaping the medieval world in 1071. Accompanying Romanus and his native Greek troops on his campaign were Byzantium's traditional allies, the Armenians and Georgians, whose homelands the expedition was approaching in eastern Anatolia. Because of court intrigue in Constantinople and the poor combat capabilities of native imperial forces, Romanus supplemented his army using mercenaries from Catholic Europe, most notably the Normans, and warriors from the Eurasian steppes, including the Bulgars, Uze, and Pechenegs, once and future adversaries of the Byzantine Empire. Protecting the emperor were members of the Varangian Guard, Swedo-Slavic warriors from the Ukraine who had served the Eastern Roman emperor since the reign of Basil II (r.976–1025) and died in large numbers trying to protect him when the Byzantine army began to disintegrate that fateful August evening.

Romanus' adversary at Manzikert, sultan Alp Arslan, was served by the greatest light cavalry corps of the age, the fleet and ferocious Seljuk steppe warriors, many of whom were the barely Islamized and often uncontrollable Turkoman raiders. These mounted warriors had plagued Anatolia for decades before the battle of Manzikert and were instrumental in the invasion of the peninsula in the wake of the Byzantine defeat. As ruler of a new sultanate that stretched from Armenia to the Oxus River and south to the Persian Gulf, Alp Arslan commanded a multi-national army capable of sophisticated military action that married the best of steppe tactics with the martial traditions of Umayyad and Abbasid warfare. The result was an Islamic army capable of campaigning on horseback over vast distances and different topographies, converging on the enemy from numerous directions, striking, and then disappearing in Central Asian fashion, or fighting set-piece battles and reducing powerful fortress cities in a manner consistent with the more infantry-focused militaries of the age.

Romanus understood how to meet and beat the mounted Seljuk army that arrayed before his combined-arms army outside the walls of Manzikert, as he was a proven general well-versed in the numerous Byzantine tactical manuals produced by past emperors and generals. But Romanus, for reasons both in and out of his control, did not heed those lessons and his poor generalship was instrumental in his army's defeat. Romanus ignored hundreds of years of Byzantine military doctrine developed fighting previous steppe societies like the Huns, Khazars, Bulgars, Magyars, and Pechenegs. But Romanus' defeat was not entirely due to bad military decisions. His expedition was sabotaged even before battle was met by the desertion of over half his army and the defection of valuable steppe allies. The betrayal of his reserves, under the command of a political rival, sealed his fate. Still, the loss was not a great tactical disaster, as only about 10 per cent of the total Manzikert expedition was lost, hardly the annihilation depicted in the primary sources and repeated by many modern historians. The Byzantine army was not destroyed, but Romanus' capture, blinding and death precipitated a decade of Byzantine civil war where Seljuk emirs and troops played instrumental roles in raising new Byzantine emperors to the purple. In the decade between the Byzantine loss at Manzikert in 1071 and the accession of Alexios I Komnenos in 1081, Byzantium's strategic position was severely degraded on all frontiers and much of Anatolia was lost to the Seljuk Turks. However, the strategic situation in Asia Minor was far from static. Beginning with Alexios, Byzantine armies retook important regions of the peninsula and Catholic crusader successes in the Levant changed the balance of power, albeit temporarily, between Islam and Christendom in this region. These modest successes so long after Manzikert reduce, but do not eliminate, the strategic importance of this battle in history.

Manzikert was an influential engagement, one referred to again and again by Byzantine historians as 'that dreadful day.'[9] A large Byzantine expeditionary force was defeated and perhaps just as importantly, the emperor of the Eastern Romans, ruler of the most powerful Christian civilization over the last five hundred years, was captured by a Muslim prince. The psychological importance of this event to the Islamic world is difficult to overestimate. Romanus' campaign in 1071 also changed the trajectory of Islamic history. Alp Arslan's long-awaited campaign against the Fatimid Caliphate in Egypt was first detoured to intercept the Byzantine army at Manzikert, and then derailed when the sultan was killed by a treacherous emir in his eastern provinces a year later. Romanus' loss at Manzikert should be seen more as a political disaster than a military defeat, one that weakened Byzantium's standing among its political and military rivals and invited challenges to Byzantine power on the edges of empire and opened central and eastern Anatolia up for a permanent Seljuk invasion and conquest in the decade ahead. In this light, the debacle at Manzikert can be seen as a symbol of Byzantine decline, even if many of the military elements attributed to the battle by sources medieval and modern did not take place.

This book endeavours to reinforce the importance of the battle of Manzikert in the history of Byzantium by echoing the findings of historians who see the engagement as a political failure and significant, but not devastating, military defeat. The battle is presented as the climax of the study, a study that begins by tracing the wars of Justinian in the sixth century and ends with a discussion of the reign of Alexios I until the origins of the First Crusade at the end of the eleventh century. Chapters one and three concentrate on the development of Byzantine warfare, while chapters two and four focus on the rise and triumph of Islam and its military institutions. Important battles illustrating Byzantine and Islamic warfare are highlighted throughout the text, as this book is designed to serve as a broad military history of the conflict between Byzantium and Islam in regions where these two civilizations were in contact. Other periods of history and theatres of operations are given attention to illustrate the martial capabilities of the Eastern Roman Empire from its territorial height under Justinian, who died in 565, just five years before Muhammad was born, and Islam from its rise under the Muslim Prophet in the early seventh century through the Rashidun, Umayyad and Abbasid caliphates until the rise of the Seljuk sultanates. Justinian's wars are explored in some detail to give the reader an understanding of Byzantine military organization at a time of transition between Roman antiquity and the medieval world, while also introducing the reader to the Sassanian Persians, who figured prominently in the emperor's Eastern campaigns and who, along with the Byzantines, were primary adversaries later in Islam's expansion into Mesopotamia and Persia in the seventh century. Moreover, Sassanian heavy cavalry would be emulated by the Byzantines, producing the famous *kataphraktoi* and *klibanophoroi* that dominated Byzantine battlefields for hundreds of years and who were present at the Greek defeat at Manzikert. Byzantine warfare during political and military crises and territorial contraction (the seventh to ninth centuries) and recovery in the tenth and early eleventh centuries is also discussed. The reigns of Alp Arslan and Romanus IV Diogenes are given special emphasis in chapter five, as is the campaign of 1071 leading to the battle of Manzikert, and the battle itself.

A variety of medieval sources are used to reconstruct the battle of Manzikert, the most of important of which is the account by the Greek chronicler Michael Attaleiates. Attaleiates was present at the battle, and his position as an advisor to Romanus gave him access and invaluable insight into the reconstruction of the battle. Attaleiates' views are present in the writings of contemporaries or near contemporaries of the event like John Skylitzes and John Zonaras. The account of Nikephoros Bryennios, who was the grandson and namesake of a Byzantine general present at Manzikert, is also used, but this history is not as detailed as Attaleiates' account. When useful, Syrian and Armenian sources are used, but often these sources were written with a strong religious providential viewpoint by historians like Aristakes of Lastiverd and Matthew of Edessa writing for a Christian audience. This author read many of the excellent translations of twelfth Muslim sources reconstructing Manzikert, but found little new information to add to the detailed Christian accounts of the strategy and tactics used in the battle.[10]

However, Muslim sources are used to reconstruct earlier campaigns during the rise of Islam in the Arabian Peninsula and in the conflict between Islam and Persia and Islam and Christian Europe surveyed in this book.

A Note on Transliterations

Because of the scope and nature of this military history, numerous languages are transliterated into English. For Greek words, *The Oxford Dictionary of Byzantium* (1991) provides the guide for most technical terms and titles, although the macrons on Greek long vowels have been omitted. Some well-known Latinized Greeks words have been retained (Constantine and Constantinople), as have Latin names where appropriate, especially when dealing with the reign of Justinian, a time of transition when Latin was still in use in the empire. *The Oxford Encyclopedia of the Islamic World* (2009) is used for Muslim, Sassanian Persian, and Turkish terms. Again, accents have been removed from these transliterated words. However, this is an imperfect solution to the challenges of writing about the military histories of so many connecting civilizations throughout Eurasia over a six hundred-year time span, and any confusion created by inconsistencies is regretted by the author of this work.

Chapter 1

Byzantine Warfare from Justinian to Herakleios

Justinian's Wars and the Early Byzantine Army

The high point of Byzantine power and territorial expansion took place in the sixth century during the reign of Emperor Justinian (r.527–565). Nicknamed 'the emperor who never sleeps', Justinian was a vigorous, intelligent and ambitious ruler who was determined to re-establish the Roman Empire throughout the Mediterranean basin, ordering Byzantine armies to fend off Sassanian Persian attacks on the eastern frontiers of Anatolia and the Levant, while also regaining parts of Italy from the Ostrogoths and North Africa from the Vandals.

In 527, Justinian inherited an empire policed by five mobile field armies and a large number of smaller regional armies (*limitanai*) located along and behind the frontiers.[1] These five field armies (*comitatenses*) were the Army of the East (a large region that included Egypt and the Levantine, Armenian, and Mesopotamian frontiers), the Army of Thrace, the Army of Illyricum, and two local imperial guard armies located in Thrace and north-western Anatolia to protect Constantinople. Each field army was commanded by a 'Master of the Soldiers' (*magister militum*).[2] Justinian added two new field armies during his reign to police his new acquisitions (the Armies of Africa and Italy) and split a third off from the Army of the East to create the Army of Armenia, reflecting the increased strategic importance of this region to Byzantium, an importance that intensified from this period to the battle of Manzikert in 1071. By the end of his reign in 565 there were over twenty-five regional commands serving as both military and police forces throughout the empire.[3]

The constitution of Justinian's Byzantine armies differed from those of their Roman predecessors in that cavalry, rather than infantry, was the dominant tactical arm. This switch in emphasis took place due to prolonged martial contacts with horse cultures from the Eurasian Steppes or the influence of these cultures on Near Eastern empires. The most formidable threat came from the Sassanian Persians who fought like their Parthian forerunners using predominately light cavalry archers and heavy cavalry lancers who sometimes carried bows.[4] Introduced into the Roman art of war by the Emperor Hadrian (r.117–138) and widely used in the East in the last years of the Roman Empire, Roman *cataphractii* and *clibanarii* (terms often used interchangeably by classical authors) mimicked their Parthian and later Sassanian heavy cavalry foes in both equipment and tactics, functioning as heavily armoured lancers or as mounted archers.[5] By the fifth century, the proportional relationship between cavalry and infantry units was 1:3 (meaning one out of three units in the Byzantine army were cavalry units, although the total number of horsemen in the army continued to be dwarfed by infantry due to the larger size of infantry units) and 15 per cent of all cavalry units consisted of heavy cavalry *cataphractii*, now called *kataphraktoi* by Byzantine authors.[6] The overall percentage of cavalry in a Byzantine army continued to rise during the reign of Justinian and into the seventh century and would be a decisive tactical arm in his wars against the Sassanians. Byzantine heavy cavalry *kataphraktoi* supplemented standard cavalry formations, deployed to reinforce the Byzantine battle line while acting as a counterbalance to similar units deployed by the Persians.[7]

Byzantine military doctrine during the age of Justinian emphasized combined-arms warfare using cavalry and infantry. Much of our knowledge of Byzantine military organization and tactics comes from an anonymous Byzantine author writing sometime in the sixth century. This author, who was probably a military engineer, stated that Byzantine infantry were drawn up in square or oblong formations, with the first four ranks in the front and flanks armed with thrusting spears, while those in rear ranks were armed with javelins. Long straight swords were a common side arm. The anonymous author goes on to write that front rank infantry were equipped with large round shields one and a half yards in diameter 'so that when they joined together they form a solid, defensive protection behind which the army can hide without anyone being injured by enemy missiles.'[8] He continues, remarking that these shields 'should have an iron circlet embossed in the centre of the shield in which a spike at least four fingers long should be fixed, both to unnerve the enemy when they see it from a distance and to inflict serious injury when used at close range.'[9] Byzantine soldiers were also protected by helmets, chainmail or lamellar armour.[10] Light infantry wore very little body armour and carried a composite bow with a quiver of forty arrows, a small shield and an axe for close combat, while those not equipped with bows used javelins.[11]

By the early sixth century, a Byzantine army's regimental organization varied widely, made up generally of three kinds of troops: *numeri, foederati* and *bucellarii*. The *numeri* were regular imperial soldiers conscripted from Byzantine territory, while the *foederati* developed from regiments of foreign allied soldiers who settled in the Roman Empire in the late fourth century and retained their own military organization and command. By the sixth century, *foederati* units could be made up of soldiers from ethnically diverse regions, much like a modern foreign legion, or of a homogenous ethnic group with special tactical capabilities.[12] Huns, Armenians, Persians, Arabs and Slavs served in these units, as did Germanic troops, depending on the theatre of operations.[13] Each 'Master of the Soldiers' also had a private guard known as *bucellarii*, paid for out of his own purse. These units could be quite large (General Belisarios' *bucellarii* guard regularly numbered over 1,000 men). By the late sixth century, these units were assimilated into the imperial army as special divisions of elite soldiers.[14] In battle, Byzantine military doctrine followed a classical model, usually placing light infantry in the front to screen the army while the heavy infantry generally formed up in the centre either in front of the cavalry, or as a second line behind the cavalry, relying on the Byzantine horse to break up the enemy formation before following up. Cavalry could also be placed on the wings, usually across from enemy cavalry formations with the intention of driving off the enemy horse and attacking the vulnerable flanks of the

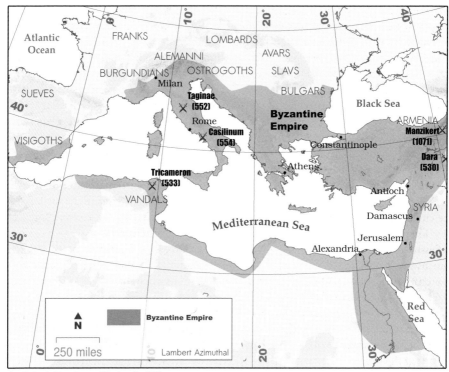

Justinian's Empire at his death, 565.

centre infantry formations. Most Byzantine generals used their personal *bucellarii* guard as a tactical reserve.[15]

Although trained as an officer, Justinian never took command in the field once he assumed the throne in Constantinople, instead relying on the battlefield genius of his two principal commanders, Belisarios and Narses, to expand his imperial possessions. Born in Thrace and of Greek or Thracian ancestry, Belisarios (c.505–565) joined the Byzantine army as a youth and rose quickly through the ranks of Emperor Justin I's (r.518–527) royal bodyguard, becoming a capable and charismatic officer.[16] Belisarios would cut his teeth in the eastern campaigns against Sassanian Persians, rising quickly through the ranks to become a commander. A major flashpoint on the Byzantine-Sassanian frontier was the strongly fortified border city of Dara (located near the modern village of Oguz in eastern Turkey). Dara was rebuilt into a fortress city by Justin's predecessor, the Emperor Anastasius (r.491–518) and was the lynchpin of the Mesopotamian defences because it covered a major trading nexus south into northern Syria and north-westwards into Anatolia.[17]

Tug-of-war in the East and the Battle of Dara

The war between the Byzantines and the Sassanians began in 527, the last year of Justin's reign, when the Christian king of the Caucasian kingdom of Iberia rebelled against the Sassanian Persian king Kavad (r.488–531), allegedly because the Persian king was trying to convert the region to Zoroastrianism. Worried for his life, the Iberian king then fled to Byzantine territory, where he was offered sanctuary. Kavad tried to ease tensions with Justin, even offering his own son and prince regent Chosroes (later king Chosroes I, r.531–579, sometimes Khusraw I), to the Byzantine emperor as an adoptive son. Justin refused and ordered an offensive against Persian-controlled Armenia, located just south of Iberia, led by the young commanders Sittas and Belisarios. After the death of Justin in August 527, Justinian tried to negotiate with Kavad, but to no avail. Sittas and Belisarios were defeated and Byzantine efforts in the region stalled in 529.[18] In 530, Justinian appointed Belisarios 'Master of the Soldiers' of the Army of the East and ordered him into the region again, leading an army of 25,000 men to Dara to keep it from being taken by the Persians.[19]

When Belisarios arrived at Dara, he arranged his army behind a series of defensive ditches dug across the main road from Dara to nearby Nisibis just outside of the walls of the city. The ditches were probably laid out with a short central section recessed behind two longer flanking sections, connected together by two transverse sections. The defensive ditches were bridged in numerous places, allowing the Byzantine forces to cross into battle. The Byzantine centre, made up of infantry, was commanded by his chief lieutenant Hermogenes. On the far-left of the Byzantine line was stationed a detachment of Heruli cavalry, fierce Germanic horsemen originally from Scandinavia who became subjects first of the Ostrogoths and then the Huns, before becoming *foederati* in service of Constantinople. To their right was another larger contingent of cavalry under the Byzantine commander Bouzes, while on their right were stationed 600 Hunnic cavalry on the left of the Byzantine centre. Another 600 Hunnic cavalry drew up right of the centre, followed by a large formation of cavalry commanded by John the Armenian, a man of considerable talent whose resolve would be instrumental in many of Belisarios' victories.[20]

Unwilling to negotiate with the Byzantines, King Kavad sent Firuz, his *mirran* (Persian *Eire-An Spahbad* or supreme commander), to Dara at the head of a Persian army of perhaps 40,000 men.[21] The attacking Sassanian host was a combined-arms force in the tradition of great classical Mesopotamian armies of the past, complete with a reincarnation of the 'Immortals' (*Zhayedan*), an elite band of Persian soldiers who served the king as a bodyguard. Like their Byzantine counterparts, Sassanian commanders used cavalry as their primary combat arm, supported by infantry and at times, war elephants.[22] Below, the fourth century Greek historian Ammianus Marcellinus, who served as a Roman staff officer under the emperors Julian the Apostate and Jovian, describes the elite Persian *clibanarii* of King Shapur II (r.309–379) and their support troops:

> The Persians opposed us with squadrons of [*clibanarii*] drawn up in such serried ranks that their movements in their close-fitting coats of flexible mail dazzled our eyes, while all their horses were protected by housings of leather. They were supported by detachments of infantry who moved in compact formation carrying long, curved shields of wicker covered with raw hide. Behind them came elephants looking like moving hills. Their huge bodies threatened the destruction of all who approached, and past experience had taught us to dread them.[23]

Ammianus continues with a description of how well protected the *clibanarii* were by their armour and how some of the horsemen were lancers:

All the companies were clad in iron, and all parts of their bodies were covered with thick plates, so fitted that the stiff-joints conformed with those of their limbs; and the forms of human faces were so skilfully fitted to their heads, that since their entire body was covered with metal, arrows that fell upon them could lodge only where they could see a little through tiny openings opposite the pupil of the eye, or where through the tip of their nose they were able to get a little breath. Of these some who were armed with pikes, stood so motionless that you would have thought them held fast by clamps of bronze.[24]

There is evidence that by the sixth century the Sassanian art of war had transitioned away from using exceptionally heavily armoured lancers to using lighter armoured cavalrymen who fought with both lance and composite bow. There may also have been specialized units who fought with only lances, and certainly there were light cavalry units who fought only as mounted archers, mostly in reaction to contacts with mobile horse archers from the steppes.[25] The elite Sassanian heavy cavalry are often referred to as the Savaran in Persian sources and were guided by a chivalry code not unlike that which was practised hundreds of years later in Western Europe by Christian knights. Savaran cavalry were made up of well-trained and well-equipped Persian nobles who excelled as lancers, wielding the long shaft with a two-handed couch. Savaran cavalry were protected by a combination of armours, including ring, lamellar plate or chainmail. Savaran noblemen wore conical helms that, as the description above suggests, incorporated protection for the face and sides of the head that often obscured the identity of the warrior. Besides the lance, Savaran cavalry carried swords, maces or javelins, and some carried composite bows and arrows. Horses were frequently armoured in leather and sometimes metal barding. The introduction of the stirrup into Sassanian Persian warfare, probably in the late fifth or early sixth century, made mounted shock tactics by lance-wielding cavalry even more dangerous, as warriors could now direct the combined weight of rider and mount into their charge.[26] Because it was the custom of the Savaran to challenge champions of an opposing army to single combat before battle, many celebrated lance-duels took place between the Savaran and Byzantine knights during the long history of conflict between these two civilizations.[27]

Firuz drew up his Sassanian forces in two dense lines, taking personal command of the centre troops in both formations. The forward Persian centre consisted of light infantry slingers, javelin throwers and archers, while behind them stood conscript infantry. He placed the king's elite Persian cavalry Immortals on both wings of the forward line, backed by their own *clibanarii* and supported by detachments of Persian and allied Arab light horse. The cavalry on his left was commanded by the 'one-eyed' Baresmanes, while the cavalry on his right was under Pityaxes.[28] Seeing Belisarios' strong defensive position behind the trench, Firuz decided to open the battle with a cavalry probe, ordering horsemen from Baresmanes' command forward against the Byzantine right, which withdrew as the Persians advanced. Fearing an attack against their flank by the Hunnic horse, the Sassanians retreated in haste, but were now counterattacked by units from the Eastern Roman left, probably made up of the fast-moving Heruli cavalry. Justinian's chief chronicler, the sixth century Greek historian Procopius of Caesarea, tells us that the Persians lost only seven men in this engagement.[29]

After the Sassanian cavalry returned to their lines, a lone Persian warrior broke ranks and rode out to challenge a Byzantine champion to a fight. This type of one-on-one duel was not uncommon in classical and medieval warfare and was practised by numerous Indo-European, Semitic, and Turkic warrior cultures. On this day the challenge was answered by a man named Andreas, an accomplished wrestler and personal attendant of Bouzes, who dropped the Persian champion with a spear thrust to the right breast, then, according to Procopius, drew a small knife and 'slew him like a sacrificial animal as he lay on his back' to the cheers of the Byzantine lines.[30] The Sassanians sent another warrior to avenge the first challenger's death, and Andreas killed him as well. Although seemingly tactically insignificant, these duels could have important morale-boosting results on the side whose champion won the challenge. Afterwards, Firuz withdrew his army back to their base at Ammodios.[31]

The Sassanian army returned the following day, this time with 10,000 reinforcements from Nisibis.[32] During the morning both sides exchanged letters. The Byzantines asked the Persians to come to the negotiation table, and the Persians refused. At midday, the two armies deployed in the same manner as the day before, with one exception; Belisarios hid a small contingent of Heruli cavalry under the command of Pharas behind a hill on the extreme left of the Byzantine position to be used if the opportunity presented itself. The battle opened with an exchange of archery fire, but despite having more bowmen, the effectiveness of the Persian volleys was hampered by strong opposing winds. Both sides suffered light casualties. Firuz then ordered his entire Sassanian line forward in a general attack. On his right wing, Pityaxes pushed forward with his Savaran and Immortal cavalry, backed by Persian and Arab horse, forcing the Byzantine left wing under Bouzes backwards. But a coordinated counterattack by 600 Hunnic cavalry from the left centre and the sudden appearance of the reserve Heruli horse from behind the hill changed the tactical situation. Struck in the flank and rear by the once-hidden cavalry, the Immortals and their allies fell back in disarray towards their second line who opened their ranks and accepted their retreating comrades. Still, casualties on the Persian right were high with Procopius recording some 3,000 dead.[33]

After a pause in the battle, the Persian *mirran* ordered his entire line forward again, but pressed his numerical advantage on his left. Here, under the command of the 'one-eyed' Baresmanes and backed by Savaran and Immortal cavalry, the Persian left pushed John and his Byzantine heavy cavalry on the right wing backwards in complete disarray. It seemed as though the Persians were about to enjoy a breakthrough when Belisarios noticed the Persian left was now detached from its centre. He ordered his two centre Hunnic units (1,200 horsemen in all) to wheel and strike the flank of the victorious Persian left wing. Belisarios seized the moment and launched his elite cavalry reserve against the beleaguered Persian left who, attacked on three sides, broke and ran for their lives, swept from the battlefield by John and his reinvigorated cavalry. Baresmanes was killed in the melee along with 5,000 other Persian troops on the collapsing left wing.[34]

Belisarios quickly recognized his fortunes had changed. The remaining Persian army in front of him was without a left wing to protect the mass of infantry in the centre. The Byzantine general ordered his mounted bodyguard and the Hunnic horse to attack the enemy's unprotected left flank, shattering the infantry formation with repeated heavy cavalry charges and *clibanarii* and light cavalry missile fire. Persian casualties

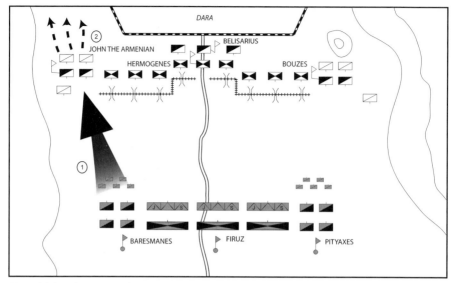

Map 1.1.1. *The Battle of Dara, 530* CE. *Phase I: Deciding against attacking the Byzantine entrenchments, Firuz opens the battle by launching Baresmanes' cavalry against the enemy horse stationed on the Byzantine right (1). The Sassanians press John's forces to the rear (2).*

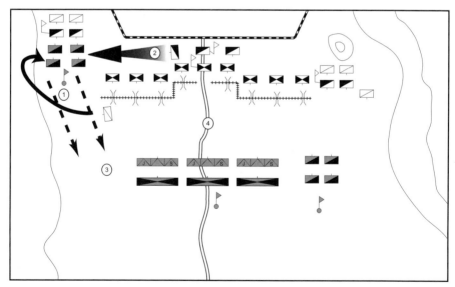

Map 1.1.2. *The Battle of Dara, 530* CE. *Phase II: Fearing a counterattack against their exposed flank, the Sassanian cavalry begins to retreat (1). As they begin this movement, they are struck by Byzantine cavalry (2), hastening their withdrawal. Losses are light and the Persians regain their position (3). A short series of duels then occurs between Persian champions and Andreas, a Byzantine warrior and Bouzes' personal attendant (4). The Sassanian fighters are vanquished, and Firuz orders his army back to camp, ending the first day's action.*

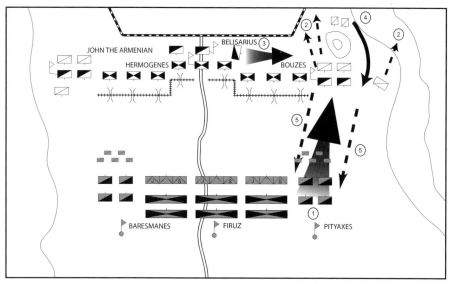

Map 1.1.3. The Battle of Dara, 530 CE. Phase III: The Sassanians return the next morning, reinforced by 10,000 men from Nisibis. Both sides deploy as they had the previous day. After a desultory exchange of archery fire, Firuz orders his entire line forward. On the right wing, Pityaxes launches an attack against Bouzes' cavalry (1). The Byzantines are pressed back (2), but as the Sassanians ride forward, they are struck on both flanks by Hunnic cavalry from the left-centre (3) and a concealed reserve under Pharas swinging around a small hill on the Byzantine left (4). Persian losses are high, and the survivors retreat (5).

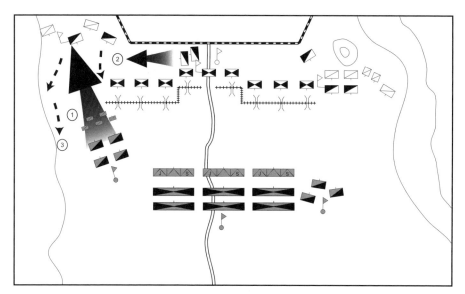

Map 1.1.4. The Battle of Dara, 530 CE. Phase IV: As the Sassanian line continues forward, Baresmanes launches a cavalry attack against John the Armenian (1), disrupting the Byzantine line and pressing them back. Belisarius orders his Hunnic cavalry against the enemy horse (2), striking their flanks and shattering the attackers. Baresmanes and 5,000 of his horsemen are killed and the survivors are routed (3).

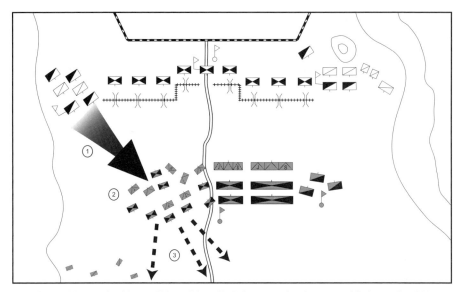

Map 1.1.5. The Battle of Dara, 530 CE. Phase V: Belisarius orders his mounted bodyguard and Hunnic cavalry to attack the now-exposed Sassanian left flank (1). Repeated assaults by the heavy cavalry coupled with mounted archery fire break up the Persian ranks (2) and a rout ensues (3). Casualties are high, with some 8,000 Persian corpses littering the field. The Immortals refuse to flee and fight to the last man. Byzantine losses are high as well, and the pursuit is halted after just a few miles.

were high, with some 8,000 men dead on the battlefield.[35] Despite the hopelessness of their situation, the Immortals fought on and died to the last man.[36] Byzantine casualties are not recorded by Procopius, although we do know that Belisarios and Hermogenes called off the pursuit after a few miles, fearing the Sassanians might regroup and counterattack, endangering the victory.[37]

After Dara, the Persians suffered several more defeats, and in 532, Kavad's successor agreed to a peace with Byzantium with no term limit, the poorly named 'Perpetual Peace'. By the unusual terms of this agreement Justinian was to pay the Persians 11,000 pounds of gold toward the upkeep of the Caucasian defences, and in return, Byzantium could keep the fortress at Dara, but not as its headquarters in Mesopotamia.[38] Both sides would return strategic strongholds captured in the decades-old war. Finally, Persia swore eternal friendship and alliance with the Byzantine Empire. The treaty lasted less than a decade, and Byzantium and Persia continue to play strategic tug-of-war in the region until the early 630s, when both empires faced a new and dangerous threat from the expansion of Islam out of the Arabian Peninsula.

The North African Campaign and the Battle of Tricameron
In 533, Justinian sent Belisarios and an expeditionary force made up mostly of soldiers from the Army of the East to conquer the Germanic kingdom of the Vandals, located in what is now modern Tunisia. Originally from north central Europe, the Vandals crossed Gaul and the Iberian Peninsula during the great Germanic migrations of the fifth century, settling in North Africa and setting up a powerful thalassocracy based out

of Carthage that controlled the sea lanes of the western Mediterranean. The reason for the invasion was a revolution in Carthage. The Vandal king Hilderic (r.523–530) was dethroned by Gelimer in 530, the great grandson of Gaiseric, the Vandal chief who so thoroughly sacked Rome in 455 that the name of his tribe has rung down the centuries as a name for destroyers of public property. Hilderic was a vassal of Justinian, and his appeal for aid from the Byzantine emperor became the pretext to launch an expedition to bring North Africa under direct imperial rule.

Belisarios' army consisted of 15,000 regular troops and 1,000 *foederati* allies and a *bucellarii* guard of perhaps a few thousand.[39] Sailing from Constantinople to a forward base in Sicily, Belisarios transported his expeditionary force on 500 ships manned by 30,000 sailors and escorted by ninety-two warships.[40] In Sicily, he waited for an intelligence report on the whereabouts of the Vandal fleet, learning that it was in Sardinia putting down a rebellion instigated by Justinian. With the formidable Vandal navy occupied, Belisarios set sail for North Africa in early September 533, landing his army south of Caputvada (modern Ras Kapudia in Tunisia), 130 miles south of Cape Bon.[41] After disembarking his army, Belisarios built a fortified camp and then sent messengers into the countryside explaining that the Eastern Roman expeditionary force was not there to punish the population, but bring the pretender Gelimer to justice. This must have worked, for Belisarios proceeded unmolested northwards up the coast toward the ancient city of Carthage. Belisarios sent an advanced guard of 300 cavalry commanded by John the Armenian to screen his march. Six hundred Hunnic *foederati* cavalry covered the main army's left flank, while the fleet shadowed on the right.[42] On 13 September, John's vanguard reached the defile of Ad Decimum (the tenth milestone from Carthage).

When word of the Byzantine vanguard's advance on Carthage reached Gelimer, he put Hilderic and his relatives to the sword, and prepared to attack the invaders.[43] Gelimer's strategy was a risky one, relying on the principles of manoeuvre and concentration. He instructed his brother Ammatus, the commander in Carthage, to engage the Byzantine van, while he took the majority of the Vandal host and attacked the rear of Belisarios' main force. The third element of Gelimer's strategy was a simultaneous attack by his nephew Gibamund, who would move over the hills from the west and attack the invader's left flank. But success would require a careful coordination of not two but three columns, a difficult feat for any army in any age.

What took place next was a product of unfortunate timing. On 13 September, Ammatus left Carthage and struck the Byzantine van before Gelimer and Gibamund were in position. Ammatus was mortally wounded and his forces panicked and fled. Gibamund struck next and was routed by the Hunnic flank guard.[44] The third Vandal column, confused by the trek through hilly terrain, missed the rear of the Byzantine main army altogether and instead struck the front of the Byzantine host, now unprotected by the absence of John and his vanguard, which was now making its way to sack Carthage. Gelimer's sudden attack pushed the Byzantines back, and it looked as through the tide had turned in the favour of the Vandals when Gelimer discovered his brother's dead body on the battlefield. Stopping his pursuit to bury Ammatus, Gelimer lost the momentum in the battle. Belisarios regrouped and counterattacked, driving the Vandals from the battlefield.[45]

Belisarios entered Carthage on 15 September and began to reconstruct the city's

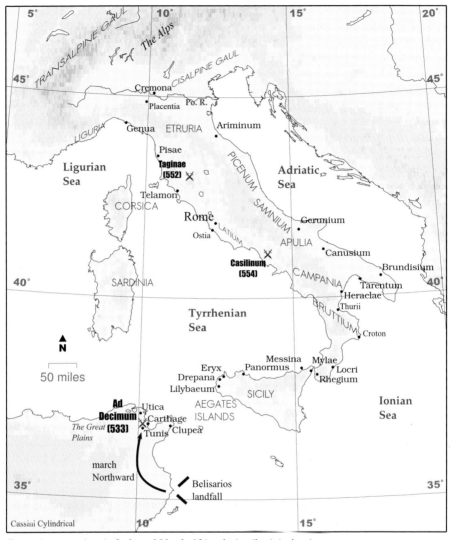

Byzantine campaigns in Italy and North Africa during Justinian's reign.

dilapidated defences for his own use.[46] Gelimer retreated west one hundred miles and recalled his brother Tzazon from Sardinia where he was putting down the rebellion. Once reinforced, Gelimer marched on Carthage, stopping eighteen miles short of his target at the village of Tricameron. Gathering intelligence on his enemy, Gelimer realized that there were strains between Belisarios and his Hunnic allies. Vandal spies offered the Huns great rewards if they would turn against the Byzantines during the next engagement. But unknown to Gelimer, Belisarios learned of this intrigue and offered the Huns a larger bribe if they stayed true. The Huns accepted Belisarios' offer, though the general realized that his *foederati*'s loyalty was now in question.[47]

Uncertain when his coalition might fracture, Belisarios decided to bring the battle to the enemy. By this time, Belisarios faced an enemy army of around 50,000 men (mostly cavalry), or about three times the size of his invading force. In mid-December, he sent nearly all of his cavalry (4,500 horse) under John toward Tricameron, following the next day with his infantry and a 500-horse reserve, camping some distance from Gelimer's position.[48] The next morning, the Vandal commander led his army out of their encampment and stumbled upon John and his cavalry preparing lunch. Instead of seizing the moment and attacking, Gelimer waited for the Byzantines to mount up. John deployed his men in three divisions and, according to Procopius, took command of the centre 'leading the guards and spearmen of Belisarios and carrying the general's standard.'[49] He then dispatched a messenger to the main Byzantine camp. Belisarios immediately led his 500 cavalry to reinforce John, leaving the Byzantine infantry to catch up at a steady march. Meanwhile, Gelimer ordered his own cavalry to mirror the enemy, deploying his horsemen into three divisions and giving command of the centre to his brother Tzazon. Procopius goes on to state that Gelimer ordered his troops to 'use neither spear nor any other weapon in this engagement except their swords', in essence favouring shock over missile combat in the upcoming fight.[50]

The battle of Tricameron began after a lengthy pause when John and a small contingent of selected Byzantine horsemen (Procopius does not record how many) crossed a brook and charged the Vandal centre, only to be rebuffed by Tzazon's forces. John attacked again with a slightly larger force and was beaten back a second time. Perhaps thinking himself charmed, John attacked a third time, this time taking the general's standard and with all of his guards and spearmen yelling at the top of their voices. In the melee, Tzazon was killed.[51] Procopius describes what took place next when Belisarios arrived on the battlefield and ordered the remaining two cavalry divisions to attack the rapidly collapsing centre.

> Then at last, the whole Roman army was set in motion, and crossing the river they advanced upon the enemy, and the rout, beginning in the centre, became complete; for each of the Roman divisions turned to flight those before them with no trouble.[52]

With the whole of the Vandal cavalry in disarray, the Huns joined in the pursuit, pressing the remaining Germanic horse back into their fortified camp. The battle was not very costly in lives. Byzantine losses were less than fifty dead, while the Vandals lost around 800 men.[53]

Knowing he could not storm the Vandal camp without his foot soldiers, Belisarios waited patiently for his infantry to arrive. Gelimer panicked as he watched the Eastern Romans begin to surround his camp. Silently, he mounted his horse and slipped out of the noose, escaping to the mountains in the west. Leaderless, the Vandals soon followed, abandoning their camp to the Byzantines. Belisarios' troops entered the camp and, breaking ranks, began to plunder. In moments, Belisarios' victorious army disintegrated into a mass of thieves, illustrating the weakness of a mostly mercenary force. It would take John another three months to hunt down and capture Gelimer.[54]

Belisarios defeated the Vandals in two battles, sending back the Vandal king Gelimer and his treasury to Constantinople, then adding the surviving Vandals as *foederati* to his new Army of Africa. In 535, Justinian ordered his brilliant young commander to invade Italy and attack the Ostrogothic king, Vitiges (r.536–540). Over the next five years,

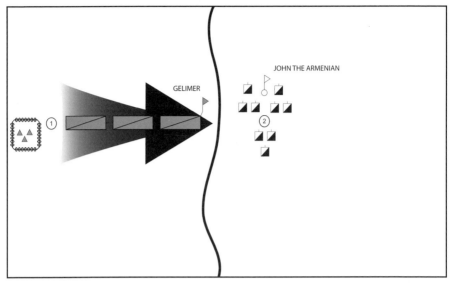

Map 1.2.1. The Battle of Tricameron, 533 CE. Phase I: As the Vandal army under Gelimer advances from their camp (1), they stumble upon Belisarius' advance guard of Byzantine cavalry under John the Armenian preparing their midday meal on the opposite side of a small brook (2).

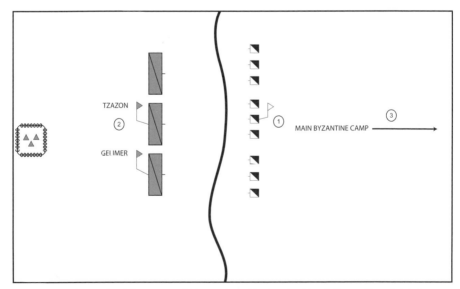

Map 1.2.2. The Battle of Tricameron, 533 CE Phase II: Inexplicably, Gelimer allows John's forces to form for battle unhindered (1). The Byzantines deploy in three divisions, a move mirrored by Gelimer, who orders his brother Tzazon to take command of the Vandal centre (2). John dispatches a messenger to Belisarius (3), who hastens 500 cavalry reinforcements to John's aid immediately, followed more slowly by the Byzantine foot soldiers. Gelimer orders his troops to stow their bows and use their swords in preparation for the impending clash.

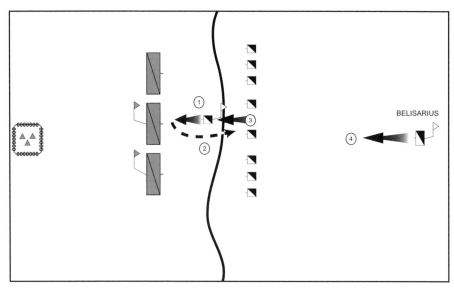

Map 1.2.3. The Battle of Tricameron, 533 CE. Phase III: John opens the battle by charging across the brook with a small contingent of Byzantine cavalry (1). The Vandals rebuff the attackers who retreat back to their starting point (2). The Byzantines regroup and launch a second assault (3), which again fails to make headway. John reforms for another assault as Belisarius approaches the fight with the cavalry contingent (4).

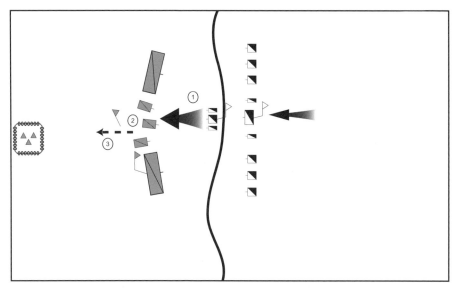

Map 1.2.4. The Battle of Tricameron, 533 CE. Phase IV: Seizing his general's standard and rallying his guards and spearmen, John launches a third attack on the Vandal centre (1). Tzazon is killed in the melee (2) and Gelimer's centre begins to give way (3).

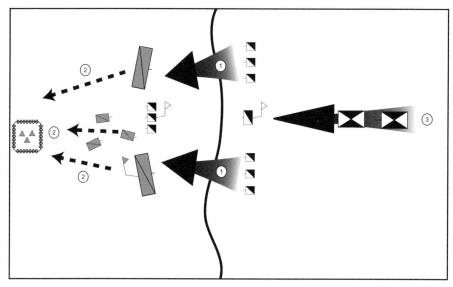

Map 1.2.5. *The Battle of Tricameron, 533 CE. Phase V: Belisarius orders the remaining divisions into action (1). The collapse of the Vandal's centre division spreads to the flanks, and they break and flee to the relative safety of their fortified camp, closely pursued by the Hunnic cavalry (2). Belisarius halts the attack and awaits the arrival of his infantry (3).*

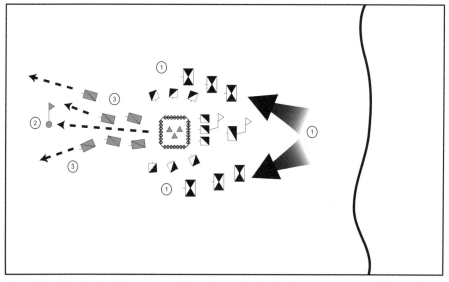

Map 1.2.6. *The Battle of Tricameron, 533 CE. Phase VI: As the Byzantine army steadily encircles the Vandal camp (1), Gelimer panics and abandons his army (2), which follows suit (3). The Byzantine army entering the camp begins to plunder, losing all cohesion. It will take John another three months to finally capture Gelimer.*

Belisarios conquered the peninsula, capturing the Gothic capital at Ravenna and all of Italy south of the Po Valley. When Justinian recalled him to Constantinople in 540 to fight the Persians after the 'Perpetual Peace' failed, Belisarios left behind a new Army of Italy and brought back the Ostrogothic king and treasury to his emperor.[55] But a devastating epidemic of bubonic plague hit Constantinople between the years 541 to 542 (Procopius states that 10,000 people were dying a day in the capital at the height of the epidemic).[56] Plague also spread by way of Byzantine port cities into the interior of Byzantine lands and weakened imperial control over its far-flung territories, precipitating rebellions over the next ten years in North Africa, Italy and the East.[57] In the meantime, Belisarios had fallen out of favour with Justinian, who dismissed him from military service in 548.[58] It would be 551 before the treasury had recovered enough to send a new army to conquer Italy from the Ostrogoths.

The Gothic War in Italy and the Battles of Taginae and Casilinus River

In the spring of 551 Justinian appointed the eunuch Narses (478–573) commander-in-chief of the armies of the West. Already in his mid-seventies, Narses had enjoyed a close relationship with Justinian for twenty years as his most trusted court advisor, but was limited in his military experience, having only served as Belisarios' co-commander in Italy in the mid-530s. The armies of Justinian had fought the Ostrogoths throughout the Italian peninsula for two decades, burning towns and cities and pillaging the countryside, but were unable to break the back of Ostrogothic power. Narses was given charge of wrestling Italy away from the Ostrogoths once and for all, landing at Salona (near Split in modern Croatia) in the fall of 551 and then marching north to Italy and then south along the Venetic coast towards Ravenna, a city taken from the Ostrogoths by Belisarios in 540 to become the seat of Byzantine government in Italy.

The composition of the Byzantine expeditionary forces in Italy changed from the time when Belisarios first campaigned on the peninsula in the mid-530s. Over the years mercenaries began to replace the Greek *numeri* and *bucellari*. By the summer of 552, Narses led an army of between 20,000 and 25,000 men, but only the core of the army was Byzantine, the rest were *foederati* troops made up of Lombard, Hunnic, Heruli, Armenian, and Arab mercenaries.[59] Even the Great Persian king Chosroes I (r.531–579) sent a small detachment of Persian cavalry as a symbol of renewed goodwill during a truce period between the Sassanians and Byzantines.[60] In June, Narses moved his multinational army from Ravenna toward the forces of the Ostrogothic King Totila (r.541–552) in central Italy. Hearing that Totila was advancing toward him, Narses made camp west of the medieval town of Taginae (Roman Tadinum and modern Gualdo Tadino) located on the Roman road Via Flaminia. Here, Narses prepared the battlefield by selecting a site straddling a local route into the Apennines from the Via Flaminia. He adopted a strong defensive position on this road into the Bono River Valley, seizing slightly raised ground with a small hill anchoring his left flank. Here, he placed his barbarian allies in the centre, a dismounted force consisting of perhaps 9,000 to 10,000 Lombard, Hunnic, and Heruli men arrayed on a slope to give them a defensive advantage. Narses then placed his Byzantine cavalry armed with lance and bow on both wings, commanding the left himself and giving the right to his trusted lieutenant Valerian. To screen the cavalry wings, Narses placed 8,000 Greek archers (4,000 per side) in front of the Byzantine horsemen, and then located a cavalry reserve

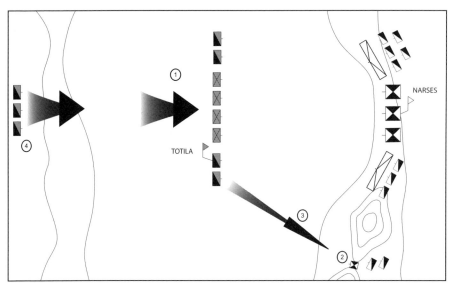

Map 1.3.1. The Battle of Taginae, 552 CE. Phase I: As Totila arrives on the field and deploys his forces (1) he spots a trail in a gully around a hill on the Byzantine left that appears vulnerable, not realizing that Narses had blocked it with a small force of heavy infantry the previous night (2). A contingent of Gothic cavalry attempts to push through the trail (3) but each charge is rebuffed by the spear thrusts of the infantry. Totila recalls his horsemen and awaits the arrival of 2,000 cavalry reinforcements (4).

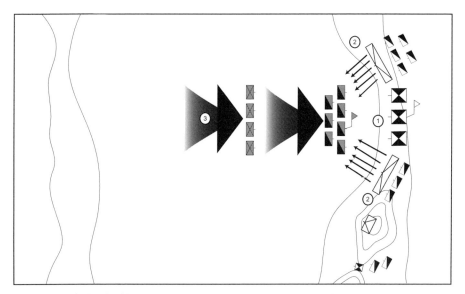

Map 1.3.2. The Battle of Taginae, 552 CE. Phase II: After several hours, Totila rearranges his army into two ranks, with the less-reliable infantry to the rear. He then launches an attack against the squares of heavy infantry and dismounted cavalry in the Byzantine centre (1). Before the charging horsemen can even get close, Narses' archers begin to loose volleys of arrows into their tightly-packed ranks (2) as the barbarian infantry slowly approaches the fight (3).

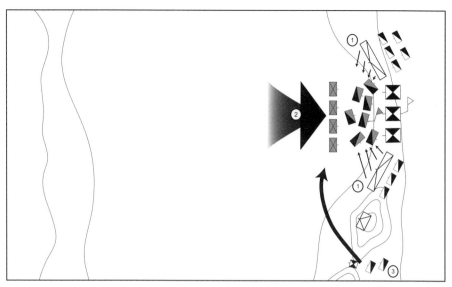

Map 1.3.3. The Battle of Taginae, 552 CE. Phase III: The Gothic cavalry fails to make headway against the foederati *infantry. As casualties mount from the unrelenting archery fire (1), the horsemen find themselves pressed from behind by their own infantry (2). Narses realizes that the battle's momentum has shifted in his favour and orders his reserve cavalry into the fray from their positions behind the hill (3).*

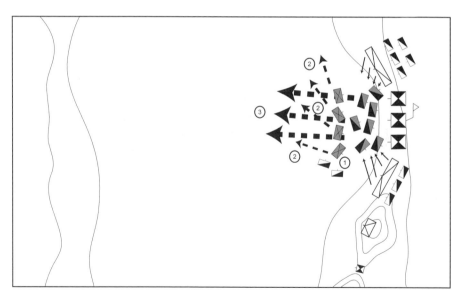

Map 1.3.4. The Battle of Taginae, 552 CE. Phase IV: Striking the exposed right flank of the barbarian infantry (1), the Ostrogoth formations crumble and soldiers begin to flee (2). Meanwhile, the archery fire continues unabated, exacting a heavy toll of the Gothic horse, which finally breaks, stampeding through their own infantry (3) as they join the rout. Totila is mortally wounded in the final action, dying later in a nearby peasant's hut.

of 1,500 horse behind his position on the left.[61] Procopius explains that 500 of these troops were to be used to reinforce the centre, while the remaining 1,000 would serve as a flanking force if the Gothic infantry attacked the Eastern Roman centre or flank.[62] The entire Byzantine army was arrayed in a slightly concave position, in effect, creating a dangerous killing zone for any enemy trying to attack the Byzantine centre.

Totila left Rome and marched towards the town of Taginae, encamping some thirteen miles south of Narses' position. Because the Goths possessed such a small standing army, Totila was forced to pull his garrisons from nearby cities to swell his ranks, in the end creating a host somewhat smaller than the invading Byzantine army and one probably padded with unreliable infantry conscripts. When Narses learned that the Gothic army had made camp he dispatched a Greek messenger to Totila, proposing either a peaceful settlement or a time for battle. Totila refused the call for peace, but countered that battle should take place in eight days. Narses, probably relying on field intelligence, realized this was a ruse designed to relax the Byzantine army and ordered his own troops to prepare for battle. This strategy proved prescient as the Gothic army was nearing the Byzantine position at dawn the following day.[63]

Totila entered the narrow valley and, according to Procopius, took up a position 'not more than two bow-shots' from the Byzantine host.[64] Totila placed his cavalry on the wings and his infantry in the centre, mirroring the Byzantine array. Totila immediately saw what he believed to be a vulnerable approach to the Byzantine lines – a track through a gully around the small hill to the left of the imperial lines. However, recognizing this weakness, Narses had dispatched fifty heavy infantrymen to defend the route the night before. When Totila tried to take the ravine with contingents of Gothic cavalry, the fifty 'standing shoulder-to-shoulder' held their ground, 'pushing with their shields and thrusting very rapidly with their spears' and beat back the enemy charges.[65]

As the morning wore on, Narses left the initiative to Totila, but the Gothic king refused to attack until the arrival of 2,000 cavalry reinforcements. As the two armies stared at one another, a Gothic warrior rode out and issued a challenge to the Byzantine side, only to be killed by the responding Byzantine warrior. Still stalling, Totila rode out between the armies and entertained the troops on both sides with his outstanding equestrian skills, parading between the lines in his ornate golden armour. Once the cavalry reinforcements arrived, Totila withdrew into his lines and changed into the armour of a common soldier and joined the ranks of the Gothic army.[66]

Totila, realizing both armies had stood at attention for hours, ordered a sudden cavalry attack against the Byzantine centre, hoping to catch the Eastern Romans and their allies off guard during the midday lunch period. The Ostrogothic king pulled his cavalry forward in one line across the entire front, keeping the less reliable infantry conscripts in one line behind. But Narses, fearing the prospect of a sudden attack, ordered his men to stay in their kits and eat standing up. Procopius tells us that, inexplicably, Totila ordered his soldiers to 'use neither bow not any other weapon in this battle except their spears.'[67] But before the Gothic cavalry could even reach the Byzantine lines a rain of arrows came from the 8,000 Byzantine archers on the flanks, killing horses and riders alike by the hundreds. Procopius also remarks that the Greek bowmen on both flanks began to turn 'both of the wings of their front as to form a crescent', in effect creating a dangerous enfilade of the Gothic position.[68] Those Gothic cavalry that did reach the Byzantine lines fared no better as the *foederati* heavy infantry, buttressed with dismounted heavy cavalry, held their ground. Aggravating the situation, the attacking Gothic cavalry soon found themselves pressed between the Byzantine defenders and their own approaching barbarian infantry. Seeing the tipping point of the battle, Narses ordered the entire Byzantine line forward and then commanded his heavy cavalry reserve from behind the hill to attack the flank of the approaching Gothic infantry, rolling up their line and driving them from the field. Surrounded and facing certain annihilation, the Gothic cavalry fled, cutting their way through their own fleeing infantry.

King Totila was mortally wounded leaving the battlefield, dying in a peasant's hut nearby. Procopius claims 6,000 Ostrogoths were killed in the battle. Those who were captured by the Eastern Romans were later massacred.[69] After the battle of Taginae, Narses pursued the remaining Goths to Rome and then farther south to Naples, killing their new king and continuing his campaign of extermination. Finally, a truce was called at Mons Lactarius (modern Monte Lettere near Monte Vesuvius) in 553 and the few surviving Goths were allowed to leave Italy and settle north of the Po River in any other barbarian kingdom they wanted.[70]

With the Ostrogothic army destroyed, Narses faced a new threat from the north by a large raiding expedition made up of Frankish and Alemanni forces commanded by the chieftains Leutharis and Butilin. The Franks were a Germanic tribe who raided Roman Gaul between the third and fifth centuries, finally settling in this region in 357 and growing into a powerful regional kingdom in the fifth century under the Merovingian dynasty (c.450–751). Under King Clovis I (r.481–511) the Franks converted to Roman Catholicism, and later Merovingian kings coveted the wealth of Italy. The Alemanni were a confederation of Germanic tribes from the Rhine Valley brought under Frankish control by Clovis and who fought for Merovingian monarchs. This Frankish–Alemmanic army entered the Po Valley at the beginning of June 553.

When Narses learned of the raiders, he dispatched a sizeable Byzantine army to intercept and hold them while he finished the capture of the city of Lucca. But the Eastern Roman holding force was decisively defeated at Parma, and Narses, despite being reinforced by a sizeable Cumae force, decided to winter in Rome and wait until the following year to engage the Frankish–Alemannic army. In the meantime, these barbarians pushed southward, easily infiltrating central Italy. Here, they split into two armies. Butilin continued to the rich agricultural lands of Campania and Bruttium in southern Italy, while Leutharis raided Apulia and Calabria. In the summer of 554, both armies began to make their way north laden with a year's war treasure. Leutharis' army was mauled by a well-laid Byzantine ambush near modern Pesaro on the Adriatic coast as it tried to escape the Italian peninsula. Butilin marched north on the west side of the Apennines towards Rome at the head of an army of around 15,000 men, but was intercepted by Narses at the Casilinus River (modern Volturno River) near Capua in south central Italy.

The Byzantine army was made up of 18,000 men, including Greek heavy cavalry *kataphraktoi* and heavy infantry, supported by Heruli *foederati*. The sixth century Greek historian Agathias of Myrina tells us that Butilin's army was struck by disease and desertion in the summer of 554, reducing its numbers from 30,000 to a number slightly smaller than that of the Byzantine host, probably around 15,000 men.[71] The

Frankish–Alemannic army faced by Narses was similar to Germanic armies faced by the Romans centuries earlier. From the early sixth century to the beginning of the eighth century, the Franks and surrounding Germanic peoples fought similarly. Infantry was by far the most prevalent combat arm in Germanic warfare, with barbarian infantry fighting in battle square formations or columns.[72] Most Frankish soldiers were armoured in leather, or at best, chainmail, and carried a round or oval shield.[73] Although Germanic nobility would most certainly be armed with either the single-edged *scramasax* or a double-edged long sword, the primary weapon of all Germanic infantry, including the Franks, was the spear. Medieval sources identify a unique Frankish spear called an *angon*, which was not only special in its design but also in its use in warfare. Agathias describes the weapon as a unique barb-headed spear of moderate length that could be used, 'if necessary for throwing like a javelin, and also in hand-to-hand combat.'[74] Besides the spear, Frankish infantry also employed a *francisca* or throwing axe which, according to Procopius, 'at a given signal and at first encounter, was thrown at the enemy' with the intent of breaking enemy shields and disrupting the enemy lines before engaging in hand-to-hand combat.[75]

In the sixth century, the Franks did employ a small number of heavy cavalry lancers, but these horsemen, devoid of stirrups and saddles with built-up pommels and cantles, were not the masters of the medieval battlefield yet. The diffusion of the stirrup from Central Asia to medieval Europe is usually credited to the Avars in the second half of the sixth century.[76] The Byzantines adopted the stirrup in this time period as well.[77] Identifying the precise time when the stirrup made its appearance in Western European

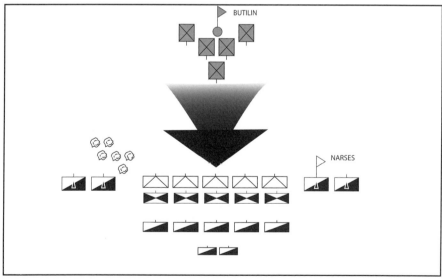

Map 1.4.1. The Battle of Casilinus River, 554 CE. Phase I: Narses forms his army into a three-rank centre with archers in the front line, infantry in the second and cavalry in the third. He leaves an opening for his foederati *troops that have yet to arrive and places a small cavalry reserve behind his centre. On the flanks he places his cavalry, with the left wing partially obscured by trees. Butilin forms his Franks and Alemanni opposite in several unarticulated battle squares. He opens the action by charging the Byzantine centre in a wedge formation, led by his well-armed and heavily armoured warriors.*

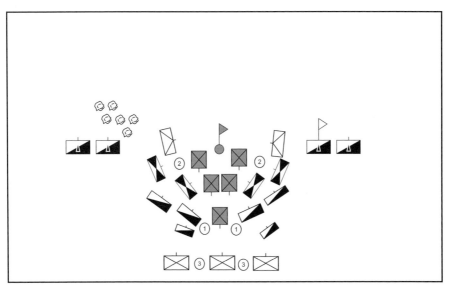

Map 1.4.2. The Battle of Casilinus River, 554 CE. Phase II: The Franks' ferocious attack breaks the first two lines and pushes the third to the rear (1), but the Byzantine infantry recovers and begins to close in on the now-exposed flanks of the Frankish/Alemanni wedge (2). At the same time, the Heruli foederati infantry arrive to reinforce the centre (3), though scattered Franks and Alemanni manage to push through to the Byzantine camp.

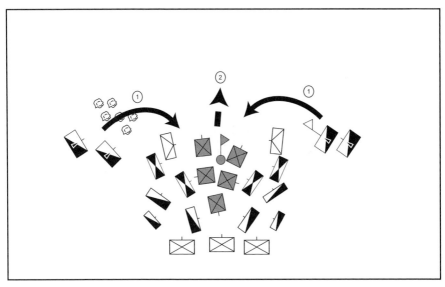

Map 1.4.3. The Battle of Casilinus River, 554 CE. Phase III: Narses orders his cavalry wings to wheel into the barbarian formations and engage them with archery fire (1). Beset on all sides, Butilin attempts to form a defensive square and withdraw (2), but his army loses its cohesion. Greek heavy cavalry charges break up the barbarian square, and slaughter ensues as the Byzantine infantry joins the counterattack. Byzantine losses are light while the Frankish and Alemanni army is annihilated.

warfare is more problematic, although most historians agree that it took place sometime in the early eighth century, probably during the rule of the Frankish leader Charles Martel (c.688–741), and was widely used throughout Western Christendom by the ninth century.[78] The Franks, like most Germanic peoples, did not have a tradition of using light cavalry in their art of war. Contacts with light cavalry archers came almost exclusively from relationships with nomadic peoples from the Eurasian Steppes such as the Huns and Avars with a strong tradition in mounted archery. Sometimes, these skills were acquired by Germanic peoples like the Heruli after prolonged interaction with steppe peoples. Later, Bulgar and Magyar penetrations into Eastern and Central Europe reintroduced Catholic Europe to the military capabilities of horse archers. Still, heavily forested Western Europe proved less than ideal for light cavalry, a fighting style that requires a great deal of open space and horse fodder to be successful. Also, mounted archery was a skill that took years in the saddle to perfect, a pastime more suited to Turkish and Mongol steppe warriors than Germanic farmers north and west of the Alps.

Butilin ordered his Frankish-Alemannic army to make camp on the banks of the Casilinus River, creating a perimeter out of the wagon wheels of this baggage train by burying the wheels up to their hubs as a continuous defensive barrier. The Frankish commander then built a wooden watch tower near a bridge over the river close to the entrance to the camp to cover a possible retreat route over the river and away from a Byzantine attack. When Narses arrived in the area he built a fortified camp and then ordered an imperial cavalry detachment to stop barbarian foraging. These horsemen succeeded in capturing several enemy wagons and setting the wooden tower ablaze by setting alight a hay-filled wagon near the structure. This action proved to be the prelude to the battle of Casilinus as the Franks and Alemanni immediately began to exit their camp and form up for battle.[79]

In response to the barbarian movements, Narses ordered his own troops from their camp and into a traditional deployment of cavalry on both wings and infantry in the centre, with a small cavalry reserve placed behind the infantry in case of a breakthrough. Narses took command of the cavalry on the right, and then placed the horsemen on the left in a position where they were partially concealed by trees. The Byzantine infantry in the centre consisted of archers in the front line and spearmen in the second line, supported by cavalry in the rear. An issue with the Heruli *foederati* delayed their deployment, but Narses reserved a place in the centre of his formation behind his infantry for these barbarian units when they finally arrived. However, Heruli deserters to the barbarians insisted that the Heruli were not going to fight emboldened Butilin, who ordered his army into the Germanic attack formation described by the Romans as the *cuneus* or wedge or boar's head formation.[80] This column placed the heaviest armoured and best-armed men in the front ranks in a narrow-fronted shield wall designed to punch through enemy lines. This wedge formation had limited offensive manoeuvrability, but presented plenty of impact power on a small frontage. The boar's head array was launched at an enemy in order to break up opposing formations in a single movement. If the initial attack miscarried before determined resistance, then the barbarians retreated in disorder, but if the boar's head was successful in breaking up the opposing formation, then individual combat ensued consistent with the Germanic fighting style.[81]

Formed up in their *cuneus*, the Frankish-Alemannic raiders charged the Byzantine centre, breaking the first two lines of infantry and pushing the third line backwards. Although the initial barbarian attack was successful, the Byzantine infantry was able to recover from the impact of the offensive, and were now closing in on the exposed flanks of the boar's head formation. At this moment, the Heruli reinforced the centre from behind, blunting the effectiveness of the attack, although some barbarians did manage to push onwards and attack the Byzantine camp. Meanwhile, Narses ordered his cavalry on both flanks to wheel into the barbarian wedge formation and engage with bows. Threatened by this double flanking manoeuvre and stopped by the engaging Eastern Roman infantry and Heruli forces, the barbarians halted their charge and formed into a defensive square and tried to fall back. In their retreat, the barbarian formation lost cohesion, and the Greek heavy cavalry charged with lance, completely outflanking and breaking up the square. A horrible carnage ensued as the Greek infantry, joined now by their cavalry, pressed their attack. Agathias tells us that the Byzantines only lost eighty men. Of the barbarian raiders, only five men survived.[82]

Narses' victory at Casilinus was absolute and Italy emerged out of two decades of Byzantine occupation ruined by war, famine and plague. The largest cities, such as Milan, Rome and Naples, were nearly depopulated and the countryside's agricultural economy devastated.[83] Eastern Roman rule would only last another fourteen years before the final wave of Germanic invaders, the Lombards, occupied the northern two-thirds of the peninsula, ending for ever Justinian's dream of imperial rule over Italy.

Strategic Challenges in the East in the Late Sixth and Early Seventh Centuries

Justinian's reign was the high-water mark for the Byzantine Empire. After his death in 565, the Eastern Roman Empire faced crisis after crisis. Constantly besieged by the Avars, Slavs and Bulgars in southern Europe, Sassanian Persians in Mesopotamia, and from the mid-seventh century onward, Islam from Africa and the Levant, the Byzantine Empire found its military and fiscal resources relentlessly stretched. Still, despite defeats that deprived it of all its African and Asian possessions except Asia Minor, the Byzantine Empire maintained itself for centuries as a formidable eastern Mediterranean power.

Byzantium's relationship with the Sassanian Empire soured in the decades after Justinian's death. His successor, Justin II (r.565–578), intrigued with the first Turk Empire (552–630), signing a peace treaty with the steppe nomads. This Turkish presence threatened the northern frontiers of the Sassanian Empire through their control of the Caucasus region and kept the growing power of the Avars in check.[84] In 572 Justin also refused to pay the tribute required in the peace with the Sassanians, precipitating renewed hostilities with the Persians that lasted until 591. During this period, a tug-of-war ensued between the Persians and Byzantines over territory along the eastern frontiers. Most of the fighting was over Armenia, which both states desired for strategic and economic reasons. In the sixth century Byzantine commanders lost access to Germanic mercenaries who were migrating west and began to rely more and more on Armenian soldiers to fill the ranks, and could not afford to let these lands fall under Persian control.[85] Hostilities opened with Byzantine raiding into Persian Arzanene, followed by a punitive Persian expedition into Syria and a successful siege of

Dara in 574. Two years later, the Byzantines successfully defeated the Persian king Chosroes I at the battle near Melitene (modern Malayta in central Turkey), who returned and sacked the city, but was again defeated by a Byzantine counterattack later in the year. In 577, the Sassanians defeated a Byzantine army in a surprise attack in Armenia. Chosroes' death in 579 did not bring peace as his son continued the war against the new and capable Byzantine emperor, Maurice, until his death in 590. Chosroes's grandson, Chosroes II (r.590–628, sometimes Khusraw II), made peace with Constantinople in 591, ending this phase of the Byzantine-Persian wars.[86]

The peace treaty Maurice (r.582–602) secured in 591 with the Sassanians yielded much of their Armenian conquests to Byzantium and it freed Byzantine resources to campaign in the Balkans where the Avars and their Slavic subjects were threatening Byzantine possessions from bases in Central Europe. Nine years earlier in 582, the Avars seized the strategically important city of Sirmium (modern Sremska Mitrovica in Serbia) and put the entire Balkan Peninsula to the torch. Slavic migrations into Byzantine territory followed in the wake of these raids. In 592 Maurice commenced large-scale operations against the Avars, crossing the Danube River several times and defeating the barbarians. But sustained operations in this remote and hostile land proved too taxing on the Byzantine troops. Ordered to spend the winter north of the Danube, they revolted and marched on Constantinople in 602, overthrowing and killing Maurice and proclaiming the half-barbarian Phocas as emperor.[87]

Although his reign was cut short, Maurice is considered to be a great Byzantine ruler, remembered for his reorganization of Western territories along military lines, conjoining civil and military authority through the creation of exarchates (imperial provinces) in Ravenna in Italy and Carthage in North Africa. This system would be later extended to Byzantium's heartland provinces of Anatolia and Greece. This system was essential to the prosperity of the Byzantine Empire for centuries to come.[88] Perhaps Maurice's most important contribution was his restructuring of the Byzantine army, although some of the reforms that bear his name probably took place before and after his reign. These reforms were written down in the *Strategikon* or *Handbook on Strategy*, one of the most important military treatises from the medieval period. Although not entirely successful, Maurice did his best to put an end to the *bucellarii* or semi-private armies that were common in the Byzantine military since the time of Justinian. Maurice also moved away from using feudal levies commanded by what were essentially warlords. Instead, superior officers were appointed by the imperial government. Maurice resurrected the Roman republican idea that the army was to serve the state, not its commanders.[89] The Byzantine army was also made more uniform, organizing the infantry and cavalry around the *bandum*, a manoeuvre unit consisting of between 300 and 400 soldiers.[90] These *bandum* would be cobbled together to form larger divisions within a Byzantine army. The new Byzantine military system also wanted to minimize the role of mercenaries in imperial service, believing that natives made superior soldiers. However, as time went on future emperors would rely heavily on Armenians, Slavs and other mercenaries to meet their manpower needs. Maurice's military system would remain virtually unchanged for more than three hundred years. In fact, the Byzantine emperor Leo VI's (r.886–912) *Taktika*, penned sometime at the beginning of the tenth century, added little to Maurice's organization.[91]

After Maurice's death Slavic penetrations continued in the Balkans and relations with the Sassanians disintegrated. The Sassanian king Chosroes II used the overthrowing of Maurice as a pretext to renew hostilities against the Eastern Romans. In 611, Chosroes, often referred to as *Parvez* (the 'Always Victorious') because of the success of these campaigns, invaded Syria, seizing Jerusalem in 614. A year later his Persian forces moved against Anatolia, pushing as far west as the Bosporus opposite Constantinople itself. In 619, they took the port city of Alexandria, and then subdued all of Egypt.[92]

The Byzantine recovery took place under Emperor Herakleios (r.610–641) who personally led a series of three military expedition against the Sassanians in 624, 625 and again between 627 and 628. During this period, Herakleios, who dropped Latin titles and adopted the ancient Greek title of *basileus* (later expanded to *basileus Rhomaion* or 'king of the Romans'), campaigned from the coast of the Black Sea in Anatolia, through the Caucusus, western Iran, and northern Mesopotamia, sacking Sassanian cities and temples along the way.[93] This type of expeditionary warfare was characterized by the location and destruction of enemy armies, not control over cities and territory, and as such, there was no linear front between the two states.[94] The death of Chosroes in 628 and the subsequent power struggle allowed the Byzantine emperor to make peace with the Persians and re-establish the old frontier of the two empires along the Khabur River.[95] This tug-of-war between Byzantium and Persia in the Levant weakened this region militarily. Cities had been sacked and defences ruined while the projected losses of Byzantine troops in this recent war with Persia is estimated at 200,000 fighting men.[96] Byzantine rule was only re-established in the region in 630 after a near twenty-year absence, just in time for the Eastern Romans to face a new and more dangerous threat emerging from the Arabian Peninsula, the expansion of Islam.[97]

Chapter 2

Islamic Warfare from Muhammad to the Rashidun Caliphate

Muhammad and the Rise of Islam

From the seventh century onward, Byzantium's greatest rival was the rise of Islam and the establishment of a new and powerful Islamic state in the Middle East and North Africa. According to Muslim tradition, in the year 570, the Prophet Muhammad (570–632) was born in Mecca to a merchant family and orphaned at the age of five. He was raised by his Uncle Abu Talib, the leader of the minor Hashim clan, part of the dominant Quraysh tribe that ruled Meccan affairs.[1] Muhammad grew up to become a successful caravan manager, eventually marrying a rich widow named Khadijah who was fifteen years his senior and also his employer. Muslim tradition states that at the age of forty, Muhammad began to experience visions that he believed were inspired by Allah, a prominent deity in the polytheistic Arab pantheon. Muhammad believed that, although Allah had already revealed himself in part to Moses and Jesus (and therefore through the Hebrew and Christian traditions), the final and perfect revelations were now being given to him. These revelations were eventually written down and formed Islam's holy book, the Qur'an, or the guidelines by which followers of Allah were supposed to live. Muhammad's teaching emphasized obedience to the will of the one-god Allah and polytheism was strictly forbidden. In fact, the word Islam literally means 'submission to the will of Allah' and one who submits is a Muslim.

Muhammad's new teachings caused friction between his newly converted Muslims and the citizens in Mecca. When his teachings openly criticized some of the business practices of Meccan merchants, the city's ruling tribe, the Quraysh, put pressure on Muhammad's Hashim clan to silence him. But the clan's leader, Abu Talib, refused to silence his nephew and the clan was subjected to economic sanctions. Abu Talib died in 619, leaving Muhammad and his followers unprotected. Without a powerful patron, over the next few years the Meccan Muslims would face increased persecution. But in 620, Muhammad met with some citizens from Yathrib (later renamed Medina, Arabic for 'the city'), a city 200 miles north of Mecca, who asked him to move there and mediate a feud between the majority Arab and minority Jewish factions. Muhammad initially refused the offer, but persecutions of his followers in Mecca and the conversion of scores of Arabs to Islam in Medina finally convinced Muhammad to leave Mecca in 622. Under the cover of darkness, Muhammad narrowly escaped the grasp of Quraysh agents sent to arrest him.

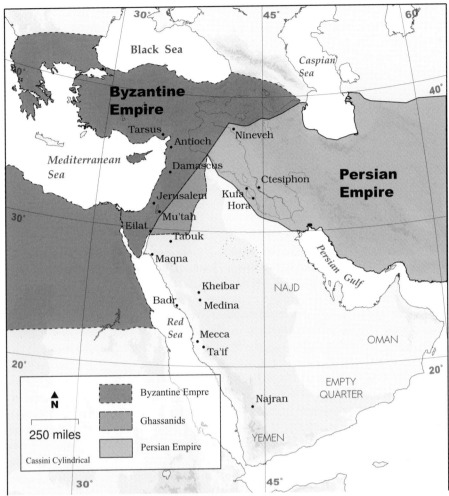

Arabia and South-west Asia at the time of Muhammad, c. 600 CE.

Muhammad's journey to Medina in 622 is known as the *Hegira* (Arabic for 'departure') and represents year one of the Islamic calendar. While in Medina, Muhammad converted Arabs from both the city and the surrounding Bedouin tribes, forming the first Muslim community or *ummah*. The Muslim *ummah* would evolve into a kind of super-tribe, based not on descent but on commitment to the new religion.[2] A charismatic man, Muhammad soon became a popular religious, political and military leader in the vein of a Bedouin chieftain or tribal *sheik*, so popular, that he was unable to support his followers in the limited arable land surrounding Medina, turning instead to raiding Meccan caravans.[3] In late 623, Muhammad began sending out larger raiding parties, but their attacks were mostly unsuccessful, apparently because a spy in the Medina camp alerted the caravans of the Muslim raiders. In January 624, he tried a new tactic. To ensure operational security, Muhammad sent out a small raiding party of twelve men with sealed orders to attack a small caravan travelling from Yemen to Mecca.[4] The men joined the caravan disguised as pilgrims, but attacked the procession during a holy month of Rejab where safe passage was guaranteed.[5] In Mecca, Muhammad was criticized for violating the truce and tensions intensified between the Muslims and Meccans. This did not stop Muhammad from continuing to raid Meccan caravans, a proclivity the Quraysh tribe used to spring a trap for him. The leading Quraysh merchant, Abu Safyan, led the richest caravan of the year from Yemen towards Mecca hoping to lure Muhammad into a decisive battle. Muhammad took the bait and in March 624 left Medina at the head of a small poorly equipped infantry army of some 314 men (the column contained only seventy camels and two horses) in search of the caravan.[6] When news arrived of the approaching Muslims, Abu Safyan requested reinforcements from Mecca to supplement his forty guards, and between 900 and 1,000 men responded under the command of Abu Jahl.[7] This army was better armed and armoured (600 of the Meccan infantry wore chainmail) and included 700 camels and 100 horses.[8] Scouting the location of the Muslim forces personally, Abu Safyan diverted his rich caravan away from the raiders and returned safely to Mecca. He then sent word to Abu Jahl of his homecoming, and when word of their master's safe arrival reached the army, about three clans or 300 of the 900 to 1,000 Meccans left the field and returned home (sources indicate that these clans refused to fight against their Muslim relatives in Muhammad's army).[9] Believing he still had the superior army, Abu Jahl decided to confront Muhammad with his reduced forces and marched twenty-five miles south-west of Mecca to the oasis and wells of Badr where the Muslims were waiting to ambush them.

Islam's First Battles: Badr, Uhud and the Ditch

Muhammad prepared the battlefield, taking the high ground on the back edge of a field of sand dunes. He seized most of the wells, stopping up the remaining wells so his thirsty enemy could not access water after their long trip from Mecca. Muhammad also picked a site where his men would be facing west and to the south, forcing the Meccans to face east. Since Bedouin warfare usually took place in the morning before the heat of the day made battle difficult, the Meccans would fight at a disadvantage with the morning sun in their eyes.[10] Abu Jahl's army moved through the southern pass and deployed across the plain to Muhammad's front, behind the sealed wells, encamping in desert sand.

In the hours before dawn on 15 March 624, the smaller Muslim and larger Meccan armies prepared for battle. According to Arabic custom, troops were organized under their own banners and commanded by their own clan chiefs. Because troops were not dressed in distinguishing uniforms or equipment, watchwords were used to determine friend or foe on the battlefield.[11] Wealthier Arabic warriors wore chainmail (*dir* in Arabic), while poorer fighters wore leather or felt padded armour or no armour at all. Both carried small round leather shields. Sometimes helmets were worn (*bayda*). Offensively, warriors preferred long straight hilted swords (*sayf*), used in either slashing or thrusting attacks. Swords were carried on baldrics or straps around the shoulder or waist in the early Roman fashion. Both thrusting spears (*rumh*) and iron maces (*amud*) were also used as shock weapons. For distance warfare, Arab warriors utilized throwing spears or javelins (*harba*) as well as bows (*qaws*). In fact, archery formed an important part of early Islamic warfare.[12] Two kinds of bows were probably present at the battle of Badr – the light Arab bow and the heavier and more effective

Persian bow. Early Islamic archers before the ninth century mostly fought on foot as light infantry, but from the ninth century on mounted archery became the backbone of the Muslim army, mostly due the influence of Central Asian military practices on Islamic warfare.[13] Before Central Asian cavalry transformed Islamic mounted warfare, Muslim Arabic cavalry utilized light lances and would float on the flanks of enemy infantry formations and exploit any tears or ride down fleeing infantry.[14]

At dawn, the Meccans left their encampment just inside the southern pass and marched forwards, deploying in front of the Muslim ranks. From his seat on a hill under a tent overlooking the battlefield, Muhammad ordered his men not to leave their defensive position. True to Arabic custom, once the Meccans had formed their ranks, three of their best warriors stepped forward and issued challenges for individual combat to the Muslims. Three Muslims from Medina answered the call, but because the Meccans were Quraysh, they refused to fight the warriors from Medina, stating 'Send forth against us our peers of our own tribe.'[15] Muhammad then sent out three Muslim converts from the Quraysh tribe, one of which was his cousin and son-in-law, Ali, a man destined to be one of his successors and the architect of the later Sunni-Shia split, and another his uncle Hazma, an experienced warrior. The three Muslim champions quickly killed the Meccans (although one of the Muslim champions later died from his wounds).[16]

The sources do not tell us who started the main engagement of the battle of Badr. We can assume that the Meccans' morale was suffering. Weak from lack of water and staring into the rising morning sun, the Meccans had just witnessed the death of three of their finest warriors and were now facing an enemy in a superior tactical position. The Meccan commander may have wanted to seize the initiative and attack before the heat of the day took its toll, or perhaps Muhammad ordered his warriors forward, seeing a weakness in his enemy. The sources do tell us that battle raged back and forth for some time (the texts are silent on precisely how long). According to the eighth century Muslim historian Ibn Ishaq, in a lull in the battle, Muhammad left his tent on the hill and addressed his troops directly, stating:

> By God in whose hands is the soul of Muhammad, no man will be slain this day fighting against them with steadfast courage, advancing, not retreating, but God will cause him to enter Paradise.[17]

Muhammad's promise of eternal salvation in heaven for those Muslim troops killed in battle was new to Arabic theology, and may have been the motivator for the outnumbered Muslims to rally and defeat the Meccans. After the speech, Muhammad reached down, picked up some pebbles and threw them at the Meccans, then ordered his men to attack. Tradition maintains (although the original texts do not support this) that a divine wind came up and blew dry sand in the faces of the Meccans.[18] The ferocity of the Muslim attack broke the spirit of the Meccans, who turned and ran. Meccan casualties are placed at seventy dead and another seventy taken prisoner, a loss of 20 per cent of the total force. Muslim casualties were fourteen dead and an unknown number of wounded.[19]

What makes the battle of Badr stand out in the annals of Arabic warfare is how the Muslims treated their prisoners after the battle ended. Bedouin warfare was traditionally

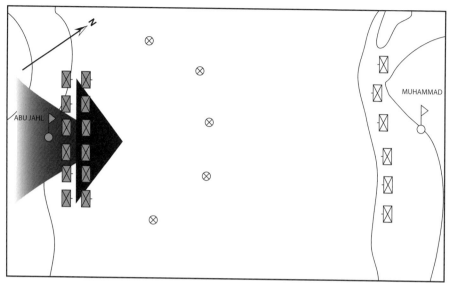

Map 2.1.1. The Battle of Badr, 624 CE. Phase I: Muhammad deploys his Muslim army on a rise overlooking a field of sand dunes, dotted with wells that his troops have blocked up. Abu Jahl's Meccan forces move up through a southern pass and form up opposite Muhammad's army. They make camp in the desert sand with the rising sun in their eyes.

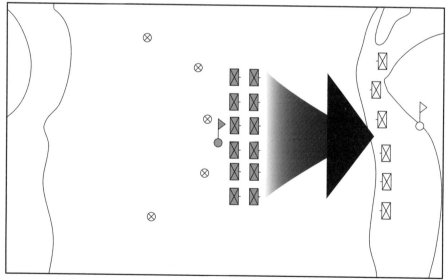

Map 2.1.2. The Battle of Badr, 624 CE. Phase II: Three Meccan warriors issue a challenge to the Muslims to engage in individual combat. The Meccans are swiftly killed. The lack of water and glaring sun goad the Meccans into motion and they march towards the high ground occupied by Muhammad's dug-in defenders.

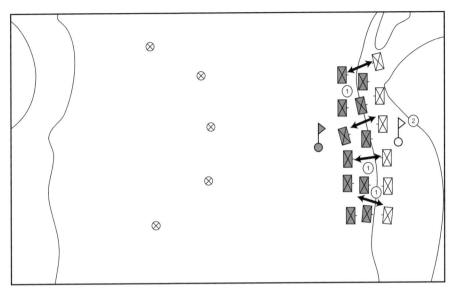

Map 2.1.3. The Battle of Badr, 624 CE. Phase III: The battle rages back and forth (1), the Muslims holding fast against their numerically superior foe. During a lull in the action, Muhammad leaves his tent (2) and addresses his soldiers, promising eternal salvation to those killed in battle.

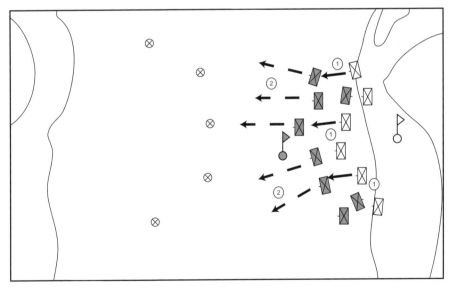

Map 2.1.4. The Battle of Badr, 624 CE. Phase IV: Muhammad's exhortations hearten his men. The Muslims rally and charge the enemy formations (1). Already weary and thirsty, the sudden shock of the Muslim attack shatters the Meccans' spirit and they break and flee from the field (2). The captured Meccans, including Abu Jahl, are beheaded by the victorious Muslims, a marked change in traditional Arab warfare.

characterized by mercy towards all who were captured, with prominent members ransomed back to their clans. After Badr, Muslims beheaded the vanquished, despite many of the prisoners being members of their own tribe, clan and family members. Even the Meccan commander, Abu Jahl, was not offered mercy.[20] In the words of one modern authority, 'Muhammad had brought a new cruelty and lethality to Arab warfare.'[21]

Muhammad's victory at Badr over a military force twice the size of his own illustrated his acumen as a battlefield commander. Muhammad had no military training prior to commanding an army in the field and as an orphan he did not have the opportunity to learn Arabic martial arts from his Bedouin father, the normal way of learning military skills in this period. Muhammad 'became an excellent field commander and tactician and an even more astute politician and military strategist.'[22] Like Philip II of Macedon, Scipio Africanus and Julius Caesar before him, Muhammad also practised removed command, selecting a strong defensive position, appointing his tactical commanders, and not participating in the combat himself.[23]

In the months after the victory at Badr, Muhammad blockaded the caravan route between Mecca and the Levant, raiding pagan tribes and forcing the Quraysh caravans to take alternative routes. Believing the Muslim blockade was now a threat to their livelihood and economic survival, the Meccan leadership selected the experienced commander Abu Safyan to raise an army and destroy Muhammad and his Muslim insurgents once and for all. By late January 625, Abu Safyan had assembled an army of 3,000 men (with 700 Meccan warriors wearing chainmail) and 200 horses, consisting of loyal Quraysh troops, Bedouin client tribes, and what the sources call 'black troops' who were probably Abyssinian mercenaries.[24] After a twelve-day march from Mecca to Medina, Abu Safyan encamped west of the city at a place known as the Two Springs on an open plain at the foot of Mount Uhud. Dispatching scouts to keep an eye on the encamped Meccan army, Muhammad convened a war council and called for a general mobilization. By the beginning of March 625 about 1,000 men reported to defend Medina, but only one hundred of them had armour.[25]

Despite pleas from his lieutenant, Abdullah ibn Ubay, to draw the Meccans into the city in house-to-house warfare, Muhammad sent his army into the field to face a large Meccan host again just outside of Medina at the battle of Uhud. In protest, Ubay withdrew his contingent of troops from the Muslim army, reducing Muhammad's force by some 300 men or one-third of the total defenders.[26] The loss of these veterans placed Muhammad's army in a precarious position. Outnumbered now by more than four-to-one in infantry (3,000 Meccans and allies to 700 Muslims) and again without a cavalry contingent, Muhammad was staking both his life and the very existence of his new Islamic religion on a battlefield engagement against a capable and numerically superior foe.

Like the battle of Badr a year before, Muhammad did prepare the battlefield, posting fifty infantry archers on the Ainain Hill (later called the 'Hill of Arrows' in Muslim sources) to protect his left flank. Ibn Ishaq tells us that Muhammad instructed their commander, Abdullah bin Jubayr, to:

> Keep the cavalry away from us with your arrows and let them not come on us from the rear whether the battle goes in favour or against us; and keep your place so that we cannot be got at from your direction.[27]

Believing his left flank was secured by the archers on Ainain Hill, Muhammad reviewed his troops from one of the few horses available to the Muslims and moved them forwards and into position on the battlefield across from the Meccan infantry, probably late in the morning on a Friday sometime in March. As was the custom in Arabic warfare, a Meccan veteran stepped forwards and challenged the Muslims to send out a champion to meet him in individual combat. One of the three champions from Badr, Muhammad's son-in-law Ali, rushed out of the ranks and killed the Meccan warrior with a single slash of his sword. For perhaps the first time in Islamic warfare, the battle cry '*Allahu Akbar*' ('God is great') rose from the Muslim ranks. The Meccan warrior's brother jumped out to attack Ali, but he was struck down by the Muslim veteran Hazma, another of the champions from Badr and Muhammad's uncle. Three more Meccans stepped forth and challenged Hazma and all three were killed. Emboldened by the actions of their champions, the Muslim army surged forward and engaged the Meccan line 'until the battle grew hot'.[28]

The intensity of the Muslim offensive succeeded in breaking the Meccan line at several points, allowing Muslim warriors to both penetrate and isolate groups of enemy warriors and kill them. The Meccan line began to falter and retreat turned into rout, allowing some of the Muslims to cut completely through the Meccan line and attack the enemy's rear, causing a complete collapse of the Meccan defence.[29] Unfortunately, the Muslims did not have a contingent of cavalry to complete the victory by picking off the scattered Meccan troops in full retreat. Seemingly with victory in their grasp, many of the Muslim infantry broke off pursuit and began to

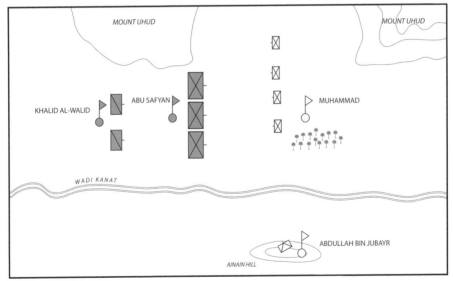

Map 2.2.1. The Battle of Uhud, 625 CE. Phase I: Muhammad deploys his outnumbered forces opposite the advancing Meccan army, covering his left flank with a fifty-man formation of archers under the command of Abdullah bin Jubayr on top of Ainain Hill, just across a shallow wadi and well within archery range of Muhammad's line. Abu Safyan's Meccan army approaches the Muslim positions late in the afternoon, trailed by Khalid al-Walid's cavalry reserve.

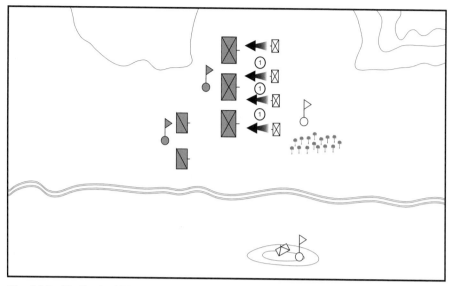

Map 2.2.2. The Battle of Uhud, 625 CE. Phase II: Having drawn near, the customary fighting between opposing champions takes place, in which the Meccans are handily defeated by their Muslim opponents. Muhammad's men, their confidence boosted by their champions' triumph, surge forward towards the Meccan lines (1).

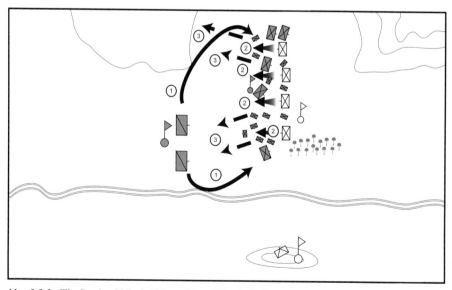

Map 2.2.3. The Battle of Uhud, 625 CE. Phase III: As the battle rages, the Meccan cavalry fans out to hover on the Muslim flanks (1). The ferocity of the Muslim assault shatters their opponents' lines in several places (2). As the Muslims isolate and destroy pockets of resistance, the Meccan infantry begins to break and rout (3).

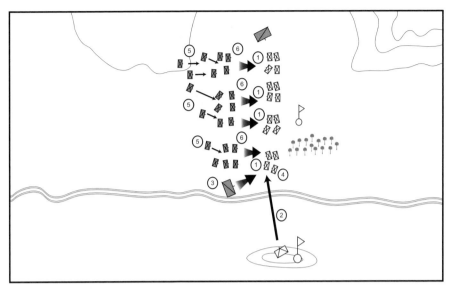

Map 2.2.4. The Battle of Uhud, 625 CE. Phase IV: The Muslims stop to loot the Meccan camp (1) and are joined by the archers on Ainain Hill (2). Khalid al-Walid orders his cavalry to charge into the resulting gap on the left flank (3) and begin to attack the looters (4). As the Muslims turn to face the horsemen, the Meccan infantry use the respite to reform (5) and advance once again (6).

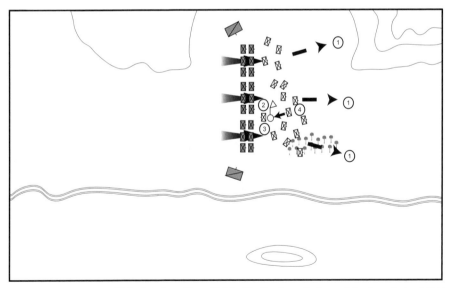

Map 2.2.5. The Battle of Uhud, 625 CE. Phase V: The Muslims lose cohesion and flee from the battlefield (1). Muhammad falls from several wounds (2), but his bodyguard stands fast by his side (3). A band of Muslims comes to the beleaguered group's relief (4), driving off the attackers. The Meccans' attack slows as they stop to celebrate their victory, giving Muhammad and his officers time to escape. They watch from a nearby glen as the victors put the wounded and captive Muslims to the sword in retribution for their defeat at Badr the previous year.

plunder the Meccan camp. It was at this moment that the tide turned against the Muslims.

The Meccan general, Abu Safyan, kept his 200 cavalry in reserve under the command of Khalid al-Walid. In typical fashion, the Arabic horse hovered on the Muslim flanks and waited to exploit any tears in the formation. The Meccan cavalry would have certainly been wary of the Muslim archers perched on the Hill of Arrows. But when the Muslim infantry broke ranks and began to plunder the Meccan camp, many of the Muslim archers left their post to join in the sack. Al-Walid rallied his cavalry and led a charge through the now unprotected gap and turned the Muslim's left flank. This action forced the Muslims to quit sacking the enemy camp and twist to face the attacking Meccan cavalry, which in turn allowed the fleeing Meccan infantry enough breathing room to stop their rout and reform and return to the battlefield. Attacked now by both Meccan infantry and cavalry, the Muslim infantry began to lose cohesion and flee.[30] The battle had turned quickly in favour of the Meccans.

Meanwhile, Muhammad, protected by forty bodyguards, was now surrounded by Meccan warriors. In the chaos of combat, Muhammad was struck in the face by a sling stone, shattering one of his teeth and perhaps pushing the cheek guard of his helmet deep into his face. The blow knocked him off his feet. He was struck again in the head by a sword stroke, knocking his helmet over his eyes. Tradition maintains that all of the Muslim bodyguard were killed in defence of their Prophet, save one – the warrior Zayad – who was disabled, before a relief force of Muslims returned and drove off the enemy. Interestingly, the Meccans may not have been aware they were even attacking Muhammad, since he had switched armour with his standard-bearer earlier in the day to disguise himself. The death of that same standard-bearer about this same time caused a rumour to spread through the ranks of the Meccans, who broke off their attacks to celebrate, giving Muhammad and his officers the opportunity to escape and hide in a nearby glen.[31] From this vantage point, Muhammad watched as Meccan troops murdered and mutilated wounded and captured Muslims as blood-feud retribution for what took place at Badr a year before. Among the notable dead was the champion Hamza, who was killed by a javelin from a hired slave-assassin for striking down one of the Quraysh champions at Badr and his body mutilated, 'his belly ripped up and his liver missing, and his nose and ears cut off.'[32] In all, around seventy Muslims and twenty Meccans were killed at Uhud, high casualties by Arabic standards.[33]

The Muslim defeat at the battle of Uhud opened the road to Medina, but Abu Safyan did not follow up on his victory and invest the city. Instead, he marched home, allowing Muhammad to rebuild his forces and fight again, using Medina once again as his base of operations. Why Abu Safyan did not hunt down Muhammad and his remaining forces that day remains a point of speculation, although the answer probably lies in the code of Arabic chivalry. To kill the Muslim leader after the battle was concluded would have been dishonourable. To Abu Safyan, war was sport and honour was essential to its practice.[34]

Over the next year, Muhammad consolidated his position in Mecca both by conducting assassinations and raids against those Bedouin tribes allied with Mecca and through adroit negotiations with other regional Arab tribes to secure alliances or neutrality. Muhammad's strategy was so successful that he was able to shut down both the northern and eastern caravan routes used by the Meccans, disrupting their trade and income to the point where another battle was inevitable. Successful raiding also attracted more converts to Islam, allowing Muhammad to replenish his losses and reputation from the defeat at Uhud.[35]

The next battle between Muhammad and his Muslim army and Abu Safyan and his Meccan forces took place in March 627 outside of Medina at the battle of the Ditch (sometimes known as the battle of the Trench) because of a long defensive work constructed by Muhammad to protect the northern approaches to the city. In reality, this battle was actually a siege. A month earlier, Abu Safyan returned to Medina at the head of a very large army consisting of 10,000 men made up of 4,000 Meccans, with the remainder coming from local Bedouin tribes, many with personal grudges against Muhammad for his actions over the past year. The sources also indicate that 'black mercenaries' from Abyssinia were also present, although their precise numbers are unknown.[36] Once again, Khalid al-Walid commanded the 200 Meccan horse, but this cavalry contingent was joined by another 400 Bedouin cavalry under their own commanders. To face this sizeable force, Muhammad pulled together 3,000 infantry and thirty-five cavalry, all under his unified command, a testimony to his ability to inspire loyalty and rebuild his forces after the loss at Uhud.[37]

Muhammad prepared the battlefield against his numerically superior foe by using the topography of the area around Medina to his advantage. Here, Medina sat in a plain with very few obstructions, surrounded on the east, west and south by old lava fields, forming a sort of peninsula jutting to the south. These lava fields were difficult to fight in, so approaching Medina from these directions was impractical, although not impossible. The distance across the widest part of this peninsula was some four miles. Muhammad ordered the construction of a hook-shaped ditch across this gap that was at least three and a half miles long, with the step of the hook anchored at a Muslim fortification called Twin Forts in the north-east and the end of the hook dug into the base of Mount Sal just west of Medina. Modern estimates place the ditch at sixteen feet wide and around six feet deep, making it a formidable obstacle to Meccan cavalry and infantry. The ditch took nearly four months to construct, with Muhammad conscripting the people of Medina for the task.[38]

In spite of being outnumbered by more than three-to-one by the Meccan forces, Muhammad and his Muslim army were in a strong defensive position. His army had sufficient food and water and had the advantage of making a stand behind a defensive barrier where interior lines could be used to move men and material against any breaches. Muhammad also pursued a scorched-earth strategy, ordering the fields around Medina to be stripped of their produce, forcing the Meccans to support themselves and their horses and camels with the fodder they brought with them.[39]

Abu Safyan ordered his army to make two camps on the north plain of Medina. Over the next month, the Meccans probed the Muslim defences along the ditch, but it seems that no large-scale offensives were launched by either infantry or cavalry. There was also evidence of archery duals. Curiously, at no time were simultaneous attacks launched along the length of the ditch, even with the obvious advantage in manpower available to the Meccans. The ditch was serving its military purpose for Muhammad and his Muslim defenders as well as highlighting the unsophisticated nature of Arab military doctrine. Despite the ditch's impressive dimensions, this obstacle would not have been an issue for contemporary Byzantine or Sassanian Persian armies and their

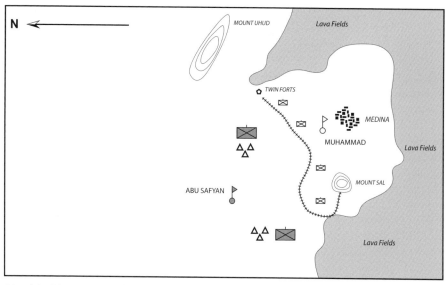

Map 2.3. The Battle of the Ditch, 627 CE. *Well supplied with food and water and protected by a sixteen-foot wide by six-foot deep ditch, Muhammad's outnumbered forces in Medina keep Abu Safyan's army at bay in a siege lasting over a month. Inexplicably, the Meccans never launch an all-out assault on multiple points of the ditch, a move that might have overwhelmed the Muslim defenders. Suffering from lack of food and water due to Muhammad's scorched-earth preparation of the area, a fierce storm buffets the besiegers and finally breaks their will. Abu Safyan withdraws from the plain outside of Medina.*

capable military commanders and engineers.[40] After four weeks of siege, only three Meccans and five Muslims were dead, despite over 13,000 combatants taking part in the action.[41] Still, lack of food and fodder for the Meccan forces was beginning to take its toll. Horses and camels were dying, and human rations were running low, despite a resupply from an allied Jewish caravan from the city of Kheibar.[42]

Another Jewish tribe, the Beni Qurayzah, was also a factor in the battle of the Ditch. This tribe was native to Medina and was allowed to stay in the southern districts of the city because it had pledged its neutrality to Muhammad. Some of the contemporary sources intimate that Abu Safyan sent his own Jewish negotiator into Medina and tried to raise a fifth column by enticing the Beni Qurayzah to attack Muhammad's forces from the city. The negotiations failed and the Beni Qurayzah remained neutral and were not a factor in the siege, although the Jews were later surrounded in their neighbourhood in Medina and after a twenty-five day siege massacred by Muhammad.[43]

The straw that broke the proverbial camel's back for the Meccan forces was a fierce Arabian storm. Abu Safyan's army was not prepared to stay in the field for a month, and contemporary sources tell us that the Meccans 'had no permanent camps' to shield themselves from the ravages of March weather on the peninsula.[44] Already weak from irregular rations and demoralized by lack of military success, the Meccans and their allies lifted their siege of Medina and returned to their homes and fields to prepare for the spring caravan season.

Muhammad's victory at the battle of the Ditch consolidated his military and political reputation. Although not a decisive engagement militarily, Muhammad had withstood a Meccan army three times the size of his own through the use of an innovative defensive barrier. Over the next two years (628 and 629), Muhammad would use his enhanced standing to either court or intimidate Bedouin tribes close to the city of Mecca. Once again, he used assassination as a political weapon to remove rivals. He also increased Muslim raiding of caravans close to Mecca, striking at the economic heart of the ruling Quraysh tribe.[45] Ultimately, this strategy proved fruitful. On 1 January 630, Muhammad set out from Medina at the head of an army of 3,000 Muslims. As the army marched south towards Mecca, it swelled to perhaps 10,000 men as Bedouin allies joined the column. It is important to note here that Muhammad's gifts of arms and armour to his Islamic troops and Bedouin allies produced a very well-equipped army, with most contingents being fully armed and armoured with helmets, breastplates and back plates.[46] The sources also indicate that the Quraysh leader, Abu Safyan, sent as an ambassador by the Meccans to Muhammad, actually intrigued with the Muslim leader to bring Mecca into Islamic hands.[47]

On 11 January, Muhammad ordered his army to surround and invest Mecca, where resistance was very light. This date is known to Muslims as the *fat'h* or Conquest. He prohibited his followers from sacking the city (a traditional means of payment in medieval warfare), and even took out large loans from Meccan bankers to pay his men and allies.[48] Muhammad then turned to the temple district of Mecca, where he ordered the destruction of false idols, leaving only the images of Abraham, Jesus and the Virgin Mary intact as an illustration of the continuity of lineage from Judaism to Christianity to the new faith of Islam.[49] Later, he ordered the destruction of idols throughout Mecca and Muslim-occupied zones in western Arabia. Many Meccans converted to Islam and the city would become the religious epicentre for the Islamic faith. Medina would remain the political centre until the rise of the Umayyad Caliphate in 661.

The capture and conversion of Mecca was an essential component to Muhammad's strategy. Over the next two years, until his death in 632, Muhammad would consolidate Islamic rule in western Arabia. This was a difficult task. Muhammad still faced armed rebellion from tribes not willing to submit to the Prophet, while many new converts were half-hearted in their allegiance to Islam, brought into the new faith by clan chiefs to accommodate Muhammad or as an opportunity for war treasure. In order to secure authentic conversions, Muhammad instituted the *Surat al-Tawbah*, translated from Arabic as 'The Repentance'. This proclamation declared war on all non-Muslims. Idolaters were given four months' grace, then Muhammad would give Arab non-believers a choice: convert to Islam or die. Christians and Jews in Arabia (and later elsewhere where Muslims ruled) were not included in this proclamation and were not to be harmed.[50] Protected Christians and Jews would later be recognized as *dhimmis* or 'People of the Book' in recognition of their shared origin with Islam as an Abrahamic faith and given a protected status in exchange for paying higher taxes. By issuing the *Surat al-Tawbah* Muhammad was articulating what would later be known as *Dar al-Islam* or 'The House of Islam' and *Dar al-Harb* or 'The House of War'. It is important to emphasize that this strategy of forcing pagan Arabs to convert to Islam under threat of death took place on the Arabian Peninsula during the last years of Muhammad's life.

When Islam exploded out of Arabia in the decades after his passing, Islam would only recognize voluntary acceptance into the faith.

Muhammad also instituted the *zakat*, a yearly tax levied on all Muslims, as a way for his faithful followers to show their allegiance to him. The payment of the *zakat* was a traditional Arab means of showing submission to a chieftain and an efficient way to raise revenue. Those who were taxed and refused payment would be killed.[51] Muhammad's threat of turning all of Arabia into a battlefield worked. Soon, tribal chiefs from as far away as Yemen were seeking audience with Muhammad and converting to the new faith. When Muhammad died in June of 632 he was arguably the most powerful man in Arabia, but he was also a man with many enemies and the success of Islam was not guaranteed.

Rise of the Rashidun Caliphate and the *Riddah* War

When Muhammad died no more than 30 per cent of Arabia had converted to Islam, and some of these converts were backsliding into their old paganism.[52] Muhammad did not name a successor or *caliph* himself, but one was elected by his lieutenants. Abu Bakr (573–634), the Prophet's most trusted and capable advisor, became the first of what Islam refers to as the 'Four Rightly-Guided Caliphs'. These four reigns would witness first the consolidation of Islam in Arabia and then the expansion of the faith into North Africa, the Levant and Persia at the expense of the Byzantine and Sassanian Persian Empires in the period between 632 and 661. Abu Bakr, together with his successors Umar (r.634–644), Uthman (r.644–656), and Ali (r.656–661), are also sometimes referred to as the Rashidun Caliphate.

Although a man of nearly sixty years when he became caliph, Abu Bakr proved to be a shrewd political and military leader. He continued with the conversion of Arab pagans by force, and also declared the *Riddah* or 'War of the Apostates', a roughly one-year campaign (summer of 632 to spring of 633) to bring all of the Arabian Peninsula, both pagan and backsliders, into the *Dar al-Islam*. In fact, the *Riddah*'s main target were those Muslims who had converted to Islam but waivered after the death of the Prophet. From this point forward, Islam strictly prohibited apostasy under punishment of death.

Most of the Muslim armies dispatched from Medina during the *Riddah* were made up of the faithful from Medina, Mecca and Taif and consisted of between 4,000 and 5,000 men, large enough to meet and defeat the smaller disobedient tribes. These conquests fell into a similar pattern. Muslim commanders would use political rivalries among local chieftains to divide and conquer, and promised war treasure to those who converted to Islam and joined the effort. Those tribes who refused to convert were defeated in war and then given the choice of conversion or death.[53] Abu Bakr did create one larger army, under the command of the newly converted Khalid al-Walid (592–642), to deal with the larger and more dangerous Arab tribes of north-east Arabia, specifically the Banu Hanifa.[54] A later tenth century Islamic scholar, Muhammad al-Diyarbakri, wrote of Khalid's success during these campaigns:

> The Arabs began to flock to Khalid out of desire to adopt Islam or from fear of the sword. Some were captured and claimed either that they had come voluntarily to submit to Islam or that they had never apostatized but rather had been stingy with their property and now would willingly pay their dues. Others, who were not

captured, either came to Khalid yielding to Islam or headed to Medina to submit to Abu Bakr.[55]

Khalid al-Walid would later become one of Islam's most celebrated commanders, nicknamed *Sayfullah* or 'the Sword of Allah', spearheading the conquest of both Byzantine Syria and Sassanian Persia. By the spring of 633, the *Riddah* was over and Arabia was firmly under the control of Islam, but the peninsula was also an armed camp full of Muslim warriors seeking glory and booty, and Abu Bakr understood that the only way to keep the fragile coalition together was to provide those opportunities to his warriors.

The military organization of the Islamic armies went through a transformation in the period between the death of Muhammad in 632 and the introduction of Turkish military institutions into Islamic warfare by the Abbasid Caliph al-Mutasim (r.833–842). The armies inherited by Abu Bakr consisted of Bedouin Muslims recruited from the faithful in the Arabian Peninsula and also of adult males without families, flocks or herds.[56] These first troops were well armed with long iron swords,

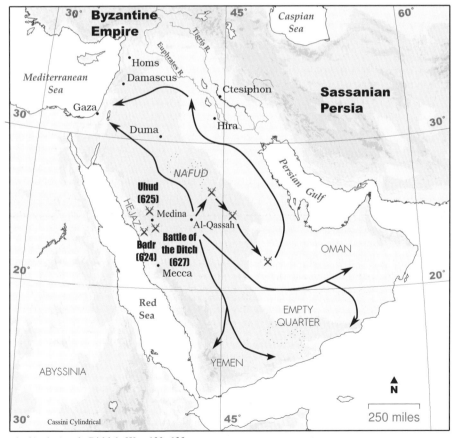

Arabia during the Riddah *War, 632–633.*

maces, javelins and bows, and were protected by felt armour (chainmail if wealthy) and small round leather shields. Bakr's forces fought in close formation, mirroring the infantry tactics of their seventh century Byzantine foe, using archers as skirmishers and to protect their flanks from enemy cavalry attacks.[57] Initially poorly equipped with horses, Islamic cavalry improved when Yemeni Najran in southern Arabia and Yamamah in north-eastern Arabia came under Muslim control after the *Riddah*, providing the caliph's army with highly prized Arabian and heavier Persian horses.[58] Early Islamic armies also made good strategic use of the camel for mounted infantry, bypassing enemy armies by travelling though deserts and then dismounting and fighting defensive battles at the time and place of their own choosing.[59]

Islamic Expansion in Syria and the Challenge of Byzantium and Persia

With the Arabian Peninsula securely under the Islamic banner by 633, Abu Bakr ordered three Muslim armies to converge on Byzantine-held territory in Syria, initiating the great Arab conquests that by 750 CE would carve out the largest contiguous empire the world had ever seen, stretching from Spain to India, and create an Islamic cultural zone that has remained mostly intact ever since. The Muslim conquest of the Levant was assisted by the fluid strategic circumstances in this region in the early seventh century. Muhammad and his successors were well aware of the opportunity this border war created for the expansion of Islam into the Levant, Egypt and Persia.

Abu Bakr placed the Rashidun armies under the command of Khalid al-Walid who invaded the Sassanian province of Mesopotamia in March 633 and campaigned up the Euphrates River Valley, taking this region for Islam by the end of the year. Before he could invest the Sassanian capital of Ctesiphon (just south-east of modern Baghdad), Abu Bakr ordered Khalid to assume command of the Syrian campaign and converge on the strategically important Byzantine city of Bosra in Palestine. In June 634, Khalid defeated the Byzantine and Christian Arab Ghassanid garrison there after a two-day battle and took the city after a one-month siege. Meanwhile, Byzantine forces were concentrating at the fortress city of Ajnadayn (just south of the modern Israeli city of Beit Shemesh) in Palestine. At the end of July, Khalid marched his army of 15,000 to 18,000 men to Ajnadayn and defeated a sizeable Byzantine army there consisting of between 9,000 and 10,000 men in a two-day engagement.[60] The battle was costly for both sides, with more senior Islamic officers dying in this battle than in any other campaign in Syria.[61]

Caliph Abu Bakr died in August, replaced by Umar ibn al-Khattab (r.634–644) who continued the campaign in Syria, directing his Muslim armies north to lay siege to Damascus and taking the city in September 635 after a one-month siege. Over the next eleven months, Muslim and Byzantine armies would spar in the region, building for a decisive confrontation. As the Byzantine host gathered for a counterthrust to retake lost territory, Khalid al-Walid ordered the evacuation of Damascus in early summer 636 and pulled back southwards towards the Jabiya region where there was abundant water and pasture.[62] A clash there in mid-July between the Ghassanids and Muslims forced the latter farther south to a position between Dara'ah and Dayr Ayyub where they could draw a line and use the local topography to their advantage to block the advancing

Byzantines. The Muslims waited there for nearly a month before the decisive battle took place as the Byzantine army made camp north of their line, delaying combat to allow their soldiers to gather intelligence and attempt to subvert the Muslims in typical Byzantine fashion using diplomacy and bribery.[63] These attempts failed and the engagements collectively known as the battle of Yarmuk River took place in a series of clashes over six days in mid-August 636 (15–20 August) along what is now the modern border between Syrian and Jordan, east-south-east of the Sea of Galilee.

Estimates of the size of the Byzantine army at Yarmuk River vary greatly depending on the source. Contemporary sources range from a fantastical 400,000 men down to 100,000 men, while modern sources vary from 150,000 men to 15,000 troops.[64] There may have been tens of thousands of Byzantine and allied troops in the Levant, but most of these troops were likely tied down in garrison roles. The Byzantine army at Yarmuk River probably consisted of around 25,000 soldiers made up mostly of Armenian, Greek, and local allied Christian Arab Ghassanids.[65] Emperor Herakleios placed this force under the supreme command of the Armenian general Vahan.[66] The different contingents would have spoken at least three different languages (Greek, Armenian and Arabic), presenting a problem with command, control and communication.[67] Additionally, the sources point towards considerable friction within the Byzantine ranks before the battle, with some clashes perhaps leading to bloodshed.[68] Meanwhile, as dissent plagued the Byzantine army, the Muslim army was being reinforced from the south by Arabian troops, mostly infantry archers from Yemen, swelling the army to perhaps 20,000 men.[69]

Vahan arrayed his Byzantine army in twenty units in four divisions across from the Muslim positions along a line some twelve miles across between the Allan River to the south and the Roman road to Jabiya to the north. Despite the size of his army, the Byzantine general was unable to cover the entire front.[70] Much of the terrain in this region was flat, sloping gently from north to south with some undulation, ideal for cavalry manoeuvres, but also possessing ditches and brush suitable for infantry. The most significant feature of the battlefield was the existence of two ravines, the Ruqquad and Allan gorges, to the south-west and south of the plain respectively where the two armies deployed. Both had banks 1,000 feet high punctuated with vertical drops between 100 and 200 feet in height.[71] The shallow Wadi Allan (Allan River) flowed north-east to south-west across the middle of the battlefield (there is no evidence it proved an obstacle in combat), finally dipping down a series of waterfalls into its deep gorge to eventually join with the nearby Yarmuk River.

Vahan took personal command of the centre, largely consisting of Armenian troops, while his right was commanded by the Armenian Gargis and included heavy infantry with large shields trained to form a shield wall and anchor the right near where the Allan River begins to dip into the gorge, leaving the left wing and the centre of the army as the manoeuvre units for the Byzantine army.[72] The left wing was commanded by a man who the sources identify by his Byzantine rank of *Buccinator*, who commanded additional Eastern Roman troops. The Ghassanid king Jabala al-Ayham's men consisted mostly of light cavalry (horse and camel). They were stationed along the front to act as scouts and skirmishers and to protect the exposed left flank of the Byzantine army. Other Christian Arab units protected the vital bridge at Ayn Dhakar two and a half miles behind the Byzantine lines.[73]

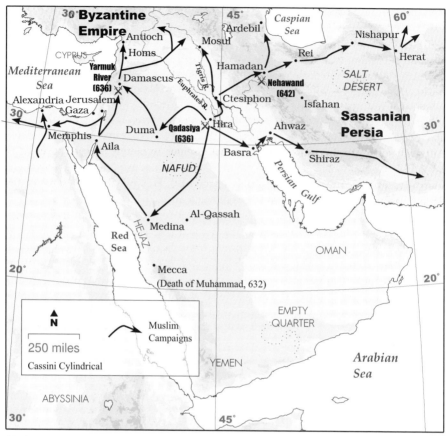

Muslim campaigns during the Rashidun Caliphate, 632–661.

When Umar became caliph in 334, he relieved Khalid al-Walid of command of the Rashidun armies in Syria, giving overall command of the Muslim army to Abu Ubaida ibn al-Jarrah (583–638), an early convert to Islam and a participant at Badr, Uhud and the battle of the Ditch. Abu Ubaida in turn gave operational control of the Muslim forces at Yarmuk River to Khalid. Khalid divided his Muslim army into thirty-six infantry units of between 400 and 450 men, forming four divisions. The Muslim army formed a thin line, only three ranks deep, but without any gaps between divisions. All of the spears available in the army were issued to the front rank to help resist Byzantine cavalry charges. Khalid then separated his cavalry into four divisions, three of equal strength of 1,000 horsemen and one larger consisting of 2,000 horse. He placed one cavalry division on each flank and one in the centre, and then kept the larger cavalry division behind the centre infantry and cavalry divisions as a mobile guard reserve, commanding it personally. Muslim archers, mostly Yemeni, were spread out along the entire front to protect the Muslim infantry formations.[74]

The Battle of Yarmuk River and the Muslim Conquest of Syria

Final negotiations broke down after Vahan met with Khalid al-Walid, offering large sums of money for a Muslim withdrawal. Khalid refused and the next morning, 15 August, the six-day battle of Yarmuk River began.[75] The first day of the battle began in the morning with Byzantine and Muslim champions exchanging blows. At noon, Vahan ordered a third of his infantry forward to test the Muslim defences. Once within bowshot of the Yemeni archers, the Byzantine troops took some casualties until both infantries locked in hand-to-hand combat. Vahan did not reinforce his forward infantry and the fighting continued until sunset with no advantage gained by either side.[76] Although some Muslim sources indicate that a senior Byzantine officer converted to Islam in a parley before the battle, only to die later in the day as a Muslim martyr (some sources identify Gargis), this is probably apocryphal. It is possible that some of the Arab Ghassanid troops defected to the Arab Muslims.[77]

That evening, Vahan convened a war council and decided to attack at dawn on day two (16 August) while the Muslims were conducting morning prayers. However, the night before Khalid al-Walid had set a strong cordon between the two armies, delaying the Christian advance long enough for the Muslims to don their armour and weapons before the main Byzantine force reached their ranks.[78] Marching to the sound of their war drums, Vahan ordered the Byzantines to advance along the entire line, but held the centre back as his wings pushed against their numerically inferior Muslim foe. This strategy worked well as the right Muslim flank gave way, allowing the *Buccinator* and his imperial troops to reach one or more of the Islamic camps. Here, Muslim wives, children and camp followers goaded and shamed their retreating husbands and protectors back into battle. A similar scene unfolded on the Muslim left flank with Gargis and his Armenian troops. In both cases, relief came in the form of the Muslim reserve mobile guard cavalry, sent by Khalid to buttress his failing flanks. At the same time, the Islamic centre counterattacked, pushing the Byzantine centre backwards. Day two ended with both sides returning to their original positions.[79]

On the third day of the battle (17 August) the Byzantine army initiated combat again, this time concentrating on the northern part of the battlefield. Once again, the Muslim left flank gave way to the *Buccinator*'s Eastern Roman troops, followed by the right centre, allowing the Byzantine army to advance to the enemy's tents, and once again the Muslim women forced their men back into the battle. One of the Muslim soldiers confided to his comrades that 'It is easier to face the Romans than our women.'[80] Like the previous day's action, the flank was shored up by Khalid's cavalry reserve, although Muslim casualties were higher this time.[81] Still, three days of Byzantine offensives had not broken the Muslim lines.

The fourth day of the battle of Yarmuk River (18 August) proved to be a tipping point in the battle and the fiercest fighting to date. Believing the Muslim line was weak after two days of Byzantine penetration, Vahan repeated this attack, sending the *Buccinator*'s Eastern Roman troops, supported this time by King Jabala's Ghassanid cavalry, against the Muslim centre right division, driving back the Muslim soldiers. Fearing a general attack along the entire front (an event he did not have the manpower to repulse), Khalid al-Walid ordered the Muslim centre left and left divisions to counterattack the Byzantine centre and right, stalling the Christian advance. At this moment, the supporting Byzantine cavalry became separated from its infantry, a dangerous

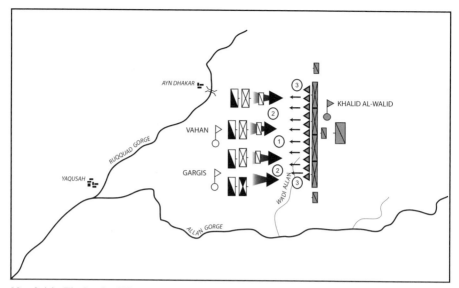

Map 2.4.1. *The Battle of Yarmuk River, 636 CE. Phase I: After a duel between Byzantine and Muslim champions (1), Vahan orders about a third of his infantry forward (2) to test Khalid al-Walid's defences. The Byzantines take some casualties to archery fire as they draw near (3) and engage the Muslim infantry in close combat. Vahan does not reinforce his initial advance and withdraws his troops at sunset. No gains are made by either side.*

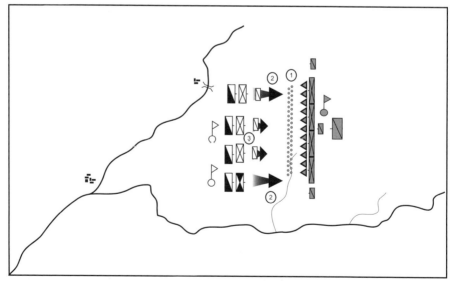

Map 2.4.2. *The Battle of Yarmuk River, 636 CE. Phase II: Early the next morning Vahan orders his army forward, hoping to catch the Muslims at prayer, but Khalid al-Walid had prepared for such an event by establishing a strong cordon between the armies (1) allowing his forces to prepare for battle. The Byzantine wings are pushed ahead (2) with the centre divisions held back (3).*

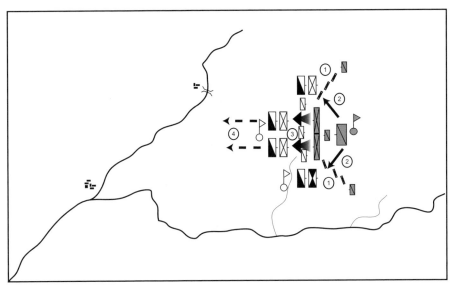

Map 2.4.3. The Battle of Yarmuk River, 636 CE. Phase III: The Byzantine wings press the Muslims back through their camps (1), but the wives and other camp inhabitants shame the men back to their duty. The rallied infantry is reinforced by cavalry from the general reserve (2) and the flanks hold. Meanwhile, Khalid al-Walid orders a counterattack against the Byzantine centre (3), which is pushed back (4). The second day ends with the armies back at their start points.

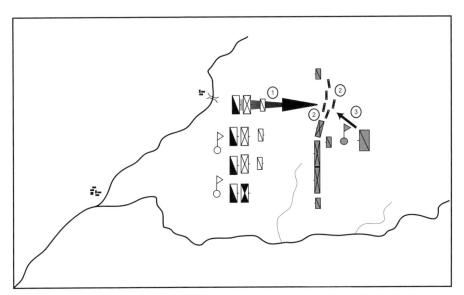

Map 2.4.4. The Battle of Yarmuk River, 636 CE. Phase IV: On the third day of battle, the Byzantines attack with their left (1). The Muslim right flank begins to crumble, and the right-centre begins to give way as well (2). As on the second day, the men are shamed into returning to the fray by the camp's inhabitants and the Muslim cavalry reserve assists (3) in restoring the status quo.

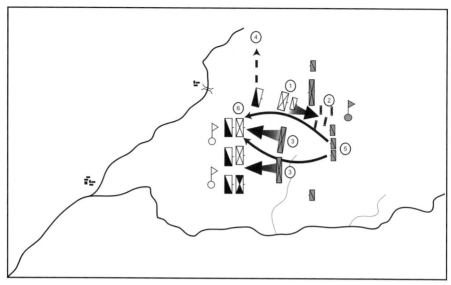

Map 2.4.5. The Battle of Yarmuk River, 636 CE. Phase V: Vahan opens the action on day four with a thrust from his left (1) against the Muslims' right-centre (2). Khalid counterattacks the Byzantine centre and left (3), slowing the Christians' attack. A gap opens between the Byzantine attackers and their supporting cavalry and the horsemen break and flee north (4). Khalid divides his cavalry reserve in two (5) and orders them to strike the Byzantines' left-centre formation (6) as the Muslim infantry assaults their front.

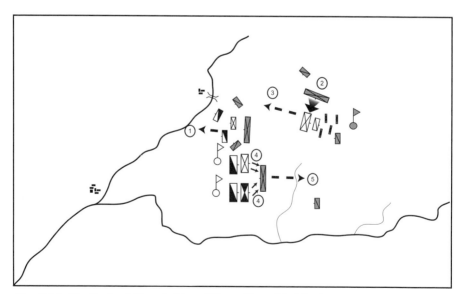

Map 2.4.6. The Battle of Yarmuk River, 636 CE. Phase VI: The three-pronged assault forces the Byzantines back (1). Meanwhile, the Muslim formations on the right turn to strike the exposed left flank of the initial Byzantine assault (2), causing them to break off the attack and withdraw (3). Vahan sees that the Muslim infantry attacking his right is without cavalry support and launches an intense archery attack against them (4), driving them back to their camp (5). The Byzantines attempt to follow up, but are driven back as the Muslim women once more rally the troops and aid them in defending their camp.

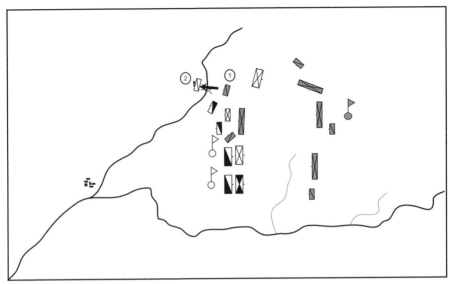

Map 2.4.7. *The Battle of Yarmuk River, 636 CE. Phase VII: Adding to the Byzantines' day four setbacks, a small Muslim cavalry detachment (1) pursues a largely Ghassanid auxiliary cavalry unit across the strategic Ayn Dhakar bridge. The Ghassanid unit dissolves, some blending into the local populace while others defect to the Muslim side. The Byzantines' main avenue for possible retreat is now severed.*

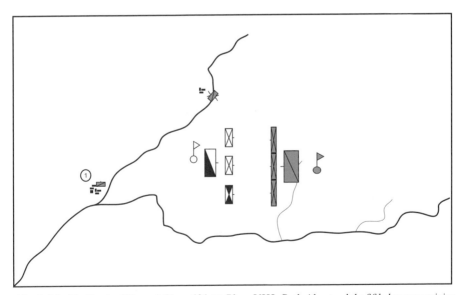

Map 2.4.8. *The Battle of Yarmuk River, 636 CE. Phase VIII: Both sides spend the fifth day reorganizing their remaining forces. Vahan and Khalid both consolidate their cavalry into one large force. Strategically, the Byzantines suffer another setback as their base at Yaqusah eleven miles to the west falls to a Muslim force (1).*

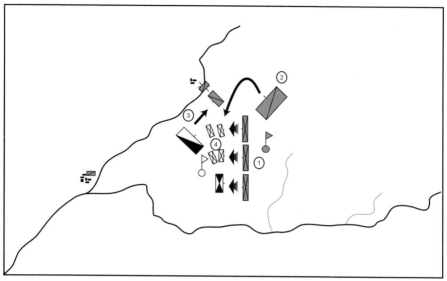

Map 2.4.9. *The Battle of Yarmuk River, 636* CE. *Phase IX: The sixth day opens with a contest between Byzantine and Muslim champions – the Armenian general Gargis against the Muslims' overall commander, Ubaida. Ubaida defeats Gargis and Khalid orders an overall Muslim advance (1) to pin the enemy's infantry while Khalid leads the Muslim cavalry in an attack against the Byzantine flank (2). While some of the Muslims block an attempted counterattack (3), Vahan's Eastern Roman front line, beset from front and flank, is disrupted and pushed back into the Armenian divisions (4).*

Map 2.4.10. *The Battle of Yarmuk River, 636* CE. *Phase X: The Muslim centre presses ahead through gaps in the fracturing Byzantine lines (1). Khalid wheels the Muslim cavalry (2) against the Byzantine horse, which are scattered and pushed from the field (3). Bereft of cavalry support, many of the Byzantine infantry attempt to surrender, but are cut down by the victors. Vahan is killed as are many of his men, some falling to their deaths in the steep ravines hemming the battlefield while others are hunted down by pursuing Muslim forces.*

predicament in combined-arms warfare.[82] Unable to return to the safety of its infantry, the Byzantine horse fled north. Seeing this opportunity, Khalid divided his mobile guard into two divisions and attacked the flanks of the Byzantine left centre, while the infantry of the Muslim centre right attacked from the front. Under this ferocious three-pronged flanking movement, the mauled Eastern Romans and Ghassanids fell back. Meanwhile, the Muslim right wing renewed its offence with its infantry attacking from the front and the cavalry reserve attacking the northern flank of the Byzantine left wing. As the Byzantine left centre collapsed under Khalid's three-pronged attack, the Byzantine left wing, now exposed on its southern flank, fell back as well.[83]

While Khalid al-Walid and his mobile guard were dealing with the Armenian front throughout the afternoon, the situation on the southern end of the Islamic line was deteriorating. Vahan, seeing that the Muslim infantry on his right were missing adequate cavalry support, ordered his archers into the fight, subjecting Muslim infantry to intense missile attacks. Perhaps some of these archers were mounted as there was little Muslim cavalry to repel this type of attack.[84] The eighth century Muslim historian Umar al-Waqidi wrote that 'the arrows fell like hailstones and blocked the light of the sun.'[85] Al-Waqidi recounts that some 700 Muslim soldiers lost an eye to Byzantine arrows, and as a result the fourth day at Yarmuk River became known in Islamic history as the 'Day of Lost Eyes'.[86] As the Muslim men fell back towards their camps, their women rushed forward to join the battle, invigorating the Muslim ranks and forcing the Eastern Romans backward toward their own lines. Although day four proved to be the worst day for Muslim casualties, the most crippling loses were born by the Byzantine centre divisions made up of the Armenians and their Ghassanid allies.[87]

To make matters worse for the Byzantines, in late afternoon a small Muslim cavalry contingent under the command of Khalid's lieutenant Zarrar followed the retreating Byzantine horsemen west two and a half miles towards the town of Ayn Dhakar. Most of these Byzantine horsemen were Ghassanid auxiliaries, who began to evaporate into the local Arab populations, while others defected to the Muslims. Ghassanid control over Ayn Dhakar was severely weakened and Zarrar was able to easily capture the strategically important bridge there, cutting off the Byzantine army from its main base at Yaqusah. Should the Byzantines need to retreat, their only options were to scramble over the rough terrain of the Allan or Ruqquad gorges or breakout northwards across barren territory now controlled by the Muslims.[88]

On the morning of the fifth day of the battle (19 August) both armies arrayed for combat, but the Byzantine army did not press forward. Still reeling from the casualties taken the day before and recognizing his army's precarious strategic position, Vahan sent an envoy to the Muslims and tried to negotiate once again with Khalid al-Walid either the withdrawal of the Muslim forces or safe passage for his own. Khalid refused the Byzantine overture, and prepared his own army for the next engagement, reorganizing his cavalry elements into one large division with his mobile guard acting as the core. Across the field, Vahan did the same with his cavalry units.[89] No major action took place on the fifth day of the campaign.

Another event of strategic importance took place during one of the nights late in the battle (evening of the fourth or fifth day of the battle), although the exact date is lost to history. That evening, the Muslims stormed the main Byzantine camp of Yaqusah, some eleven miles west of Ayn Dhakar on the road to the Sea of Galilee, seizing the base from their Eastern Roman defenders. If this event took place on the evening of the fourth day of the battle, it would have given Vahan more incentive to negotiate during the fifth day, since he had now lost his principal base in the region.

The sixth and final day (20 August) of the battle of Yarmuk River began like the first day, with champions riding out between the two armies. As the morning sun rose over the plain, the Armenian general Gargis rode out in front of the Muslim ranks and offered a direct challenge, asking for 'none but the commander of the Arabs', Abu Ubaida.[90] Gargis, a large and skilled soldier, had approached with the mission of killing the Muslim commanding general in hope of breaking the spirit of the Islamic forces and raising those of his own side. Although the Muslim rank and file would have preferred the experienced Khalid al-Walid to respond to the challenge, Ubaida donned his armour, and giving the army standard to Khalid, shouted, 'If I do not return you shall command the army until the caliph decides the matter.'[91] He then galloped off to meet the Byzantine champion. The two generals duelled on horseback, circling one another as the Muslim and Byzantine ranks watched flashes of steel from the centre of the field. After a few minutes, Gargis broke off and cantered back towards the Byzantine line as the Muslim troops shouted in victory. Calmly, Ubaida urged his mount forward to slowly overtake the retreating Gargis, who turned swiftly and raised his sword against the pursuing Muslim general, his feigned withdrawal a success. But Gargis was struck at the base of the neck by Ubaida, who watched the large Armenian fall from his horse to the ground, then turned and rode back to the Muslim front.[92] Having witnessed the triumph of his commanding general from the front ranks, Khalid galloped off to take control of the cavalry division. He gave the order for a general attack and the entire Muslim army surged forward.[93]

The Muslim centre and left engaged the Byzantines divisions on their front, but did not press their attack, probably in a move designed to hold these troops in position as the consolidated Muslim cavalry division swung to the north, galloping around the flank of the *Buccinator*'s imperial left division. Khalid broke off a cavalry unit to delay the relieving Byzantine cavalry as he turned the remainder of his horsemen into the flank of the Byzantine left wing in a magnificent 'hammer and anvil' manoeuvre.[94] Caught between the charging Muslim horsemen and the now advancing Muslim front line, the Eastern Romans attempted to repel the attack from their front and flank, but without support from their own cavalry, these foot soldiers fell back into the centre division of the Byzantine lines. These mostly Armenian troops, commanded by Vahan, did their best to receive the retreating Eastern Romans, but they too, fell into disorder. The Muslim centre pressed forward, exploiting the gaps forming in the now jumbled Armenian-Greek lines. Khalid now wheeled his large cavalry division again and engaged the imperial horsemen directly, pushing them from the battlefield. With their Byzantine cavalry now missing in action, the remaining Christian infantry lost desire and attempted to surrender, casting down their arms and sitting waiting to be captured, but most of the Muslim victors offered no quarter.[95] Vahan was probably killed on the battlefield or as he fled.[96] Others tried to escape by climbing steep slopes and cliffs in the area, falling to their deaths. Most of the Byzantine troops who escaped probably fled along the valley or scampered up the southern slopes into Jordan.[97] Contemporary accounts describe Muslim units chasing and cutting down Byzantine troops as far as Damascus and Emesa (modern Hims) to the north in modern Syria.[98]

Muslim casualties were light compared with those taken by the Byzantines, but exact numbers are impossible to know because of the inflated total numbers of troops before the battle provided by both Muslim and Byzantine primary sources. What is certain is the relentlessness and ruthlessness in which Muslim forces exploited their victory after the battle, making the six-day engagement a decisive military event. After Yarmuk River, the Byzantine field army in Syria effectively ceased to exist and there was no concerted Byzantine challenge to Islamic rule in Syria and Palestine, and over time, the remaining Byzantine garrison and fortress towns succumbed to Muslim advances through either siege or negotiation.[99] With the Byzantine threat neutralized, the armies of Islam now concentrated on the Sassanian Persian threat in the region.

The Battle of al-Qadisiya and the Conquest of Persia

After Khalid al-Walid was called away from western Mesopotamia by Abu Bakr in 634 to take command of Islamic forces attacking Syria, the remaining Muslim army of about 5,000 men was defeated by a larger Sassanian Persian army at the battle of the Bridge in October along the Euphrates River near Kufa in southern Mesopotamia in what is now modern Iraq. The well-equipped Persian army was commanded by a capable *mirran*, a man named Rustam Farrokh-Zad who carried with him the *Derafsh-e-Kaveyan* ('Standard of Kaveh'), the great tiger-skin standard of the Persian kings, measuring over forty yards long by six yards wide. Rustam's army included heavy cavalry Savaran and an unknown number of elephants, who seemed to have terrified the Muslim cavalry, allowing Persian archers to devastate the Muslim ranks.[100] The Muslim commander, Abu Ubaid, was trampled to death while attacking an elephant, while the small number of surviving Muslim soldiers, under the command of a man named Muthanna, disappeared into the desert. The battle of the Bridge was the worst defeat the Muslims suffered in the early years of the conquests.[101]

After the battle, Islamic activity in the region reverted to raiding along the desert margin. This would change, however, when the newly elected caliph, Umar, made avenging the battle of the Bridge a priority. Umar believed the time was right to expand Islamic influence in Mesopotamia, especially since the Sassanians were now ruled by the grandson of Chosroes II, the young and untested King Yazdgird III (r.632–644), who became emperor when he was just sixteen and was still consolidating his rule after a contentious accession to the throne. Yazdgird understood the Muslim threat hovering on his western border and concluded an alliance with an unlikely ally, the Byzantine emperor Herakleios, in 635 with the intention of joining the Eastern Romans in their campaign against the Muslims in Palestine. This combined Byzanto-Persian army never materialized, and after the devastating loss at Yarmuk River a year later, Byzantium was in retreat and the armies of Islam were gathering to push eastward into Mesopotamia, forcing the Persian king to prepare for the coming invasion.

Caliph Umar began to assemble a Muslim expeditionary army, but manpower shortages were beginning to take their toll on the Islamic war effort. The campaigns in Palestine and Syria against Byzantine forces required multiple field armies and the continuing threat of Persia pulled additional reinforcements from Arabia. Umar sent another army from Arabia to the region under the command of Saad ibn Abi Waqqas, an early convert to Islam and cousin of the Prophet. After the decisive Muslim victory at Yarmuk River in August, Umar ordered elements of the Syrian army to Iraq, including a contingent of veterans from Khalid al-Walid's Euphrates expedition, soldiers both familiar with the region and with victory in battle. Because of his seniority, Saad took overall command of a Muslim army that probably numbered between 6,000 and 12,000 men.[102]

Rustam's Sassanian army left Ctesiphon and crossed the Euphrates to engage the Arabs sometime in the autumn of 636, now encamped on the western bank of the tributary Atik River on the plains of al-Qadisiya south-west of Kufa. The Sassanians fielded a large army. Exact numbers are unknown but most historians agree that it was three times the size of the invading Arab army, somewhere between 18,000 and 36,000 men.[103] Many of these troops were raw recruits hastily conscripted into the Persian army and were not well trained or well motivated. The core of the Sassanian army consisted of the remaining Savaran heavy cavalry, archers, fierce Daylami (sometimes Dailamite) infantry from the forests of northern Persia, and thirty-three war elephants. Daylami warriors fought with a distinctive two-pronged javelin, but also used heavy swords and battleaxes for hand-to-hand combat and bows and slings for distance warfare. These soldiers fared well against Roman legionaries in the late Roman imperial period and were highly praised later by Arab Muslim commanders, who actively sought to recruit them into their armies, even paying them more than Arab troops.[104]

Even though the Persian host outnumbered the invading army three to one, Rustam sent emissaries to Saad to seek a negotiated settlement, one that would compel the Muslims to leave Persian territory. The Arab response was typical in negotiations between Muslims and their enemies, offering the Sassanians conversion and submission or war, and giving the Persians three days to consider the offer.[105] Rustam rejected the offer and the ensuing four-day battle is known to history as the battle of al-Qadisiya.

Sometime in mid-November Rustam ordered his army to cross a well-protected bridge across the Atik River and deploy for battle in front of the smaller Muslim host. According to the tenth century Muslim historian al-Tabari, the Sassanians formed up in three divisions, with war elephants with accompanying cavalry in mixed battle groups in the front line and archers, Daylami, and the less reliable conscript infantry in the second line. The Persian *mirran* placed eighteen elephants in the centre formation and seven and eight on the two wings respectively. Rustam overlooked the battlefield from his elevated seat in a shaded command post behind the right centre divisions, protected by his personal guard. At his side waved the Persian king's tiger standard.[106] Saad's Muslim army was already drawn up in typical fashion in three divisions with infantry in the forward line and cavalry in the second line.[107]

Rustam opened the battle of al-Qadisiya with an attack by the combined Savaran and war elephant battle group on his left. The Arab right initially fell back under the weight of the onslaught, but Muslim troops accustomed to fighting pachyderms pushed through the elephants' escorts and gutted the animals while simultaneously attacking the turrets. The Savaran were also overwhelmed by Arab archers, some of whom were using a modified bow called *majra* (sometimes called *nawak*) that shot darts at high velocities.[108] Al-Tabari tells us that the engagement continued past sunset until Rustam, fearing the collapse of his left flank, called back his Persian troops.[109] The first day of the battle of al-Qadisiya is known as the 'Day of the Concussion' by Arab sources.[110]

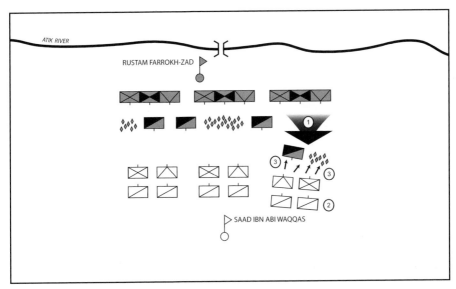

Map 2.5.1. The Battle of al-Qadisiya, 636 CE. Phase I: Rustam opens the battle with an attack by his left-wing Savaran/war elephant battle group (1) that succeeds in pressing back the Muslim right (2). Muslims familiar with combating elephants soon infiltrate the groups, gutting the animals while engaging their turrets with archery fire (3). The fight continues past sunset, when Rustam recalls his troops to reconsolidate his flank.

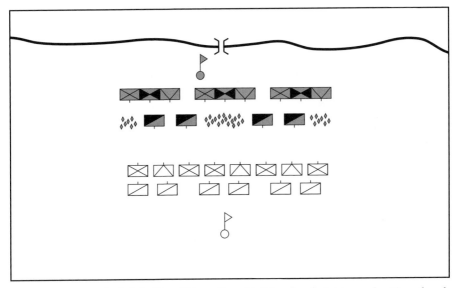

Map 2.5.2. The Battle of al-Qadisiya, 636 CE. Phase II: Other than duels between champions, the only action on the second day is the arrival of Muslim reinforcements that include Persian defectors familiar with pachyderm warfare.

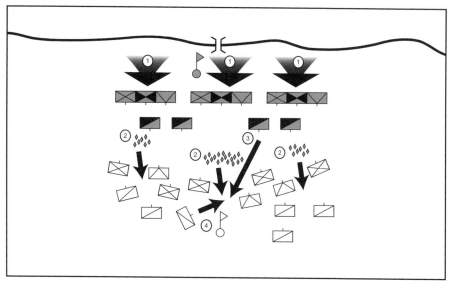

Map 2.5.3. The Battle of al-Qadisiya, 636 CE. Phase III: Rustam, perhaps worried at losing his numeric edge, orders a general advance (1). The assault is led by the Sassanian war elephants (2) that disrupt the Muslim ranks and open gaps in their formations. Into one of these gaps, Rustam orders one of his elite Savaran cavalry units (3) to assault Saad's headquarters, located in an abandoned castle to the rear, but they are intercepted and driven back by a swift cavalry counterattack (4). Muslim troops adept in countering elephant attacks swiftly restore order, mutilating the animals and causing them to stampede off of the field.

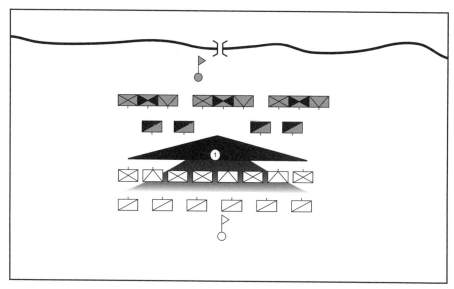

Map 2.5.4. The Battle of al-Qadisiyya, 636 CE. Phase IV: Saad regroups his forces and orders a general counterattack (1), but the Sassanian line holds. Darkness falls and the armies disengage. Muslim raiders harass the foe through the night by raiding the Sassanian camps.

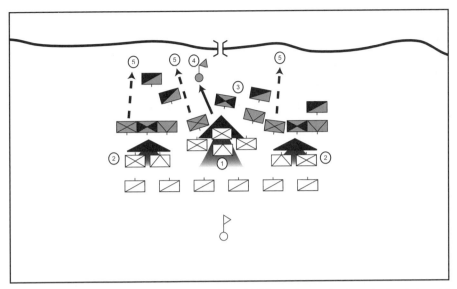

Map 2.5.5. *The Battle of al-Qadisiya, 636 CE. Phase V: The Arabs open battle on the fourth day with an assault by their centre (1) followed by the remainder of their line (2). The attack breaks the Sassanian formation (3) and Muslim troops overrun the enemy headquarters, killing Rustam and scattering his guard (4). Panic begins to grip the Sassanians and the ill-trained conscript infantry begins to break for the river (5).*

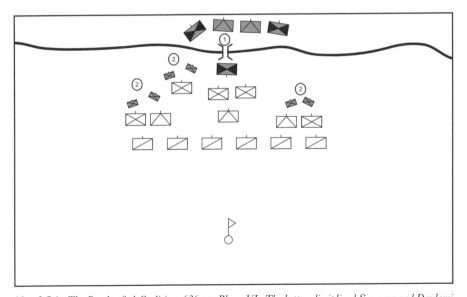

Map 2.5.6. *The Battle of al-Qadisiya, 636 CE. Phase VI: The better-disciplined Savaran and Daylami soldiers manage to make an orderly withdrawal across the bridgehead (1), while the scattered groups of routed conscripts are hunted down and killed by the victorious Muslims (2).*

The second day of the battle, known to Muslims as the 'Day of Succours', was consumed with champion duels and no major action took place between the two armies. However, Saad's army was reinforced on the second day by Arab veterans from the Levant, ex-Byzantine spearmen and Persian defectors familiar with fighting elephants.[111] Probably wary of additional Muslim reinforcements altering his numerical superiority, Rustam ordered a general attack along his entire front on the third day of the battle. All three Sassanian divisions surged forward, led by the war elephants supported by infantry and cavalry units. The elephant advance had the desired effect, frightening both Arab soldiers and horses. As the Muslim army fell back in disarray, Rustam ordered an elite Savaran unit to breach the developing gap and assault an old palace where Saad had set up his headquarters in the Muslim rear. But the Savaran knights were intercepted by a strong Muslim cavalry guard and driven from the field. Aware of the damage being done by the Persian elephant corps, Saad called forward soldiers specialized in fighting pachyderms who blinded the beasts or severed their trunks, causing the mutilated creatures to stampede through their own ranks towards the safety of the river. By noon none of the elephants were engaged in battle. Saad followed up this confusion by ordering a general counterattack, but the Persian lines held, despite the absence of their war elephants. Finally, as the afternoon turned to evening, the two exhausted armies disengaged. But darkness did not deter Saad from organizing small Arab raids into the Persian camp throughout the night until dawn. The evening of the third day into the fourth day of the battle of al-Qadisiya is known to Muslim chroniclers as the 'Night of the Rumbling Noises'.

At dawn on the fourth and final day of the battle of al-Qadisiya, the Muslims prepared a final attack against the Sassanians. The historian al-Tabari recounts that one of Saad's commanders, al-Qaqa ibn Amr, walked among the exhausted Muslim troops exhorting:

> He who resumes the fight against the Persians will defeat them in an hour. Endure for [another] hour and launch the attack, because victory comes with endurance. Prefer endurance to fear.[112]

An hour later the Arab centre struck first against the Persian centre, followed by a general attack along the entire Muslim front. Eventually, the Muslim centre was able to break through and Arab warriors swarmed the Sassanian headquarters, killing the *mirran* and seizing the royal Standard of Kaveh, despite an elite Persian guard dying to the last man to protect it. News of the death of Rustam quickly spread throughout the Persian ranks, destroying their morale.[113] Part of the Persian front, most probably the ill-trained infantry conscripts, simply collapsed and ran towards the river only to be slaughtered by the pursuing Muslims. Other Persian contingents, most likely the well-trained Savaran and Daylami troops, were able to withdraw in good order across the Atik bridgehead and make their escape. Later, many of these troops would defect to the Arab invaders and convert to Islam, becoming the point of the spear for deeper penetrations into Iraq, Persia and beyond.[114]

After the Persian loss at al-Qadisiya, central Iraq lay open to Muslim invasion. Arab troops defeated the remnants of the Persian forces near the ancient ruins of Babylon, and then turned their attention to the Sassanian capital at Ctesiphon, which was nearly deserted when the invaders arrived. Yazdgird and what remained of his court had escaped east across the Zagros Mountains to northern Persia, leaving all of Mesopotamia to the Muslim invaders. Over the next few years, the Sassanians would launch raids into Muslim-controlled Iraq, but the Arab victory at Nihawand in 641 opened the way for a Muslim conquest of Persia. In 642, Caliph Umar ordered his Arab armies into central Persia, taking the Sassanian strongholds of Isfahan and Tabaristan. Over the next two years, Muslim armies marched south, seizing Fars, and then pushed east to Kerman and Makran in the south-east and Sistan in the north-east through what is now southern Afghanistan and western Pakistan. Umar ordered his armies to the edge of Hindu lands on the Indus River, declaring this waterway the eastern border of *Dar al-Islam*. Meanwhile, Arab armies pressed north-west into Azerbaijan and then west into Persian-controlled Armenia (Byzantine Armenia was captured by the Arabs between 638 and 639), taking these regions by 644. Only Khurasan remained under Sassanian control. This ancient region, made up of what is now modern north-eastern Iran, north-western Afghanistan and southern Turkmenistan, was the Sassanian's second largest province. Yazdgird made a final stand here in the summer of 644. He was defeated in the battle of the Oxus River, but escaped to Tang China as an exiled king. He would eventually return to Persia, only to be killed in 651 by a local miller for his purse, officially ending the last Sassanian dynasty. However, by the end of 644 the Sassanian Empire as a political entity had ceased to exist and Umar declared the Oxus River the north-eastern border of Islamic territory.

The conquest of Persia presented the Muslims with a religious problem concerning the status of the subjugated population. Most of the Persians practised Zoroastrianism, an ancient religion that included idol worship and elements considered polytheistic to Islamic orthodoxy. But the prospect of killing entire Zoroastrian communities for not converting to Muhammad's faith proved distasteful and the Arab conquerors of Persia soon tempered their religious enthusiasm with political pragmatism. Over time those Zoroastrians who did not convert to Islam would be protected as *dhimmis*, an act of compassion and political and economic expediency that would become a model when Islam pushed farther east into Central Asia and South Asia.

Civil War and the Sunni-Shia Split

Even while the conquest of the Levant and Mesopotamia was taking place the Rashidun caliphs organized their newly conquered territories into taxpaying provinces. These Arab rulers continued to rule from Medina and showed little interest in governing the new lands directly. Instead, they kept in place the old governmental systems (newly converted kings, governors and their administrations) to administer the newly conquered territories. The Arab conquerors were present, although they often lived apart from the conquered peoples in garrison cities (*amsar*) military districts (*ajnad*) and military monasteries (*ribat*). The Rashidun rulers also understood their manpower pool as all able-bodies Muslim men were required to register in the *diwan* (Arabic for register). Muslim soldiers enrolled for life in the *diwan* and were entitled to quarters, monthly rations, and an annual cash stipend.[115]

By the mid-seventh century problems arose over succession, precipitating a power struggle in Islam between Ali, the last of the four 'Rightly Guided' caliphs, and the governor of Syria, Muawaiyah Umayyad. Ali, the Prophet's son-in-law and champion at the battles of Badr and Uhud, was assassinated in 661 in the city of Kufa in Mesopotamia. Soon, the internal dissention over who should rule the *ummah* created a split in Islam between the Shia, who only accepted the descendents of Ali as the true rulers of Islam, and the Sunni, who claimed that the descendents of Muawaiyah should lead the faithful. This Shia–Sunni division would continue to complicate politics in the Islamic world throughout the period under study here and to the present day. Muawaiyah became the first member of what would become the hereditary Umayyad Caliphate (661–750). Muawaiyah moved the capital of the new Islamic empire from Medina to Damascus and ushered in the next phase of Islamic conquests.

Chapter 3

Byzantine Warfare in an
Age of Crisis and Recovery

'Enemy at the Gates': The Arab Sieges of Constantinople

The expansion of Islam in the seventh century fundamentally changed the political and strategic landscape of the Mediterranean basin. Muslim armies swept north into Palestine and Syria and Mesopotamia, defeating the Sassanians at al-Qadisiya in 636 and destroying their Persian Empire by 651. Arab armies then pushed west across North Africa to the Atlantic Ocean, swallowing up Byzantine possessions in Egypt, Libya and Tunisia along the way. By 700 all of North Africa was under Islamic control. In the Levant, the devastating Byzantine loss at Yarmuk River in 636 forced the Eastern Romans to pull their field armies from Palestine first to Northern Syria and Mesopotamia, and then to the natural Anatolian frontier line consisting of the Taurus and Anti-Taurus mountain ranges in south-eastern and eastern Turkey. Further east, the Byzantine capital of Constantinople weathered two determined Muslim sieges between 674 and 678 and again in 717–718, illustrating the vulnerability of the heart of the Eastern Roman Empire.

The first Umayyad Caliph Muawaiyah (r.661–680) resumed attacks against Byzantine-controlled Anatolia in 663, just two years after settling the Muslim civil war. Over the next fifteen years the Arabs would launch annual raids deep into Eastern Roman territory, reaching as far west as Chalcedon on the north-west coast of Asia Minor. However, the ultimate prize was the city of Constantinople, and Muawaiyah, as governor of Syria before becoming caliph, recognized the Byzantine capital could only be taken if control of the sea was established in the Aegean and the Sea of Marmara. So to that end, the caliph continued the Muslim conquest of strategic islands. Cyprus, Rhodes, Cos and Chios fell to Arab fleets, while in 670, the strategic Cyzicus peninsula on the southern shore of the Sea of Marmara was taken, providing an excellent base to begin the blockade of Constantinople by sea. Over the next two years, the blockade continued as more Muslim bases were established on the western and southern shores of Anatolia in preparation for the direct attack on the capital.[1]

In early 674 the main action began when a Muslim squadron of ships appeared before the southern seaward walls of Constantinople in an attempt to blockade the city by sea as an Arab army laid siege to the massive Theodosian Walls on the landward side to the west. Completed in 423 during the reign of Theodosius II (r.408–450) and rebuilt after a massive earthquake in 447, the Theodosian Walls were a sophisticated defensive system separating the small triangular peninsula where Constantinople was built from the mainland. This defensive work ran about four miles from the Golden Horn waterway in the north to the Sea of Marmara in the south and consisted of three lines of defence (a sixty-feet wide water-filled moat, outer wall and inner wall) flanked by 192 towers.[2] Over its thousand year history, the Theodosian Walls protected the Byzantine capital from sieges by the Avars, Persians, Arabs, Bulgars and Slavic Rus, although the city succumbed in 1204 to the Catholic Crusaders during the Fourth Crusade and finally to the cannons of the Ottoman Turks in 1453, ending the Byzantine Empire.

The Muslim blockade and siege of Constantinople of 674 lasted all summer and was led by Muawaiyah's son and eventual successor, Yazid I (r.680–683). For the next three years the Muslim flotilla blockaded the city by sea during the summer, and then retired to Cyzicus for the winter. The blockade was finally lifted in 678 after the Byzantines employed a secret weapon known to history as Greek Fire invented by Kallinikos (sometimes Callinicus), an architect-turned-engineer and refugee from Arab-held Syria.[3] The precise recipe for Greek Fire is unknown, but probably the substance itself was a mixture of olefins and naphthalenes or a distillation of petrol obtained naturally from the oil-rich Caspian Sea region. This mysterious recipe was heated to increase its flammability and then siphoned through bronze pumps to a nozzle over a match or lantern to ignite it. Once alight, the oil was discharged as a jet stream creating a medieval flame-thrower. Greek Fire continued to burn even on the surface of water, making it an ideal naval weapon. Greek engineers mounted these weapons on a swivel, usually on the bows of ships, so that it could be aimed in an arc.[4] Armed with this devastating new weapon, Byzantine ships sailed out of the safety of Constantinople's harbour walls and dispersed the Muslim fleet, setting many of the ships on fire and forcing Yazid to lift the siege on land and sea. To make matters worse, much of the remaining Muslim fleet was destroyed in a powerful storm on the voyage back to Syria.[5]

The Arabs returned to Constantinople in late summer 717 with a large land army of 80,000 men commanded by Maslama bin-Abd al-Malik, son of the short-reigned Umayyad caliph Sulayman bin-Abd al-Malik (r.715–718). On 15 August, Maslama laid siege to the Theodosian Walls and two weeks later, on 1 September, a huge Muslim armada consisting of 1,800 ships from all over the caliphate dropped anchor below the sea walls of Constantinople.[6] Many of these ships were carrying supplies for the sieging army, and as such, were heavily laden and bunched together as they prepared to empty their holds. Seeing this, the Byzantine emperor Leo III 'the Isaurian' (r.717–741) ordered his ships armed with Greek Fire out of their protected harbours, setting alight many of the vulnerable Muslim vessels.[7] The early ninth century Byzantine monk and chronicler Theophanes the Confessor remarked that:

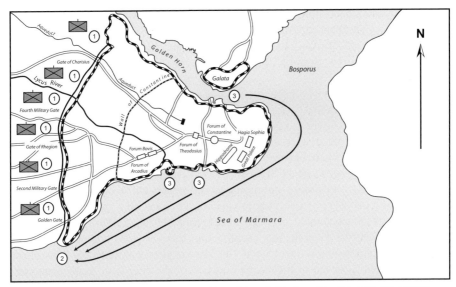

Map 3.1.1. The Siege of Constantinople, 717–718 CE. Phase I: Maslama bin Abd al-Malik's 80,000-man army besieges Constantinople's walls in the late summer of 717 (1). On 1 September, a fleet of 1,800 Muslim ships drops anchor below the sea walls (2) to supply their forces ashore. The Byzantine emperor, Leo III, orders warships armed with Greek Fire to sally forth from their protected harbours (3) and attack the thickly-packed Muslim ships. Many vessels burst into flames, while others collide with the sea walls and each other before sinking. Thousands of besiegers die from exposure, famine, and disease in the ensuing winter.

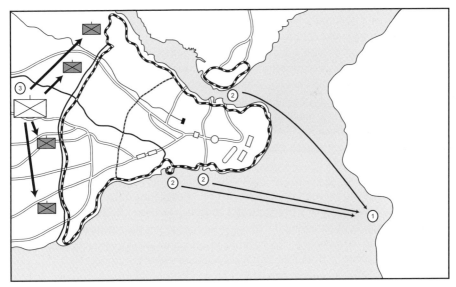

Map 3.1.2. The Siege of Constantinople, 717–718 CE. Phase II: In the spring of 718, a Muslim supply fleet arrives from Egypt and North Africa, concealing itself along the Asiatic shore (1). The Byzantines learn of the fleet's location from defecting Coptic Christian sailors and Leo dispatches his warships once again (2) destroying the enemy vessels and seizing the supplies meant for the besieging army. The final straw is the arrival of a Bulgar relief force that attacks the siege lines (3), killing 20,000. In August, the new caliph, Umar II, lifts the siege and withdraws his forces.

Some of them still burning smashed into the sea walls, while others sank in the deep, men and all and others still, flaming furiously, went as far as the islands of Oxeia and Plateia [modern Princes' Islands located about 10 miles south-east of old Constantinople in the Sea of Marmara].[8]

The Muslim host wintered outside the walls of Constantinople, but was ravaged by a hard winter with thousands dying from cold, famine, and disease.[9] Reinforcements and supplies arrived from Egypt and North Africa in the spring of 718 on 660 ships, but the newly arrived ships stayed clear of the Byzantine capital's sea walls, instead staying hidden on the Asiatic shore of the Sea of Marmara. But the new flotilla's location was discovered by Leo when Coptic Christian sailors from the Muslim fleets defected. Leo dispatched his Greek Fire ships and destroyed the vessels and seized their supplies on shore, denying the sieging army vital provisions. The final blow came from a Bulgar relief army that attacked the Arab siege lines, killing 20,000 Muslims.[10] The siege was finally lifted in August when the new caliph, Umar II (r.717–720), ordered Maslama to retire. Once again on the return voyage, the Muslim fleet was destroyed by a storm. Only five vessels returned to their native ports.[11] In the end, both Arab sieges were thwarted on land by Constantinople's massive fifth-century Theodosian Walls and the application of Greek Fire against Muslim ships at sea. The siege of 717–718 would be the last time a Muslim armada would reach the Sea of Marmara before the late eleventh century.[12]

The Byzantine Army in Transition in the Wake of the Islamic Conquests

Byzantium's territorial contraction required adjustments in its field army placements. Emperor Constans II (r.641–668) settled his remaining field armies in specific districts called *themata* or themes. The new organization of themes introduced regionalized army groups under the command of a *strategos* who replaced the 'Master of the Soldiers' and served as both a senior general and governor. The *Opsikion Theme* was made up of the two former praesental armies and was pulled back to its original bases in north-west Anatolia and Thrace.[13] The *Anatolikon Theme* was made up of the former Army of the East and protected south-central Turkey, while the *Armeniakon* and *Thrakesian Themes* were made up of the Armies of Armenia and Thrace.[14] The *Anatolikon Theme* protected south-central Turkey while the *Armeniakon Theme* defended the dangerous eastern and northern districts of Asia Minor.[15] However, when determined Arab attacks forced the Byzantines to abandon the region of Cilicia (south-central Anatolia adjacent to Muslim-controlled Syria) at the end of the seventh century, imperial strategy shifted from trying to control a clearly defined frontier through pitch battles and territorial rollback to a strategy known by the Easter Romans as 'shadowing warfare', consisting of harassing the invaders and attacking their logistical lines.[16] The net effect of this strategy was the creation of an economically unstable and lawless frontier region between Byzantine and Umayyad controlled territories.[17]

The thematic system military provided both regional frontier troops and mobile field armies through the creation of a dedicated militia. These troops became the legal holders of the land itself, a development that came in the form of imperial land grants that were similar to the land grants during the early Roman Empire that settled legionaries in newly conquered regions. Although the Byzantine soldiers did not work

The Byzantine Empire in the early eighth century.

the fields or run farms on a full-time basis, their ownership (and that of their heirs) brought about a personal stake in the defence of their theme and provided the emperor with manpower for his campaigns. The thematic system had an added benefit of removing soldiers from the imperial payroll through the substitution of a land grant at a time when the contracting empire was running out of money to pay its soldiers.[18]

Because if its militia nature, a theme's primary role was that of a defensive force, but Constantine V (r.741–775) would take an interest in regaining lost territory and, to fulfil this aim, created an imperial guard consisting of elite cavalry and infantry units called *tagmata* (Greek for 'the regiments'). Constantine originally used these troops as a reaction to a rebellious theme in north-west Anatolia, and then later for offensive campaigns against the Arabs and Bulgars.[19] *Tagmata* soldiers were recruited, equipped and paid a salary directly by the state and were under the direct command of the emperor. These well-trained and well-disciplined professional soldiers provided the core units of an imperial expeditionary army when supplemented by less reliable but more numerous local thematic militia. The most important of these imperial regiments were the Scholai, the *Exkoubitoi*, the *Artihmos* and the *Hikanatoi*, under the control of a commanding general or *domesticus* rather than a *strategos*. The *domesticus* of the *Scholai Tagmata* usually assumed supreme command of Byzantine expeditionary armies if the emperor was not present on campaign.[20]

The Byzantine army used the same organization of units whether they were troops from the *themes* or from the *tagmata*. The size of units on the battlefield varied depending on tactical need and there is no scholarly consensus on the numerical makeup of Byzantine armies. What is known is that the smallest unit was a *bandum* normally consisting of about 300–400 soldiers, which was commanded by a tribune or count.[21] Five to eight *banda*, roughly 1,500–3,200 men, formed a *turma* under the command of a *turmarch*. Each *turmarch* had his base in a fortress town and was responsible for the defence of his district and served as an important military and civic leader in his theme.[22] Normally, two or three *turmae*, roughly 4,500–9,600 men, formed a thematic army commanded by a *strategos*, although this number could vary widely. When imperial *tagmata* were added to thematic troops, the resulting expeditionary army could consist of tens of thousands of troops.[23]

The role of cavalry and infantry in Byzantine military doctrine also slowly changed from the time of the great Muslim victories in the mid-seventh century. At that time, both the Byzantine and Arab armies used large infantry contingents in their arts of war as illustrated by the role of infantry in the signature battles of this period. Cavalry, especially light cavalry, became the dominant arm because of its strategic mobility, especially important in defending the broad expanses of the Balkans and Anatolia, and utility when fighting mounted Bulgar and Muslim raiders.[24] Byzantine cavalry, like cavalry in most periods of history, tended to be of noble birth and were better trained and equipped than their usually common-born infantry counterparts. From the eighth century on Byzantine thematic infantry was better suited for garrison roles and irregular combat in difficult terrain as they were often the most unreliable troops on the battlefield. These troops did not perform as well as the infantry of Justinian and Herakleios' time owing to a lack of discipline and poor equipment. Quality heavy infantry would not return to the Byzantine art of war until the tenth century.

Crisis on the Northern Frontier: The Early Bulgar Wars

The Byzantine Empire faced new difficulties in the Balkans with the arrival of the Bulgars, a people of Turkic origin. Byzantine emperors had enjoyed good relations with the Onogur-Bulgar confederation since the reign of Herakleios, but the arrival of the Khazars from Central Asia in the middle of the seventh century destroyed this alliance. Some of the Bulgars submitted to the invaders, while several Bulgar tribes migrated west from their homeland in the Volga River basin, settling at the mouth of Danube in the 670s. Emperor Constantine IV (r.668–685) personally led an expedition against the Bulgars, but was unsuccessful in compelling the barbarians to battle. The Byzantines were attacked when they attempted to cross the Danube back into imperial territory, suffering heavy losses. The Bulgars followed up this victory by putting the Eastern Roman district of Varna to the sword. The Bulgars would settle in this heavily Slavic region and create a powerful Slavo-Bulgarian Khanate that stretched from the Balkan range north to the Danube River.[25] It is significant to note that this new barbarian khanate, carved out of Byzantine territory, required the Byzantine emperor to pay an annual tribute that was, in the words of Theophanes the Confessor, 'to the great disgrace of the Roman name'.[26]

By the eighth century the power of this Bulgar Khanate was regularly threatening Byzantine Thrace, requiring military responses by successive Byzantine emperors. Constantine V (r.741–775) spent two decades campaigning deep into Bulgar territory in an effort to bring the barbarians under Eastern Roman control. Although nearly successful, the Bulgars proved resilient and even bounced back by the end of the century under the leadership of Kardam Khan, threatening Byzantine Thrace again. Constantine VI (r.776–797) and his mother, the Empress Irene (r.797–802), went on the offensive again in an attempt to shore up the Thracian frontier, but these efforts lead to a stalemate and a tenuous truce with Kardam. Irene's successor, Nikephoros I (r.802–811), campaigned aggressively against the Bulgars, initiated a reorganization of the Byzantine Empire by adding new themes in the Balkans and resettling Greeks from Anatolia in Greece in a policy of re-Hellenization of the region.[27]

Nikephoros refused payment of tribute to the powerful Abbasid Caliph Harun al-Rashid in Baghdad, precipitating a new war with the Arabs. Taking the field at the head of his imperial army, Nikephoros was soundly defeated by the Muslims at the battle of Krasos in Phrygia in 805. A year later, al-Rashid sent a huge Abbasid army into Anatolia, forcing the Byzantine emperor to sue for peace and pay tribute. But al-Rashid's death in 809 and the following succession problems allowed Nikephoros to turn his attention to his northern frontiers where the Bulgars, now under the command of the capable Krum Khan (r.803–814), were raiding Byzantine territory, even sacking the Byzantine city of Serdica (modern Sofia and the future capital of modern Bulgaria), destroying the fortress there and massacring the garrison. In 809 Nikephoros launched a punitive expedition against the Bulgar capital at Pliska, putting the city to the sword and burning down the khan's palace. Two years later in 811 Nikephoros returned to the region with a large army and imperial retinue determined to finally destroy the Bulgar threat once and for all.[28]

Confident of an easy victory, Nikephoros launched a surprise attack into Bulgar territory in July, dividing his army into three columns that converged on the capital of Pliska, defeating the garrison and a relief force. The Byzantine emperor seized Krum's treasure, distributed some of the booty to his soldiers, and put the city to the torch again. He then proceeded to plunder and the burn the countryside as he pursued the retreating Bulgars south-west towards Serdica. The pursuing Byzantine column entered a wooded valley watered by one of the many rivers flowing from the Balkan range. An anonymous contemporary of the battle of Pliska mentions that Byzantine troop morale was high but discipline within the column was lax and that the emperor did not heed the warnings of his senior officers to proceed with caution as they marched deeper into enemy territory.[29] Moreover, advance reconnaissance was very poor, an important element of any expedition. While marching in a south-westerly direction through difficult terrain, the Byzantine army found itself the victim of a Bulgar trap with its path blocked by a wooden palisade and trench constructed across the road. Because it was now afternoon, Nikephoros ordered the column to make camp for the night instead of commanding a retreat back through the valley.[30]

As per Byzantine military doctrine, each thematic division made their own camp some distance from one another, encamping on the south side of a winding stream and marsh in the valley. Nikephoros encamped with his imperial guard, the *tagmata*, and thematic troops were sent out to secure supplies from the countryside. A cordon was set up and guards posted, but there were a number of desertions among the Byzantine officer corps, a clear indication that trained officers did not like the strategic position the encamped Eastern Roman army found itself in.[31]

These deserting troops proved prescient as shortly before dawn on 26 July Krum Khan launched a full-scale attack directly against the *tagmata* division and the imperial tents. Far from having a broken army, Krum's forces had been reinforced by a call to arms earlier in the summer to his allied Slavs and the remnants of the Avars who still lived in the Hungarian Plain after the destruction of their confederation by the Frankish king Charlemagne (r.768–814) in the 790s.[32] Under the cover of darkness Krum's troops penetrated the Byzantine cordon and fell on the imperial guard and

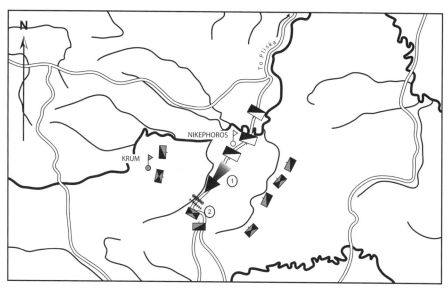

Map 3.2.1. The Battle of Pliska, 811 CE. Phase I: After sacking Pliska, Nikepheros' army pursues fleeing Bulgar forces into rugged terrain cut by numerous streams and rivers (1). Unbeknownst to the Byzantines, they are advancing into a trap. Confronted by a moat and palisade blocking the road (2), they can proceed no further.

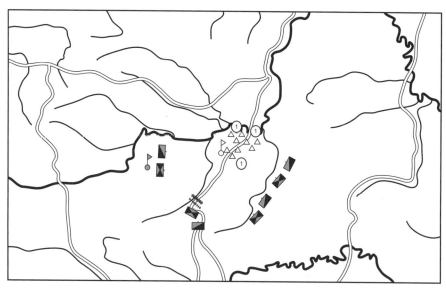

Map 3.2.2. The Battle of Pliska, 811 CE. Phase II: Nikephoros pulls back from the obstacle and orders his column into camp. Each thematic division makes its separate camp (1) in marshy terrain just south of a winding stream. Even though cordons are established and sentries posted, a number of Byzantine officers desert during the night, signalling dissatisfaction with the strategic position in which they find themselves.

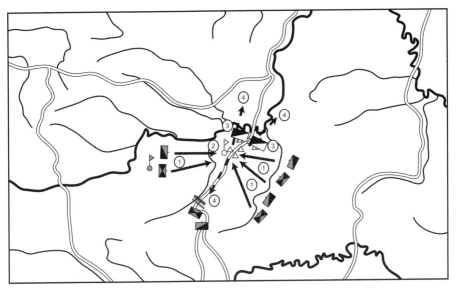

Map 3.2.3. The Battle of Pliska, 811 CE. Phase III: Just before dawn, Krum Khan launches a fierce attack against the tagmata division and the imperial encampment (1). His army, heavily reinforced by Slavs and Avars, pierces the cordon and catches the imperial guard and many others asleep. Nikephoros is killed (2) and the tagmata's attempt at a counterattack collapses when the news reaches their ears. The nearby thematic divisions attempt to form up (3), but the fleeing survivors of the assault and news of the emperor's death bring about a general rout (4).

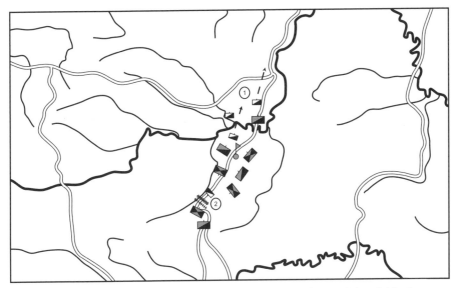

Map 3.2.4. The Battle of Pliska, 811 CE. Phase IV: The Byzantines' escape is impeded by the streams and swamps. Many perish trying to cross the marshes while others are hunted down by Krum's forces (1). Some of the fugitives attempt to scale the palisade blocking the road (2), but most fail, falling from the obstacle to their death. An attempt to burn the wall fails as well as the moat remains to block their escape. The Byzantine army is destroyed.

retinue, many of whom were still asleep. Within minutes elements of the *tagmata* organized a counterattack, but it collapsed when news of the death of their emperor spread throughout the camp. Nikephoros probably died in the first minutes of the attack along with a great many high-ranking court officials. The commander of the *tagmata* and other senior officers also perished.[33] By this time troops from the nearby thematic divisions began to form up and march towards the imperial encampment only to be met by fleeing guardsmen and the sacking of the camp by the Bulgars and their allies. When news of the emperor's death reached the nearby camps, a general rout began as Byzantine soldiers tried to escape. Some men were hunted down and drowned in the nearby marsh and river. Below, the anonymous author writes that some Byzantine soldiers:

> Could not find immediately a ford to cross, and pursued by the enemy, fell into the river. Because they entered [the river] together with their horses and could not go out, they were bogged into the mud and were trampled by those, coming from behind. As they fell upon each other, the river became so filled with people and horses that the enemy passed over them safely and pursued the rest....[34]

Still, other Byzantine soldiers were killed trying to climb over the palisade. The anonymous author continues, writing that these troops:

> Avoided their death in the river, reaching the rampart built by the Bulgars which was very strong and very hard to climb. Since they could not overcome it with their horses, they dismounted, climbed with their hands and feet and hung on the other side. On the outer side, however, a deep moat was dug out, and when they fell from the height, their limbs broke. Some of them died immediately, others walked a little, and as they could not continue, fell to the ground and perished, tortured by hunger and thirst. At other places, the rampart was put on fire. When the ties burned and the rampart fell upon the moat, the running soldiers unwarily fell down and came into the moat together with the fire.[35]

Although the exact number of Byzantine casualties at Pliska is unknown, the contemporary accounts indicate the Eastern Roman army was destroyed in the mountain passes. According to tradition, Krum Khan had the Byzantine emperor's skull lined with silver to keep as a trophy and use as a drinking cup.[36]

The Byzantine defeat at Pliska was both unexpected and complete, and its demoralizing impact on the Eastern Roman psyche was similar to that experienced over four hundred years earlier when Valens was killed fighting the Visigoths at the battle of Adrianople in 378.[37] Moreover, the Bulgar victory emboldened Krum to attack deep into Byzantine territory, twice reaching Constantinople and once sieging the capital in 813. Nikephoros was succeeded immediately by his wounded son, and then by his brother-in-law, who ruled briefly as Michael I (r.811–813). Michael ordered a Byzantine army into Bulgar territory where the enemy host was located near Versinikia in June 813. After weeks of delay one of Michael's generals ordered an attack that was not supported by the emperor or his other divisions. The result was a second Byzantine defeat and the deposition of Michael and assumption of one of his generals to the

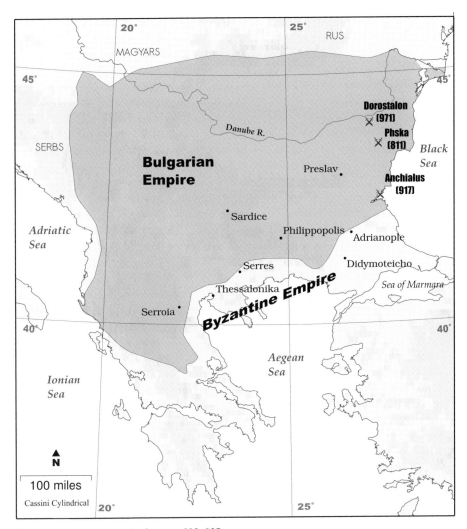

The Bulgarian Empire under Symeon, 893–927.

throne as Leo V (r.813–820) 'the Armenian'.[38] Krum's death in 814 and Leo's victory over the barbarians at the port city of Mesembria (modern Nesebar, Bulgaria) on the Black Sea the following year ushered in a peace with the new Omurtag Khan. Relations between the Bulgars and Byzantines stabilized for most the remainder of the ninth century, but tensions sparked up again in the late ninth and early tenth centuries, with disastrous consequences for Byzantium.

During the reign of Basil I (r.867–886), the first emperor of the ambitious and effective Macedonian dynasty (867–1056), the Bulgar khan Boris-Michael converted to Greek Orthodox Christianity, taking the title of Czar (Caesar). Boris-Michael presided over a strong pro-Christian, pro-Byzantine Bulgar court that smoothed out relations between the two states. However, when Symeon (r.893–927) ascended the Bulgar throne he renewed hostilities with Constantinople, initiating a war that would last with some breaks for decades until the 920s and even witnessed the Byzantine capital under direct siege. Initially, Symeon had success against the Byzantines and their emperor Leo VI 'the Wise' (r.886–912) in campaigns in the mid-890s, resulting in an annual tribute to the Bulgar czar. But after Leo died in 912, relations quickly deteriorated and the Bulgars threatened war again. Symeon's major grievance with Constantinople began in 914 when a palace coup ended his hope of extending his power over Byzantium through a marriage alliance between his daughter and the young *basileus Rhomaion* Constantine VII, then a boy of eight. Constantine's mother, the dowager empress Zoe, seized control of the court and called off the marriage alliance. Infuriated, Symeon invaded Thrace later that year and forced Adrianople to surrender, and then laid waste the districts surrounding Dyrrachium (modern Durres in Albania) and Thessalonika in northern Greece.[39]

The Byzantine response was to assemble an army under Leo Phokas, *domesticus* of the *Scholai Tagmata* and supreme commander of the Eastern Roman army. After extensive preparations over 916 and into the summer of 917, Leo launched an attack against Bulgar territories all along the Black Sea coast. His strategy included resurrecting an alliance with the nomadic Pechenegs (sometimes Patkinaks), a Turkic people who had arrived in the region from Central Asia. Previously, Leo VI had used the Pechenegs to fend off more dangerous enemies like the Magyars, another Central Asian tribe who would eventually settle on the Hungarian Plain and found the Christian kingdom of Hungary, and the Rus, a powerful Swedo-Slavic state emerging north of the Black Sea.

Leo Phokas used the imperial fleet to transport the Pechenegs across the Danube River to its south bank to attack the Bulgars from the north while his imperial army of perhaps 30,000 men consisting of imperial *tagmata* and thematic divisions assembled from Thrace, Macedonia and Anatolia. In August, the Byzantine army pressed westwards from the Black Sea coast to the Aheloy River near the ancient Greco-Roman port city of Anchialus (modern Pomorie in Bulgaria). Symeon, aware of the Byzantine attack, managed to muster a large army (contemporary sources do not tell us how large) and marched towards the imperial army where he took up position in the hills overlooking the coastal plain where the enemy was encamped.[40]

The battle of Anchialus began on 20 August after the two armies deployed for battle. The contemporary sources indicate that Symeon launched the first attack, but the Eastern Roman forces absorbed the assault and inflicted heavy casualties. As the battle unfolded in favour of the Byzantines, the commanding general, Leo Phokas, took a moment to dismount near a stream in the rear of the action to refresh himself. However, while dismounted, his distinctive horse spooked and ran off behind the Eastern Roman lines and through the imperial camp, sparking a rumour that the general was dead. Panic spread among some of the Byzantine troops and the offensive against the Bulgar line began to falter. Symeon, watching his change of fortunes from the nearby hills, ordered his army to halt their retreat and turn and attack the enemy. The renewed Bulgar effort first halted the Eastern Roman advance along the entire front, and then pushed the Greeks backwards. Retreat quickly turned to rout as the Bulgarians cut down the fleeing invaders. Leo Phokas was able to retreat to friendly Mesembria, but the battle cost Byzantium a number of its senior officers. Cut off from a land retreat

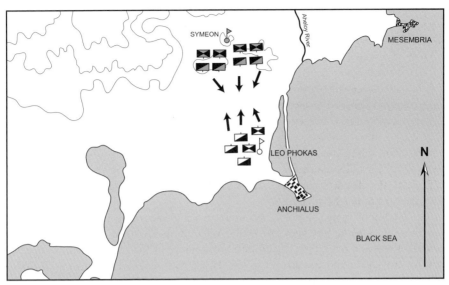

Map 3.3.1. The Battle of Anchialus, 917 CE Phase I: Symeon and a large Bulgar army arrive on the heights overlooking the coastal plain near Anchialus to face Leo Phokas and his Byzantine forces. Both sides deploy and ready themselves for combat (1).

Map 3.3.2. The Battle of Anchialus, 917 CE. Phase II: Symeon opens the battle with an assault against the Byzantine army (1). The Eastern Roman troops hold fast and counterattack (2), soon gaining an advantage over the Bulgars. As the tide begins to turn, Leo Phokas takes a moment to water his horse just to the rear of his lines. The general's distinctive mount spooks and bolts through the imperial camp (3), and a rumour spreads that the general has been killed.

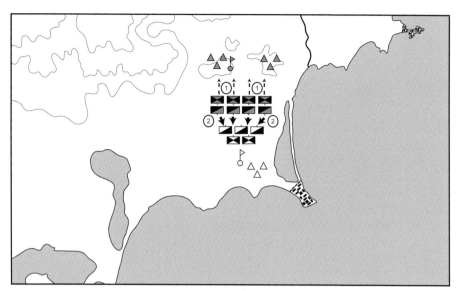

Map 3.3.3. The Battle of Anchialus, 917 CE. Phase III: The Bulgars begin to retreat (1), but the rumour of Leo Phokas' death spreads and the Byzantine attack begins to falter. Observing from the hills, Symeon observes the discomfiture of his foe and orders his troops to advance once again (2).

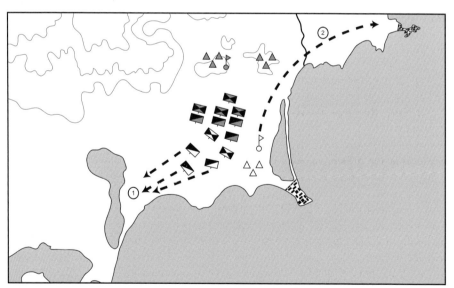

Map 3.3.4. The Battle of Anchialus, 917 CE. Phase IV: The Byzantines begin to retreat, but as Bulgar pressure mounts, retreat turns into rout (1) and the Eastern Romans flee the field. The Bulgars cut down many of the fugitives. Leo Phokas slips away to Mesembria (2) and subsequently returns to Constantinople by sea, but many other senior officers are lost in the action.

back to Constantinople, Leo was forced to return to the capital by sea. The sources do not record what the total Byzantine casualties were at Anchialus, but the victory opened up the land between Bulgaria and Constantinople to Symeon, who quickly pressed south to the Theodosian Walls. In October, Symeon destroyed a combined Byzantine and Serbian army in a surprise night attack outside of the city of Catasyrtae, near the walls of the capital.[41]

In 918, Symeon invaded northern Greece and pressed southwards to the Gulf of Corinth. He was now the master of the Balkan Peninsula but faced a new threat in Constantinople with the rise of Romanus I Lekapenos (r.920–944), a talented statesman and adroit political operator who pushed the dowager empress aside and ruled as co-emperor with the young Constantine VII. Romanus bided his time safe behind the walls of his capital as Symeon intrigued with the powerful Fatimid Caliphate (909–1171) centred in Egypt. Symeon wanted the Muslims to use their formidable navy to blockade Constantinople as he threatened the landward walls. His plan was thwarted by Byzantine diplomacy when Romanus offered the Arabs gifts and regular tribute not to assist the Bulgar czar. Unable to take Constantinople, Symeon turned his attention to the growing threat of the Serbians who were now backed by Byzantine coin. Symeon defeated the Serbs, but was humbled by the Catholic Croats in 926, who dealt him his greatest defeat.[42] Symeon's death in May 927 changed Byzantium's strategic situation seemingly overnight when Romanus signed a peace treaty with the new Bulgar czar, calming this frontier for the next forty years. He also dealt with the growing threat of Magyar raiding into Moesia and Thrace through diplomacy and annual payments. In 944, Romanus concluded a treaty with the Rus, who twice threatened Constantinople in the early 940s and were raiding Byzantine shipping on the Black Sea.[43] With his western and northern frontiers stabilized, Romanus turned his attention to the East, initiating a tenth-century Byzantine recovery at the expense of Islamic territories.

Byzantium Resurgent: Military Reforms and Tenth Century Territorial Expansion

Romanus appointed an outstanding young officer, John Kourkouas (c.900–946) *domesticus* of the *Scholai Tagmata* in 923 and ordered him to expand Byzantine power in the east. Romanus wanted to exploit changes in the strategic circumstances in eastern Anatolia and Armenia since the 860s. A Byzantine victory in 863 at Lake Lalakaon against the Emir of Melitene, a powerful Abbasid vassal, opened the way for more successes. By 912 the Muslims were pushed back again east of the Taurus-Anti-Taurus frontier. During this time the Armenians had switched their allegiance from Baghdad to Constantinople and were once again enlisting in the Eastern Roman army, increasing the pool of quality soldiers available to the emperor.[44] The border Muslim emirates of Melitene and Kalikala in central and south-eastern Anatolia were conquered between 926 and 944, extending Byzantine control to the upper Euphrates Valley and across western Armenia, restoring the imperial boundaries lost some three centuries before to Muslim expansion. John Kourkouas' campaigns illustrate a departure from the previous defence-minded strategy and highlighted the new capabilities of the Byzantine army.[45] His skilful generalship earned him comparisons with Trajan and Belisarios during his lifetime and his tenure marked the beginning of a new line of competent Byzantine military leaders who expanded the imperial borders in the tenth and eleventh centuries.[46]

One of the primary reasons for the renewed success of Byzantine military operations was a rededication to sound military principles and organization and the adoption of new arms and armour. Several new military treatises were authored in the tenth century reflecting these changes centred on a revival of disciplined heavy infantry capable of fighting on their own against enemy infantry and cavalry or operating with their own heavy cavalry using combined-arms tactics.[47] Leo VI's reign initiated a renaissance in the study of military doctrine. His *Taktika* preserved those elements of Maurice's *Strategikon* that were still relevant and added new lessons learned in the ninth century from wars against the Bulgars and Islam. In the second half of the tenth century two other important treatises were written. The first, commonly known by its Latin title *Praecepta Militaria* (*A Composition on Warfare*) was either written by or for Emperor Nikephoros II Phokas (r.963–969) and emphasizes the practical elements of infantry and cavalry warfare, encampment and use of spies. The second treatise, also entitled *Tactika*, is attributed to Nikephoros Ouranus and expands on earlier Byzantine manuals, but reveals the lessons learned during his generalship in the wars of Emperor Basil II in the late tenth and early eleventh centuries.[48]

Four types of infantry served in Byzantine armies in the second half of the tenth century. The lightest of the four were the *psoloi*, unarmored javelineers and slingers used as skirmishers and to screen the heavier infantry and cavalry in battle. The second type of infantry consisted of archers (although some sources lump bowmen into the *psoloi*) wielding a powerful short composite bow adopted through contacts with steppe peoples. Some of these bows were modified into a powerful dart thrower called a *solenarion* that utilized a hand-held grooved channel or tube held up against the side of the composite bow. The dart's length was between a normal arrow and the later crossbow bolt. This weapon is identical to the Islamic *majra* or *nawak* first seen in Muslim sources in the seventh century and used with great effect at the Arab victory at al-Qadisiya. A *solenarion* was an effective weapon because its dart was fired at such a high velocity that it could puncture any armour, had a long range, and was fired so quickly that the naked eye had a difficult time seeing it.[49] Archers in support of heavier units wore light chainmail or lamellar armour, while others wore padded armour or no armour. A small round shield, twelve-inches in diameter, was also carried for defence. On campaign, each bowman was required to carry two bows, four bowstrings, two quivers (one with sixty arrows, the other with forty), a sling, a one-handed war axe (*tzikourion*), and a sword if available.[50]

Infantry bowmen held a central place in Byzantine military doctrine as an effective counter to enemy mounted archery, whether it came from old enemies like the Arabs, Avars, Bulgars, Pechenegs and Magyars, or new ones like the emerging threat of the Seljuk Turks. However, in practice, Byzantine commanders did not have access to quality native bowmen. Military archery had been in decline since the eighth century, so much so that Leo VI proposed in his *Tactika* the reintroduction of mandatory archery practice and ordered his *strategoi* to ensure that every household possess a bow and forty arrows. Despite this initiative, native Byzantine archery remained a neglected military art.[51]

A third kind of infantry called *peltastoi* also served in the Eastern Roman army, named after the heavy thick-necked javelin employed by these troops as either a missile or close-quarters weapon. *Peltastoi* were hybrid troops who acted as a bridge between light and heavy infantry and were used to either screen heavier footmen and cavalry or act as shock units when fighting alongside their heavier armed and armoured brothers-in-arms. *Peltastoi* wore lamellar armour or chainmail when available and carried round shields. When armour was not available, a thick-quilted gambeson (*kavadion*) was worn instead made of thick cotton wadding in a raw silk cover.[52]

The heaviest of these four infantry formations consisted of *skutatoi*, named after their large shield or *skuta*. Each *skutatos* wore a pull-on chainmail hauberk or scale armour and metal helmet, some of which were of the *spangenhelm* variety in favour in Western Europe and the Baltic region in the tenth century. The manuals of the period also suggested wearing limb armour to protect forearms (vambraces) and lower legs (greaves). Their namesake shield was originally oval shaped, although this began to change as soldiers adopted a tear-drop shaped and then a kite-shaped shield reminiscent of the famous shields used by the Normans in the eleventh century. *Skutatoi* who served in the forward ranks used a thirteen-foot long pike or *kontarion* tipped with an eighteen-inch socketed spearhead. These front-line troops wielded their pikes against enemy cavalry in both offensive and defensive action and could be deployed either in a line or in a wedge formation to break up enemy attacks. *Skutatoi* positioned in the rear ranks used shorter spears. By the end of the tenth century specialized pike-wielding *skutatoi* made up 10 per cent of a 1,000-man regiment, integrated with 400 *peltastoi* and ordinary *skutatoi*, 300 archers and 200 psilos armed with javelins and slings.[53] Both *peltastoi* and *skutatoi* carried one of two types of swords. The *paramerion* was a sabre-hilted, slightly curved single-edged sword whose design was probably influenced by contacts with the steppe peoples, while the *spathion* was a straight double-edged long sword dating back to the late Roman Empire. Tzikourions were also used in conjunction with shields. Maces were not usually a part of the infantryman's arsenal.[54]

Byzantine commanders fielded four types of cavalry in the late tenth century. Light cavalry horse archers continued in their traditional role of pursuit and harassment of enemy forces and were an essential combat arm when facing similar mounted foes originating on the steppes. The *kataphraktoi* remained the premier heavy shock cavalry, although some of these heavy troops continued to employ short composite bows for missile combat. Under Nikephoros II some *kataphraktoi* were up-armoured into a super-heavy cavalry called *klibanophoroi* reminiscent of Byzantine and Sassanian *cataphractii* seen during Justinian's wars in the sixth century. Armour and barding was very heavy, with the rider covered in chain or lamellar armour with the additional protection of a padded overcoat. He wore an iron helmet with coif and chain mask that covered the entire face except for the eyes. Mounts were protected by an iron headpiece and chest barding made of ox-hide lamellar split at the front for ease of movement and leaving only the eyes, nostrils and lower legs unprotected from the front.[55] Both heavy cavalries utilized a short lance or *kontarion*, although this weapon was about eight feet in length, much shorter than the *skutatos'* infantry pike and shorter than the cavalry lances in favour later in Catholic Western Europe. The shortened length of the *kontarion* indicates lance work was not stressed; instead riders carried multiple edged and contusion weapons. The *Praecepta Militaria* suggested wearing two swords into combat, both the single-edged *paramerion* and the double-edged *spathion* suspended on waist belt and baldric. However, contemporary sources indicate the cavalry mace was the Byzantine heavy cavalrymen's primary hand-to-hand weapon, with up to two spare maces carried holstered on the saddle.[56]

The new tactical manuals reemphasized the role of the *kataphraktos* and *klibanophoros* at the point of attack, but the weight of the armour for both rider and horse meant these troops could only be used over short distances. In battle, these heavy horsemen drew up in a wedge formation, with twenty men in the first rank, twenty-four in the second and four more in each successive rank through the tenth and last rank, creating a formation of 384 heavy cavalry. Weight could be added to the attack by creating a larger wedge formation twelve ranks deep (504 horse). Light cavalry armed with bows were added to this formation at a ratio of about one horse archer per four lancers. *Kataphraktoi* and *klibanophoroi* would remain important to the Byzantine art of war until the debacle at Manzikert in 1071, after which these types of heavy cavalry became less important.[57]

A fourth type of medium cavalry was also used by Byzantine commanders. Known as *koursores*, these mounted troops were expected to fill the role between light cavalry archers and heavy cavalry. *Koursores* engaged other medium or light cavalry or were used to run down detached or fleeing infantry. Riders wore chain or lamellar armour, carried a round shield thirty-two inches in diameter, and were armed with short *kontarion* (worn slung across the back when not in use), composite bow, one sword of either variety, and one or two maces. *Koursores* rode smaller faster horses capable of longer endurance and usually without barding.[58] It should be noted that Byzantium's access to the rich horse lands of Phrygia and Cappadocia in Anatolia helped secure quality cavalry mounts throughout the early medieval period.[59] Byzantine expansion into Armenia in the tenth century increased that access and helped fuel the recovery. The permanent loss of most of Anatolia and its valuable horse lands to the Seljuk Turks after Manzikert ushered in a period of decline the Eastern Roman Empire never recovered from.

Byzantine cavalry, which had held the central role in Eastern Roman warfare since the rise of the *tagmata* in the eighth century, now had an equal partner on the battlefield with the return of well equipped and well disciplined infantry. In fact, the new Byzantine manuals emphasized combined-arms cooperation between infantry and cavalry reminiscent of the 'mixed formations' mentioned in Maurice's *Strategikon*. In battle, infantry and cavalry worked together in a new formation, essentially a hollow battle square or rectangular (depending on the terrain) where heavy and light infantry used pikes, spears and missile weapons to cope with encircling enemy cavalry while also providing a base for attacks and safe refuge for Byzantine cavalry units.[60]

Under Romanus II (r.959–963) Crete was recovered from the Arabs, taking away an important base for Muslim pirates in the eastern Mediterranean. Romanus' successor, the soldier-emperor Nikephoros II Phokas (r.963–969), continued the reconquest of south-eastern Anatolia, defeating the Emir of Tarsus and recapturing Cyprus in 964 and reorganizing these lands into new themes. He went on to expel any Muslim who did not convert to Christianity and then invited Armenian and Syrian Christians to homestead in the newly depopulated but fertile lands. Nikephoros used these new bases

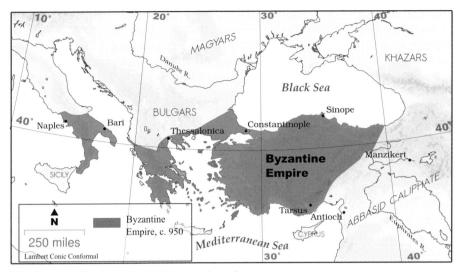

The Byzantine Empire and its neighbours in the tenth century.

to invade northern Syria, conquering both Edessa and Antioch, while his Christian Armenian allies raided and sacked the capital of Muslim Armenia. However, successes along the Eastern frontier were balanced by souring relations with the Bulgars. Rather than divert his attention from his war in Syria, Nikephoros intrigued with Svyatoslav (r.945–972), the Rus Grand Prince of Kiev, convincing him to attack the Bulgars from the north in 967. Svyatoslav easily defeated the Bulgars, taking their czar captive and incorporating eastern Bulgaria into the Rus state. Although a successful campaigner, Nikephoros' reign was weakened by three years of plague and he was murdered by his wife and replaced by John I Tzimiskes (r.969–976), a brilliant general of Armenian descent.[61]

The Rise of the Rus and the Battle of Dorostolon, 971

The new Byzantine emperor wanted to follow up his predecessor's successes in Syria but first had to deal with the growing threat of the Rus on his northern frontier. Beginning in the late eighth century, Swedish Vikings known first to the Finns and then to the Eastern Slavs as the Rus made their way down the rivers and estuaries of Eastern Europe in an attempt to establish trading links with the Byzantine Empire. Under the command of their leader Rurik (c.830–c.880), these Rus soon became involved in the Slavic civil wars, eventually dominating the native peoples and setting up powerful regional trading centres, most notably in Novgorod and Kiev.[62] Over the tenth century more Scandinavian adventurers, now known as Varangians (*Varingjar* in Old Norse, *Varjazi* in Slavonic, or *Varangoi* in Greek), joined the Rus and expanded the territory of Kiev until this principality encompassed the lands between the Danube and Volga rivers and the Baltic and Black seas.[63]

In battle, the Rus were influenced by Scandinavian, Slavic, and later Byzantine combat styles. Weapons consisted of sword or battleaxe, spear, and a round, wooden shield thirty-to-forty inches in diameter with a central iron boss. Chiefs and veterans might also wear a leather helm or metal *spangenhelm* (a forerunner to the Norman conical helm) and ring-reinforced leather jerkin or mail hauberk.[64] The Rus, like their Viking contemporaries, preferred the sword as their primary offensive arm, though the expense of this weapon often forced warriors to use axes and spears.[65] Viking sword blades were usually pattern-welded and double-edged, averaging thirty-two inches in length, with a shallow fuller on each side to reduce the weight of these hefty blades.[66] The axe, which had been nearly abandoned in warfare in the rest of Europe, found favour again in the hands of Vikings and accompanied them when they conquered Eastern Europe. Three types of battleaxe were used during this period: the *skeggox* or 'bearded axe,' so-called because of its asymmetrical blade and used in the eighth century; an intermediate type usually referred to as a 'hand-axe'; and the *breidox* or 'broad axe', first seen at the end of the tenth century and made famous in the eleventh century by the Anglo-Saxon royal bodyguard or *huscarles* at the battles of Stamford Bridge and, later, Hastings against the Normans in 1066. The broad axe took its name from the blade's distinctive crescent shape, large size (usually twelve inches along its curved edge), and five-foot haft.[67] This long hafted axe also became the signature weapon of the famous Varangian Guard.[68]

Rus spears were of light and heavy varieties, the former were thrown as javelins and had narrow blades and slim shafts, while the latter were used for shock combat and had broad, leaf-shaped blades and thicker, often iron-shod shafts. Both types of spear blades were socketed and some had short, side lobes jutting out just above the socket. This last type is often referred to as the Viking 'winged' spear.[69] Finally, archery also held an important, if ancillary, place in Viking warfare, as can be seen by the role missile fire played in both land and naval engagements. The bows themselves were of various types, including short and long varieties of self-bows. Composite bows were also used, perhaps due to contacts with steppe peoples.[70]

In battle, the Rus attacked and defended in typical Indo-European fashion. Offensively, they utilized the 'boar's head' wedge array, concentrating the shock impact of the attack on a small frontage and hopefully breaking through the opponent's formation. Once the enemy's line had been breached, Rus warriors broke into individual combat, cutting and slashing with their swords, or swinging their two-handed axes. Defensively, the Rus formed a shield wall five or more men deep, standing close enough to lock shields and presenting a frontage of only one-and-a-half feet per man. If archers and javelineers were present, they usually stood behind their companions and fired over their heads at the enemy.[71]

With the occupation of eastern Bulgaria, the power of the Rus was at a highpoint under Svyatoslav, who now wanted to expand further at the expense of Byzantine territory. In the spring of 970, Svyatoslav, together with Bulgarian and Pecheneg allies, invaded Thrace, sacking the Byzantine fortress of Philippopolis (modern Plovdiv in Bulgaria) and seizing the road to Constantinople.

Realizing that his military obligations in the east were pulling most of his manpower away from dealing with the immediate Rus threat, Emperor John hastily dispatched an elite force of between 10,000 and 12,000 men to delay the invaders. Under the command of Bardas Skleros, the Byzantine army successfully ambushed the Russo-Bulgarian host at the battle of Arcadiopolis, killing thousands and blunting any further Rus offensives in 970. Svyatoslav withdrew to the northern fortress city of Dorostolon (modern Silistra in Bulgaria). Over the winter, John ordered more Byzantine forces from Anatolia to cross into Thrace and prepared for the upcoming campaign. By April 971, a large Byzantine expeditionary army of perhaps 30,000–40,000 men was assembled, setting off and marching through the Bulgarian frontier with the *basileus Rhomaion* at its head.[72]

The Byzantine army was supported by a sizeable fleet of 300 ships as it marched towards the ancient city of Dorostolon. Founded by the Romans in the early first century during the reign of Tiberius, the walled city of Dorostolon was located on the southern bank of the lower Danube River and served as a haven for Svyatoslav and an estimated 60,000 Rus and allied soldiers, although this number is probably exaggerated because of limitations of terrain present at the battle site.[73] Emperor John's column was able to cross the numerous mountain passes through enemy territory unmolested, probably because the Rus were occupied in the far north with a Bulgarian rebellion. The Byzantines seized numerous small fortresses along the way and only received resistance as they approached Dorostolon. Here, Byzantine cavalry scouts were ambushed and killed, probably while reconnoitring a suitable encampment for the imperial army. John sent out Byzantine soldiers to comb the forests, successfully catching an unknown number of enemy ambushers. The emperor then put these prisoners to death.[74]

Once in the vicinity of Dorostolon, John established a base camp sometime in the middle of July 971. Imperial scouts relayed to him that the large Rus and allied army was arrayed in a long dense line in front of the city's walls waiting for battle, their shield wall bristling with the spears and long-hafted axes favoured by the barbarians. Leo the Deacon, a contemporary eyewitness to the battle, commented that this Rus army was devoid of cavalry.[75] To exploit this weakness, John intended to use his own powerful cavalry force and drew up his army in three divisions to match the enemy frontage, placing his heavy cavalry *koursores*, *kataphraktoi*, and *klibanophoroi* on the wings in two lines, and his heavy infantry in the centre, supported by a second line of light infantry archers and slingers. By midday both armies were arrayed for battle. Once in range, John ordered his second line bowmen and slingers to rain down shafts and bullets on the enemy shield wall. Perhaps due to mounting losses, the Rus launched a general attack all along the front. John committed his entire first line to meet the Rus assault, but kept his second line in reserve. Byzantine soldiers did break through briefly at various points along the front, but were always repulsed by barbarian counterattacks. The battle lines seesawed back and forth for an hour, and then both sides broke and returned to their original lines. After a brief rest, the Rus launched a second attack along the front, but this time John ordered his fresh cavalry on both wings into the fight. The cavalry attack on the edges of the Rus line succeeded in breaking through the shield walls and rolling up the Rus flanks. When this action was combined with a renewed push by Greek infantry in the centre, the Rus' entire line began to falter and a general rout ensued. Here, Byzantine cavalry was put to use cutting down the fleeing barbarians as they tried to reach the safety of Dorostolon's gates. Eventually, the Rus Grand Prince ordered the gates closed, fearing a Byzantine breach, and the killing continued until John ordered his army back to camp.[76]

On the second day John ordered his Byzantine soldiers to probe the city's defences, launching attacks against various points of the fortress. These attacks were met by barbarian bows and slings, with neither side getting the upper hand. After a day of unsuccessful attacks, John withdrew his troops back to camp. That evening, the Rus sent out a contingent of horsemen to test the Byzantine cordon, a move that surprised Leo the Deacon who commented that this was the first time he had witnessed the Rus using horses in the campaign. But the Rus' inexperience with cavalry was also commented on by Leo, who wrote that the Rus:

> Emerged from the fortress on horseback, making at that time their first appearance riding horses for they had always been accustomed to advance into battle without cavalry since they were untrained in mounting on horses and fighting the enemy.[77]

However, this sortie had little effect as the Rus cavalry were easily scattered by their more experienced mounted enemy, sending the barbarian horsemen back to the safety of the city gates.

Three days after the Byzantine army made their initial camp, their supporting flotilla of 300 vessels (supply ships, troop ships and war ships) arrived, many of the last armed with Greek Fire. John's troops were now directly supported by these naval vessels, which had sailed the mouth of the Danube to their position, cutting off any chance of the Rus retreating north across the river. Understanding the significance of this new strategic situation and wanting to break the siege before the new Eastern Roman troops and supplies had an impact, Svyatoslav led his army into the field again on the fourth day, but the outcome of engagement was precisely the same as the first day of the battle with Byzantine cavalry attacking the barbarian flanks and precipitating a rout back to the safety of the fortress walls.

The next day John ordered his siege equipment to be brought up and the formal siege of Dorostolon began. The Rus sent out sorties in attempts to burn the siege equipment, but were unsuccessful. On the sixth day Svyatoslav sent his army again into the field and once again John permitted his opponent to form up for a set-piece battle. This time the Byzantine emperor arrayed his infantry in a continuous division matching the long Rus shield wall. Once again, Greek cavalry was placed on the wings, while archers and slingers were placed in the second line behind the centre heavy infantry formation. The Rus attacked first and pushed the Byzantine centre backwards, inflicting heavy casualties before his mounted shock troops, including the up-armoured *kataphraktoi* and *klibanophoroi*, broke the Rus assault, sending the barbarians racing back inside the defences. One notable casualty of the day's engagement was Svyatoslav's second-in-command, killed by a member of John's imperial bodyguard. That evening under a near full moon, the Rus exited the gates of Dorostolon to collect their dead. There, in front of the walls they built huge funeral pyres, sacrificing captives, both male and female, before setting the pyres alight.[78]

Surrounded by enemy siege engines, blockaded by an enemy fleet and beaten on the battlefield three times, Svyatoslav held a war council that evening and decided to fight to the death.[79] Later that night, a sizeable contingent of some 2,000 men left the fortress in small boats, slipping the Byzantine blockade to forage for much-needed supplies. While returning to the city walls along the river bank with supplies, the Rus fell upon a Byzantine cavalry detachment watering their horses, killing all of them before escaping back into the fortress. When John heard of this lapse in security he threatened to execute his admirals should the blockade be breached again.[80]

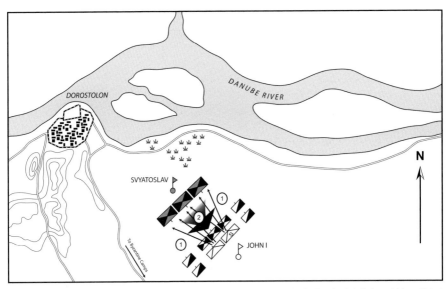

Map 3.4.1. *The Battle of Dorostolon, 971 CE. Phase I: Both armies deploy for battle by midday. John's Byzantine archers and slingers open the action with missile fire against Svyatoslav's Rus shield wall (1). Unable to respond in kind, Svyatoslav orders a general assault on the Byzantine line (2).*

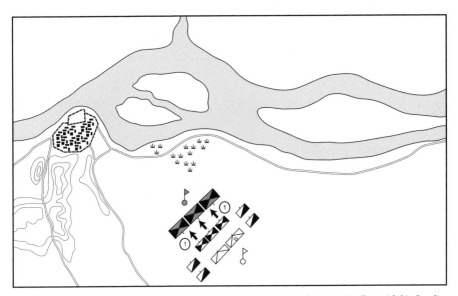

Map 3.4.2. *The Battle of Dorostolon, 971 CE. Phase II: John meets the oncoming Rus with his first line (1), leaving his archers and slingers in reserve. Though the Byzantines manage to break through in several places, Rus counterattacks always manage to drive them back. Neither side can gain advantage and both return to their original start point after an hour of close combat.*

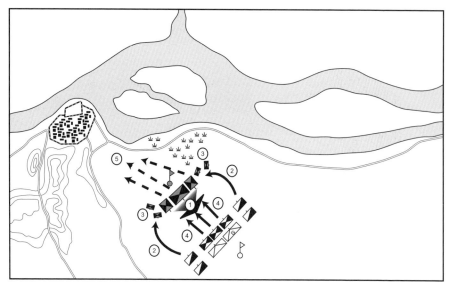

Map 3.4.3. The Battle of Dorostolon, 971 CE. Phase III: After resting and regrouping, Svyatoslav orders another general assault (1). John counters with an attack against both Rus flanks using his fresh cavalry (2) that breaks the shield wall and begins to roll up the enemy line (3). The Byzantine infantry renew their attack on the centre (4), and a rout ensues (5) as the Rus line breaks apart. The Byzantine horse pursue the fleeing survivors to the gates of the city, which are eventually closed for fear of a breach. Many Rus survivors are hunted down and killed.

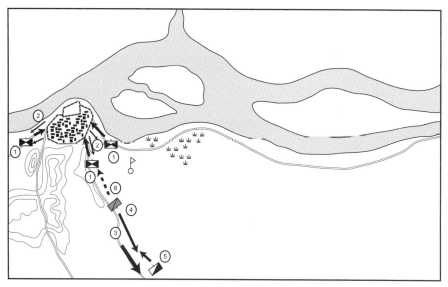

Map 3.4.4. The Battle of Dorostolon, 971 CE. Phase IV: On the second day, John's forces probe the city's perimeter (1). The defenders reply with slings and bows (2). Neither attacker nor defender gain the advantage and John breaks off his attacks and withdraws to camp (3). That evening, the Rus send forth a small cavalry detachment to probe the Byzantine cordon (4), but the inexperienced horsemen are countered by Byzantine cavalry (5) and are easily driven back to the city (6).

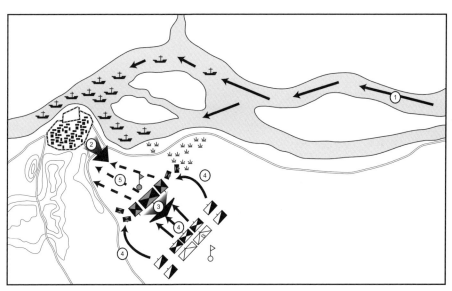

Map 3.4.5. *The Battle of Dorostolon, 971 CE. Phase V: On the third day, John's fleet of warships, transports, and supply vessels arrives (1). Svyatoslav recognizes the dire threat posed by the enemy flotilla and takes the field once again (2) in an attempt to defeat the Byzantines before additional troops, supplies, and siege equipment can be put ashore. As on the first day, the attack (3) is met by a combined infantry/cavalry counterattack (4) that drives the Rus from the field yet again (5).*

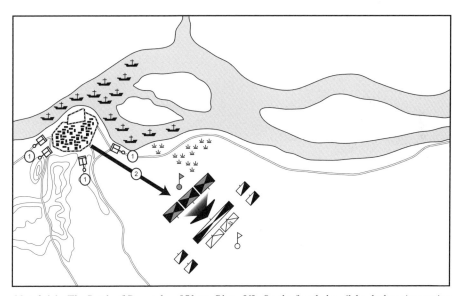

Map 3.4.6. *The Battle of Dorostolon, 971 CE. Phase VI: On the fourth day, John deploys siege engines around the city (1) to begin pounding the walls. Rus sorties fail to destroy the equipment. On the sixth day, Svyatoslav advances from the city with his army (2), a move allowed by John. The Byzantine infantry forms a continuous line to face the oncoming Rus formations with cavalry once again on the wings.*

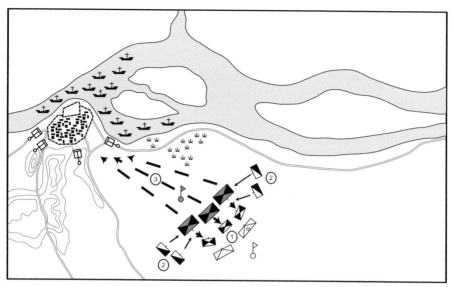

Map 3.4.7. The Battle of Dorostolon, 971 CE. Phase VII: The initial Rus assault pushes the Byzantine centre back with heavy losses (1) before the Greek heavy cavalry strikes from the flanks (2), breaking up the Rus formations and routing the barbarians (3). That night, Svyatoslav holds a council of war. The decision is made to fight to the death. Late that night, a Rus foraging party of 2,000 slip past the Byzantine blockade in small boats. Returning with desperately needed supplies, they surprise and kill a Byzantine cavalry picket along the river before re-entering the city.

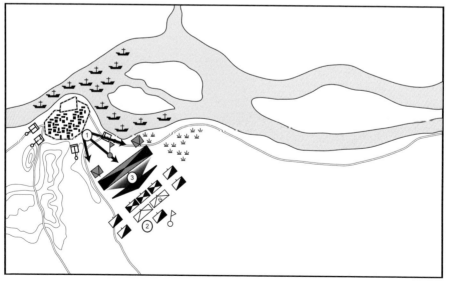

Map 3.4.8. The Battle of Dorostolon, 971 CE. Phase VIII: The following afternoon the Rus army sorties again (1), its flanks protected by archers as well as a marsh on the left and a small copse of trees on the right. John deploys much as before (2), with an added cavalry reserve behind the infantry centre under his personal command. Svyatoslav opens the battle with a general assault on the Byzantine centre (3).

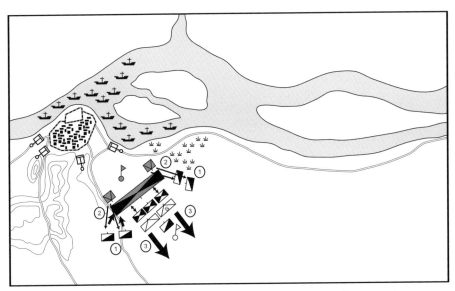

Map 3.4.9. *The Battle of Dorostolon, 971 CE. Phase IX: The Byzantine cavalry once again attempts to roll up the Rus flanks (1), but this time they are stopped in their tracks by archery and javelin fire (2) and impeded by the constricted terrain. The horsemen suffer heavy losses. The Greek line holds, but John decides to withdraw (3) to more open terrain that will allow greater mobility for his cavalry.*

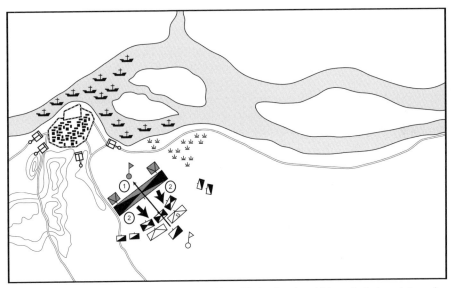

Map 3.4.10. *The Battle of Dorostolon, 971 CE. Phase X: During the withdrawal, the imperial cavalry reserve surges forward to assist the infantry in breaking contact with the Rus. Their commander, Anemas, manages to fight his way through the enemy's line to the grand prince's position (1). He knocks the prince from his horse before he is dragged from his saddle and killed. Viewing the action, Rus morale soars and they launch a vicious attack against the Byzantine centre (2), which begins to collapse.*

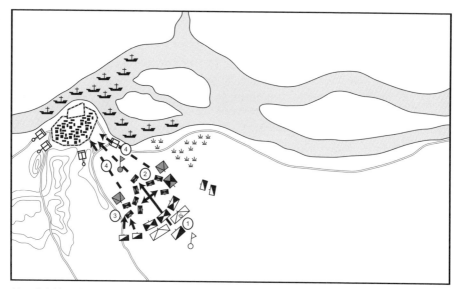

Map 3.4.11. The Battle of Dorostolon, 971 CE. Phase XI: John orders his cavalry reserve into action. The imperial horsemen stabilize the Byzantine centre (1), penetrate the Rus line (2), and begin to roll up the flanks from the inside. At the same time, one of the Byzantine cavalry wings manages to turn one of the Rus flanks (3), hastening the collapse of the line. The Rus rout back towards the city gates (4), but the Byzantine cavalry are well positioned and easily ride down the fugitives, killing 15,000 Rus and allied warriors. Svyatoslav reneges on his pledge to fight to the death and asks the emperor for terms. In return for leaving the city intact and abandoning their plunder, John allows the barbarians safe passage across the Danube. Svyatoslav is killed in a Pecheneg ambush while en route to Kiev.

The following afternoon, Svyatoslav's army emerged again from the city gates and formed up in a single deep shield wall, but this time the Rus lined up closer to the walls in an attempt to narrow the front, anchoring their left flank on a marsh and their right flank on a stand of trees to lessen the chance of enemy cavalry rolling up their flanks. The Grand Prince placed the bulk of his archers to further protect his wings against the inevitable cavalry onslaught. John ordered his army to form up across from the barbarian line, well aware of the disadvantage to his mounted troops. Staying with imperial doctrine, the Byzantines formed up in three divisions, with infantry in the centre and cavalry on the wings, and the emperor himself commanding a cavalry reserve behind the footmen in the centre. Once again, the Rus initiated battle by rushing the centre, but this time the Greek cavalry counterattack on the wings was met with concentrated javelin and archery fire, severely mauling the horsemen. Leo the Deacon writes 'once the battle broke out the [Rus] stoutly attacked the Romans, harassing them with javelins and wounding their horses with arrows and hurling their riders to the ground.'[81]

Although the Byzantine lines were holding, John recognized his troops were suffering from the heat of the late July afternoon and ordered watered-down wine rations to be distributed to his soldiers. When it became apparent that the battlefield prepared by his enemy was proving too costly in men and horses, John commanded a withdrawal back to a broader plain where his cavalry had more room to manoeuvre. The imperial troops were able to disengage and fall back to a better position. During this orderly retreat, the mounted imperial unit surged forward to assist in the withdrawal. Here, the commander of the unit, a man named Anemas, fought his way to the Grand Prince's position and knocked him off his horse before he was himself pulled from his mount and murdered under a flurry of spears, swords and axes.[82]

Anemas' death invigorated the Rus who launched a fierce attack against the Byzantine centre, pushing the Greek infantry backwards with such ferocity that the elite *klibanophoroi* guard behind them began to balk. Seeing this at first hand John immediately committed his cavalry reserve to the fight, first stabilizing the centre and then breaking through to run the barbarian flanks. Contemporaries also remark that this last phase of the battle was accompanied by a thunderstorm and strong winds blowing into the faces of the Rus, no doubt assisting in the Byzantine breakthrough.[83] To make matters worse for the Rus, at this same moment one of the imperial wings, commanded by Bardas Skleros, was successful in turning one of the flanks of the shield wall (history does not record which flank), precipitating the collapse of one side of the barbarian line. The entire Rus effort collapsed and, once again, warriors made for the safety of the Dorostolon's walls. But this time, Byzantine cavalry was in an excellent position to cut down the fleeing men. Some 15,000 Rus and allied warriors were killed, compared with 350 imperial casualties.[84]

His army broken, Svyatoslav went back on his pledge to die to the last man and asked the emperor to negotiate. John allowed the remaining barbarians safe passage across the Danube if they left Dorostolon undamaged and their plunder behind. The Grand Prince agreed, but was killed in a Pecheneg ambush on his return to Kiev.[85] John left a strong garrison at Dorostolon and returned to Constantinople, where his victory was celebrated in a triumphant parade. John then expanded Byzantine borders into Bulgar territories recently held by the Rus, adding this region to the empire and dividing it into six new themes. In a short four-month campaign John was able to defeat a powerful northern opponent and secure the Byzantine Danubian frontier for the first time since the seventh century. With this frontier secure, John turned his attention to the east where he raided Arab Mesopotamia and invaded Syria in 975, using the Byzantine base at Antioch to press southwards to the edge of Muslim-controlled Tripoli. John intended to invade the rest of Palestine and free Jerusalem but died unexpectedly in 976, leaving his co-emperor, the eighteen-year-old Basil II (r.976–1025), sole ruler.[86] Basil immediately faced a long rebellion led by Bardas Skleros, who controlled the Byzantine armies of Anatolia. Meanwhile, the Danubian frontier acted up with the Bulgars invading Byzantine territory and defeating Basil in 986 at the battle of Sophia. Facing internal and external threats, Basil turned to the Rus for assistance.

Varangians, Bulgars and the Wars of Basil II – 'The Bulgar-slayer'
Despite the war with Svyatoslav Byzantine relations with the Rus would warm in the late tenth century with both states developing strong religious, economic and military ties. In 987, the Kievan Grand Prince Vladimir I's (r.958–1015) conversion to Greek Orthodoxy established a formal religious union with Constantinople. To strengthen political ties and secure a much needed ally Basil II offered his sister's hand to Vladimir in exchange for a force of 6,000 Varangian soldiers to assist the Greek emperor with the

Anatolian rebellion and shore up his failing Bulgar frontier.[87] Byzantine emperors were quite familiar with these Viking warriors having hired small bodies of these mercenaries for expeditions as early as 911 when Rus soldiers assisted the Eastern Romans in their attack against Arab-controlled Crete.[88] However, Basil greatly increased the involvement of these northerners in imperial politics when he created a personal bodyguard called the Varangian Guard in 988. These Varangians, lacking military lands, proved loyal to Byzantine emperors who paid them very well.[89] With the assistance of his new Viking guard, Basil was able to crush the rebellion in a three-year civil war. By 990 Basil was once again in control of his empire.

Basil proved to be an ardent campaigner and master politician. His first action was to attack the Caucus kingdom of Iberia for supporting the rebels, removing its king and absorbing the territory into the empire. He then launched a war against the Bulgars, who during the rebellions had retaken the majority of eastern Bulgaria under their ambitious czar, Samuel (r.997–1014), who was also expanding at the expense of the Croats and Serbs. Basil had to interrupt his Balkan campaigns to tend to his eastern frontier when raiding by Muslim soldiers from the Syria emirates, now sponsored by the powerful Egyptian Fatimid dynasty (909–1171), threatened Byzantine possessions in Syria. After calming this region, Basil returned to battle the Bulgars, retaking all of eastern Bulgaria and periodically raiding deep into western Bulgaria to keep Samuel on the defensive.[90] Despite years of annual campaigns, Basil was unable to bring the war to a favourable conclusion. That changed in the spring of 1014.

In May of that year, Basil launched a sizeable raiding expedition (the sources do not say how large) north into Bulgarian territory using the Strumitsa River Valley as its access point.[91] Samuel, reduced to protecting what remained of his empire after nearly twenty years of Eastern Roman incursions, used the well-established military practice seen earlier at Pliska in 811 to build wooden walls and ditches across the gorges to block the Byzantine invasion. Samuel picked the area around Kleidion (modern Klyuch in south-western Bulgaria) to build his defensive works. When the Byzantine army first encountered the high wooden palisade it attempted to storm the defensive position, but suffered heavy casualties. Basil pulled his army back and sent scouts to see if the army could easily skirt the obstacle by marching east or west. His men returned with news that the Bulgars had similar defensive works blocking other routes north, news that threatened to derail the campaign of 1014. At this time one of Basil's trusted generals, Nikephoros Xiphias, commander of Philippopolis, volunteered to take a small elite force over the mountains and attack the present position from behind. Basil agreed and orchestrated small raids against the palisade to occupy the Bulgars as Nikephoros' flanking force found a narrow and difficult trail west of the pass across the area of Mount Balesca. At dawn on 29 July, Nikephoros' ordered his men to attack the rear lines of the unsuspecting Bulgars, sending the barbarians into a panic. At the same time, Basil launched an assault against the palisades, overcoming the defenders and tearing down the obstacles. Caught between two Byzantine forces, some of the Bulgars were killed, but most of them surrendered. In the chaos Samuel avoided capture, whisked away from the battle by his son, Gabriel.

Having crushed the Bulgarians, Basil was said to have captured 15,000 prisoners and blinded 99 of every 100 men, leaving 150 one-eyed men to lead the defeated army back to their czar. On viewing his mutilated soldiers, Samuel reportedly suffered a stroke and

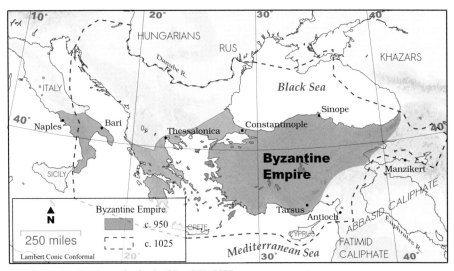

The Byzantine Empire at the death of Basil II, 1025.

died two days later. Although the extent of Basil's mistreatment of the Bulgarian prisoners may have been exaggerated, this brutal incident helped give rise to Basil's nickname of *Boulgaroktonos*, 'the Bulgar-slayer', in later Byzantine tradition.[92] The Byzantine victory at Kleidion effectively ended any large-scale organized resistance by the Bulgarians and over the next few years Basil completed the conquest of Bulgaria, once again making the Danube River the northern frontier of the Byzantine Empire.

Basil died in 1025 after ruling for forty-nine years. At his death the Byzantine army was the most powerful military force in the Eastern Mediterranean. The Byzantine resurgence under the Macedonian emperors, especially Nikephoros II, John I and Basil II, had nearly doubled the size of the empire since the 860s.[93] But in the decades following Basil's passing the House of Macedon was poorly served by a succession of weak emperors who attracted internal revolts and neglected the army. Unable to trust their own Greek commanders, these Byzantine emperors relied more and more on foreign mercenaries and allied auxiliaries for security, but even these troops were not always loyal. The mid-eleventh century witnessed the growing influence of the Varangians on the Byzantine court and military, while the Normans, who first fought against imperial interests in southern Italy beginning in 1017, later found employment in the Byzantine army as mercenaries, fighting alongside Varangian soldiers from Sicily to Georgia by the mid-century. In fact, this growing reliance on foreign mercenaries would erode Byzantium's ability to meet a powerful new enemy massing in the east in the eleventh century, the Seljuk Turks.

Chapter 4

Islamic Warfare from the Umayyads to the Coming of the Seljuk Turks

The Expansion of Dar al-Islam under the Umayyads, 661–750

The first thirty years of Islamic conquest under the Rashidun caliphs (632–661) witnessed the expansion of Arab power over the Levant, Mesopotamia, Egypt and Libya, precipitating the collapse of the Sassanian Persian Empire and great territorial contraction for the Byzantine Empire. During the first decades of the Umayyad Caliphate (661–750) these spectacular victories continued in the east with the conquest of Transoxiana and the Sindh (the region near the mouth of the Indus River in what is now southern Pakistan). In the west, Muslim armies swept across North Africa, and then used bases there to invade the Iberian Peninsula (Spain and Portugal) and Septimania (Mediterranean coast of south-western France). By 750, the armies of Islam controlled the largest empire in world history up to that date, stretching from the Atlantic Ocean to the Indus River, an area of some five million square miles and an estimated thirty million inhabitants.[1]

Central to the success of the wider Islamic conquests was the establishment of regional armies known as *junds*. Traditionally, the first organization of *junds* is attributed to the second Rashidun caliph Umar (r.634–644), although in reality it should be credited to the first two Umayyad caliphs, Muawaiyah (r.661–680) and Yazid (r.680–683).[2] These *junds*, like the later Byzantine thematic armies, were organized around fortified provincial cities, the first being Damascus in Syria, Tiberias in Jordan, and Jerusalem, Ascalon, and Homs in Palestine.[3] The earliest Syrian *junds* were closely tied to the caliphs and probably served as an elite guard similar to the role the *tagmata* would serve for Byzantine emperors. However, as Islam swept across south-west Asia and North Africa, new *junds* appeared with non-Arab Muslim converts (*Mawali*) forming the majority of the Muslim armies, although Arab Muslims, especially those from Arabia and Syria, made up the officer corps, with senior members of the Umayyad family often holding command positions, and later, governorships.[4] These *jund* armies made possible the expansive and extended campaigns of the early Umayyad Caliphate.

Of all of the Islamic campaigns of conquest in the first century of the faith, the fighting in Transoxiana was the hardest and longest in duration. Historians usually break these campaigns into four phases. Phase one consisted of intermittent Muslim raids across the Oxus River between the 650s and 705, with Arab commanders nearly always returning to their base in Merv before the beginning of winter, leaving no permanent garrisons behind. The second phase took place in the decade between 705 and 715 when Arab commanders invaded Transoxiana and established garrisons in important Central Asian cities like Bukhara and Samarkand. However, the third phase between 716 and 737 saw military reverses for the Arabs at the hands of the resurgent Turks and local allied princes, while the fourth and final phase (737–751) witnessed Arab governors and local princes reaching a compromise that left the region officially under the Islamic banner but with local princes exercising control.[5] This period ended in 751 with the new Abbasid Caliphate's victory over a Tang Chinese army at the important battle of Talas River, checking Chinese expansion west and opening Central Asia for further Islamization eastward.[6]

During these same decades Muslim generals were pushing east from their Persian bases into the Indian frontier. In 664 Muslim generals began raiding the Hindu-controlled Punjab region of what is now Pakistan and between 711 and 712 a large Arab expedition led by the brilliant young Arab general Muhammad bin Qasim (695–715), the son of a local Arab governor, brought the Sindh under Umayyad control, marking the beginning of the Muslim conquest of the Indian subcontinent. Further Muslim penetrations were halted in 738 with a Hindu victory at the battle of Rajasthan, establishing once again the west bank of the Indus River as the border of *Dar al-Islam*. But the conquests in India presented a new a problem for the victorious Muslims. Most of their new subjects were either Hindus or Buddhists, two faiths that worshipped a plethora of images and statues, a practice considered to be idolatry by the Muslims. Normal practice was to offer subjugated populations the choice of conversion to Islam or death, options not practical in South Asia. In order to rule the Sindh (and later deeper into India), the Muslim conquerors moderated their views as they had earlier with the Zoroastrians in Persia, allowing the Hindus and Buddhists to keep their lives, property and religious practices, and even began to consider these populations members of the *dhimmis*.[7]

In the west Umayyad armies used their bases in Libya to launch an invasion of Byzantine and Berber-controlled North Africa beginning in 665, but this did not become a serious endeavour until the end of the century. The Umayyad caliph Abd al-Malik Marwan (r.685–705), after successfully putting down a series of internal rebellions, allocated 40,000 men for a westward push across North Africa.[8] In 698 a combined Arab land and sea assault forced the evacuation of the Eastern Roman provincial capital of Carthage and then put the city to the torch. Byzantine resistance crumbled after a second Arab victory at Utica. This region, won back for Eastern Rome from the Vandals by Belisarios in 533, was now for ever lost to Islam. The Muslims would later found the city of Tunis in this region and use its harbours to establish a powerful Islamic maritime presence in the western Mediterranean.

By 708 North Africa from Egypt to Tunisia was under Arab control, but the region west corresponding to modern Algeria and Morocco was still very much a 'wild west' with Berber tribes controlling the hinterland and Muslim armies garrisoning major coastal cities like Tangiers. Eventually, the Berbers would convert to Islam, but even they were not always content with Arab rule, as the rebellion of 740–741 illustrates.[9] Still, Berber troops entered the service of Arab commanders in large numbers in the

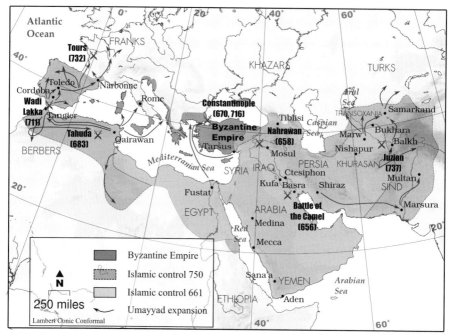

The Umayyad Caliphate in 750.

early eighth century and would provide the backbone of the Muslim invasion force sent to conquer Spain in 711.

The Muslim Invasion of Catholic Europe and the Battle of Tours, 732

In the early summer of 711, the Umayyad caliph Al-Walid I (r.705–715) ordered the conquest of Christian Spain. An Arab-led Berber army of some 12,000 *jund* infantry and 300 Arab cavalry under the command of Tariq ibn Ziyad crossed from Morocco to the southernmost tip of Spain, landing near a huge rock the Arabs named after their commanding general, *Jebel Tariq* ('Rock of Tariq'), from which the modern day Gibraltar derives its name.[10] The Muslim army swept north, defeating the new Christian Visigothic king Rodrigo's (r.711) army at Guadelete in July, then marched north and seized the Christian capital at Toledo. Visigothic resistance melted away and by 714 nearly the entire peninsula lay under Arab rule. The Arab conquerors quickly established an Islamic state in what they called *al-Andalus*, also known to history as Moorish Spain. Within a year of conquering the Iberian Peninsula, the Muslims began raiding north of the Pyrenees. These initial raids were relatively minor, but in 732, a large Muslim army led by the dynamic and popular governor or emir of Spain, Abdul Rahman al-Ghafiqi, crossed the Pyrenees and invaded Aquitaine. After crushing the duke of Aquitaine's army near the city of Bordeaux, the invading army advanced north towards the city of Orleans in the kingdom of Burgundy.[11]

Abdul Rahman's army was not an army of occupation, but rather a large expeditionary force of between 20,000 and 25,000 cavalry, supported by a small contingent of infantry.[12] The high percentage of cavalry present indicates a raiding, rather than occupying force, rebuffing a popular belief that the Muslims were bent on including Western Europe in their empire. The Muslim army that marched toward Frankish territory in 732 was a well-armed, disciplined and experienced army of plunderers.

Islamic cavalry in the early eighth century consisted of both light and heavy units and was relatively lightly armoured and mobile. Heavy lancers balanced by stirrups were not yet common in North Africa so mounted shock combat consisted of charges with sword and light lance. And unlike their Byzantine counterparts, Muslim heavy cavalry were comfortable dismounting and fighting on foot next to their infantry.[13] Light cavalry were also present, using tribal weapons like light lances, javelins and bows as their primary offensive arms.

Word of the Muslim invasion reached the Frankish leader Charles Martel while he was engaged in operations along the upper Danube River, forcing him back to Austrasia to evaluate the situation. Grandfather of Charlemagne, Charles 'Martel' ('the Hammer', c.688–741) was the *major domus* or mayor of the palace for the Merovingian Frankish kings. Between 717 and 732, Charles secured himself as the de facto ruler of the Franks (the actual kings were now seen as mere figureheads), subjugating Bavaria and Alemannia in the south-east and making war against the Saxons in the north. Charles was an experienced and capable campaigner, well aware of the growing Moorish threat in Iberia. To meet this threat, Charles created a small professional army financed, in part, by land and property seized from the Catholic Church.[14]

Charles Martel's army included his loyal nobles, their retainers and servants, as well as Neustrian and Austrasian allies, those Aquitainians who has escaped north to fight, and a large number of infantry conscripts swelling the ranks to protect their homes. The total number varies from 30,000 to 80,000, but only 15,000 to 20,000 were actually mounted, and it was this mounted contingent that actually rode towards the Arab forces early in October 732.[15] Most, if not all, of the Frankish nobles and their retainers were mounted, which gave Charles the strategic mobility he required to move from Austrasia to the area near Tours in pursuit of the Muslim army. The Frankish army was primarily a force of mounted infantry who dismounted to fight, with men from the same estate or towns standing together and feudal vassals gathered around their lords.[16] Still, Charles did possess some heavy cavalry as shock troops, perhaps as many as a few thousand.[17] The wealthier noble horsemen wore mail hauberks, helmets and carried round convex shields and used their long swords as frequently as their lances for attack, while lesser vassals wore little or no defensive protection, usually just a helmet and carrying a shield and employing a light lance, long sword or *scramasax*.[18] These less armoured heavy cavalry often employed javelins as well. Stirrups, if present at all, were certainly not a common feature on Frankish cavalry in the early eighth century.[19]

The duke of Aquitaine, who escaped the debacle at Bordeaux, urged the mayor to move south immediately to intercept the Muslims, but Charles, perhaps knowing something of the nature of Muslim armies, wanted to wait until they were over-encumbered with plunder.[20] Islamic armies had a tendency to acquire large amounts of treasure, slowing the pace of the raid. Muslim commanders were reluctant to discourage looting because the majority of their troops fought solely for that purpose.

As the encumbered Muslim army neared Poitiers, the Frankish mayor readied his army to meet them.

As Charles secretly moved his army to intercept the invaders, the Muslims halted temporarily by the fortified city of Poitiers. Leaving part of his army to invest the city, Abdul Rahman advanced to the Loire River, near Tours, plundering en route. The sack

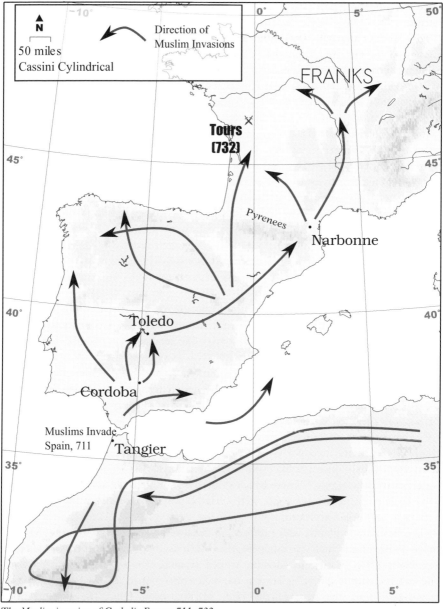

The Muslim invasion of Catholic Europe 711–732.

of Poitiers undoubtedly provided the Arab commander's army with a great deal of plunder, adding to the considerable amount of treasure acquired since the invasion began. But the Muslim army became disorganized while besieging Poitiers. Discipline was suffering due to the greed for spoil, and they were totally oblivious to the approaching Franks.[21] Abdul Rahman was preparing to besiege Tours when his scouts suddenly discovered Charles Martel's army marching towards the city. Rather than expose his plunder to danger, Abdul Rahman dispatched it south in a wagon train, then lifted the siege of Tours and withdrew slowly back to Poitiers. Martel pursued the retreating Muslim army, almost certainly with his mounted contingent.

For six days the Muslims withdrew, fighting delaying actions and pressing for Poitiers. Using his superior mobility, Martel finally outmanoeuvred the Arab general by bringing his mounted army parallel the Muslim's escape route, forcing Abdul Rahman to offer battle. The Muslims made camp between Tours and Poitiers, probably near Cenon on the Vienne River.[22] The Franks encamped near the Muslims and prepared for the coming engagement.

As dawn broke Charles Martel deployed his troops on some high ground, forming his dismounted infantry into a number of large battle formations. Charles realized his mounted warriors were no match for the skilled Muslim horsemen, therefore he dismounted most of them to strengthen the resolve of his footmen. He did, however, maintain a small contingent of cavalry in order to counter the Muslim's greater mobility and plug breaches in his infantry lines. The Frankish mayor harboured a realistic fear that his conscript infantry would break under the ferocity of Muslim charges, so he placed his veteran heavy infantry in the very front ranks of the battle lines to better resist the Muslim mounted attacks.[23]

The Muslims opened the battle just after dawn with several cavalry charges. These attacks were subsequently repeated all along the lines, but their piecemeal nature made little impression on the Frankish shield walls. The Muslims enjoyed much more success using their horse archers against the lightly or unarmoured conscripts in the centre of Charles' battle squares. Throughout the morning and afternoon, groups of Arabs and Berbers threw themselves again and again at the Frankish lines, but the defenders' shield walls held. Unable to coordinate a unified and cohesive charge against the Franks, Abdul Rahman lost many of his horsemen in small unit charges. As evening approached, the exhausted Frankish veterans in the front ranks began to fail and the Muslims opened several breaches in the lines, cutting their way into the vulnerable centre of the Frankish army.[24]

At the very moment when the battle seemed to be turning in favour of the Muslims, word spread among those hacking their way into the Frankish centre that the Franks were looting their camp. Whether by accident or design, a contingent of Frankish horse rode around the Muslim's right flank and rear, using the terrain to mask their approach, and began attacking the raiders' tents and wagons.[25] More concerned with their booty than the battle at hand, the Muslim attack wavered, with some horsemen breaking away from the fighting in order to rush back and protect their threatened base. Sensing a change of fortune, Charles ordered his troops onto the offensive. The force and suddenness of the Frankish counterattack surprised Abdul Rahman and he was left exposed as he attempted to rally his retreating troops. Here, the eighth-century chronicler known to history as Isidore de Beja wrote:

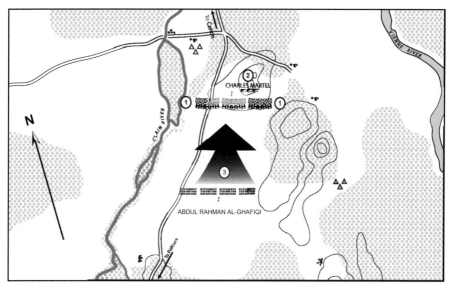

Map 4.1.1. The Battle of Tours, 732 CE. *Phase I: Charles Martel forms his Frankish army on some high ground astride the Roman road to Poitiers. His dismounted infantry deploys into several large formations with his veteran heavy infantry in the front rank to stiffen the resolve of the conscripts behind them (1). A cavalry contingent remains mounted to the rear of the line (2). Abdul Rahman al-Ghafiqi's army approaches the Franks' position (3). His forces are mounted with a considerable number of horse archers in their ranks.*

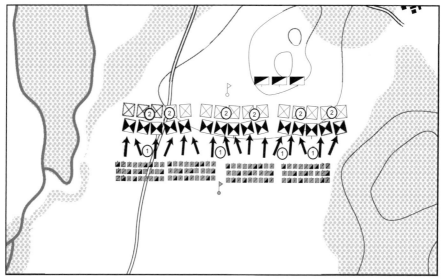

Map 4.1.2. The Battle of Tours, 732 CE. *Phase II: Abdul Rahman opens the battle with several charges against the Frankish line (1), but the attacks are piecemeal and uncoordinated. The Muslim horse archers make themselves felt and casualties amongst the lightly armoured conscripts begin to mount (2).*

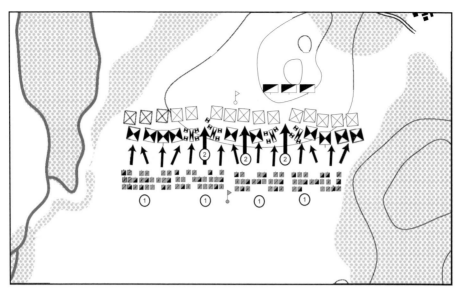

Map 4.1.3. The Battle of Tours, 732 CE. Phase III: Muslim losses mount (1) as the lack of cohesion amongst the attackers takes its toll. As evening approaches, exhausted Frankish veterans begin to waver and Abdul Rahman's horsemen are able to penetrate the line in several places (2).

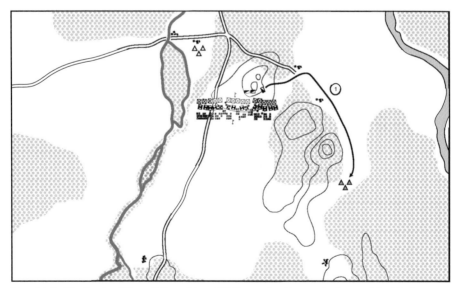

Map 4.1.4. The Battle of Tours, 732 CE. Phase IV: Just as the tide turns in favour of the Muslim army, a contingent of Frankish cavalry strikes out in a looping arc around the Muslim right and rear to strike at their camp and wagons (1).

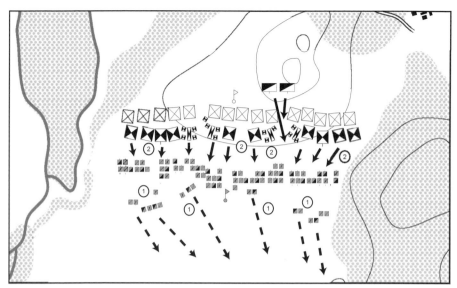

Map 4.1.5. The Battle of Tours, 732 CE. Phase V: As word of the raid on their camp spreads, the Muslim attack wavers. Some horsemen begin to break for the rear (1), worried that their plunder stored in the camp is at risk. Charles recognizes the shift in his fortunes and orders a counterattack (2).

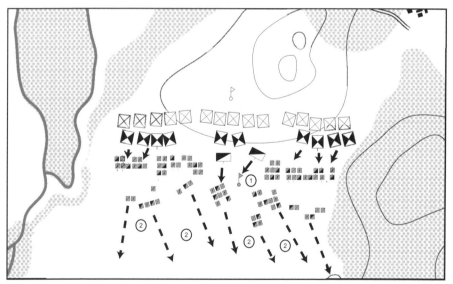

Map 4.1.6. The Battle of Tours, 732 CE. Phase VI: The sudden reversal of momentum takes Abdul Rahman by surprise and, momentarily exposed during the melee, he is cut down (1) while trying to rally his troops. News of his death sparks a general rout (2) and the Frankish onslaught drives the Muslims back to their camp as darkness falls. The Franks break off the action and return to their own camp, posting sentries in anticipation of a counterattack. The following morning Charles deploys his army for battle only to find that the Muslim army decamped during the night, abandoning their plunder. Charles opts not to pursue, taking the treasure for himself and his army.

The Austrasians [Franks], vast of limb and iron of hand, hewed on bravely in the thick of the fight; it was they who found and cut down the Saracen king.[26]

News of Abdul Rahman's death turned a frantic Muslim withdrawal into a general rout. As darkness fell, the furious Frankish counterattack forced the Muslim army back into its camp.

The Franks returned to the protection of their own camp and spent an uneasy night on constant alert to a Muslim nocturnal attack. But, to their great surprise, the Franks discovered the next morning that the Muslims had fled during the night, abandoning all their plunder. In all, perhaps 10,000 Arabs were killed at Tours. Most of the Muslim wounded were offered no quarter, given their previous record of murder and pillage in Christian territories.[27] Frankish casualties went unrecorded, but were probably moderate. Charles refused to pursue the fleeing Muslims, preferring instead to take the treasure for himself and his army, and consolidating his power over his political and military rivals at home and abroad.[28]

Along with the successful repulsing of Arab forces from the walls and harbours of Constantinople in 717, the Frankish victory at Tours fifteen years later represents a blunting of Islamic penetrations along the periphery of Christian Europe. Tours signalled the high-water mark for the Muslim advance into Western Europe with Muslim armies never again reaching as far north. However, the Frankish victory in itself did not save Western Europe from the onslaught of Islam. Charles Martel would face other Muslim raiders in southern France at Avignon in 737 and Corbières in 738 and a persistent Islamic presence north of the Pyrenees would not be vanquished until his son, Pepin III ('the Short'), pushed the Muslims from Septimania in 759. The armies of Catholicism and Islam would continue to battle south of the Pyrenees for another seven centuries, with the last Islamic outpost of Granada in Spain surrendering to Isabella and Ferdinand in January 1492, ending nearly 800 years of Moorish Spain.

Changes in Islamic Warfare in the Late Umayyad and Early Abbasid Caliphates

In 750 the Umayyad Caliphate was overthrown in a bloody civil war by Abu al-Abbas (r.750–754), a direct descendent of Muhammad's youngest uncle and founder of the Abbasid Caliphate (750-1258). Abu al-Abbas used his Arab power base in Islamic Khurasan and local non-Arab Muslim supporters (*Mawali*) to build an army and challenge the last Umayyad caliph, Marwan II (r.744–750). Muslim discontent with Umayyad rule had been growing for decades due to political and moral corruption in Damascus and poor treatment of *Mawali* by selfish governors in the provinces. Moreover, the Umayyads, who claimed no direct descent from Muhammad, were disliked by the powerful and influential Shia sect, who saw Abu al-Abbas and his Sunni Abbasid dynasty as a more legitimate alternative. In January 750 the Abbasid army, joined by their Shia allies, defeated Marwan and his larger Umayyad host at the battle of Zab River in northern Iraq, ushering in five hundred years of Abbasid rule.

Abbasid interest in Asia over the Mediterranean world became immediately evident when the great Muslim victory over Tang China at the battle of Talas River in 751 opened Central Asia and its lucrative Silk Roads to Islam. In 762, a new Muslim capital was established in Baghdad on the Tigris River, a move that continued the shift in

Islam's political interests eastward while relieving some of the military pressure on Byzantium and Catholic Western Europe. The Abbasid court in Baghdad was filled with *Mawali* from all over the caliphate, with Persians taking a central role in governing. The office of *vizier* was created, shifting the day-to-day executive power from the caliph to his chief Persian advisor. Slowly the caliph was transformed into a figurehead more interested in his harem and court life than providing the political, religious and military leadership once associated with Muhammad's successors. Eventually, weak Abbasid rulers would invite succession and numerous smaller Muslim dynasties would spin off from Baghdad and create rival and sometimes even more powerful Islamic states.

Under the Umayyad Caliphate Islamic armies began to mirror their enemies in tactics, equipment and organization. The last Umayyad caliph, Marwan II, is credited with standardizing his army, sub-dividing his forces into smaller units (*kardus*), each including heavy infantry, light infantry archers and heavy cavalry lancers. Muslim infantry fought in the Byzantine fashion, placing the better-armoured foot soldiers in the front. But unlike Byzantine horsemen, Islamic cavalry would dismount and fight as infantry, using their lances as pikes. Muslim heavy cavalry mounts were protected with felt barding, while their riders wore coifs and hauberks and were armed with maces, straight-hilted swords and the large *khanjar* or daggers. In order to better stabilize these heavier warriors on their mounts, the leather loop stirrup was replaced by metal ones.[29]

These martial trends continued into the Abbasid Caliphate (750–1258), though persisting contacts with Central Asians began to impact the Islamic way of mounted war. Abbasid generals increasingly utilized Khurasani (eastern Persian) and Turkish horse archers, armoured in lamellar cuirasses and round leather shields, and armed with lance and short composite bow.[30] Turkish influences continued to grow in the ninth century as *junds* were augmented by *ghulams* or Turkish regular troops. Later, some of these *ghulams*, purchased as slave children then trained and converted to Islam, would serve the Abbasid caliphs as their personal bodyguard.[31] And like the Roman Praetorian Guard before them, these slave-soldiers were seldom employed against Islam's external enemies, becoming instead caliph-makers and architects of palace intrigue.[32] *Ghulam* heavy cavalry were the finest in the Islamic world, marrying elements of steppe warfare (use of bow and lasso from horseback) with those of traditional mounted Islamic warfare (use of Arab lance and sword).

Islamic infantry under the Umayyad and early Abbasid caliphates often fought using indigenous weapons and armour and according to regional tactics. The first North African infantry were poorly equipped with large leather shields and javelins and if swords were carried, they were of poor quality. These men fought as free warriors, but later Islamic North African dynasties (most notably the Tulunids and Fatimids of Egypt) would utilize slave-warriors taken from Saharan tribes.[33] In the Islamic east, Umayyad and Abbasid caliphs relied heavily on Daylami soldiers, first recruited into Arab armies after the Muslim victory at al-Qadisiya. Daylami warriors fought as heavy infantry behind shield walls, advancing slowly and using javelins to break up enemy formations before engaging with their distinctive two-pronged spear, battleaxes and maces. The Khurasan region also provided Muslim commanders with excellent professional soldiers well versed in combined-arms tactics and, equally important, siegecraft.[34]

Although the Abbasid caliphs would continue to be the symbolic leaders of Islam until the Mongol destruction of Baghdad in 1258, by the ninth century, the centralized empire enjoyed by earlier caliphs was replaced by political fragmentation. At the turn of the millennium, Turkish influence on Islamic warfare would increase dramatically with the appearance of the Seljuk Turks, who converted to Sunni Islam and overran Afghanistan and eastern Persia in the 1040s and entered Baghdad in 1055, becoming the de facto rulers of Abbasid holdings. The Great Seljuk Empire reached its zenith in the 1070s with the defeat of the Byzantine emperor Romanus IV Diogenes (r.1068–1071) at Manzikert in 1071, robbing the Eastern Roman Empire of its prime Anatolian lands and precipitating the First Crusade. By the year 1000, Islamic warfare was no longer controlled by the Sunni successors of Muhammad, but was now the enterprise of the various converted peoples led by their commanders and political leaders.

One of the most powerful of these new Islamic states was the Fatimid Caliphate (909–1171) centred first in Tunisia, and then in Egypt, founding the city of Cairo in 969. This Shia caliphate was named after Muhammad's daughter Fatimid from whom the founder of the dynasty, Abdullah al-Mahdi Billah, claimed descent. At the height of their power, the Fatimids controlled a vast empire that stretched westward across the North African Maghreb to the Atlantic Ocean, south into the Sudan and western Arabia (where they controlled both of the holy cities of Mecca and Medina), and north-east to the edge of Byzantine Syria and Abbasid domains in Mesopotamia.[35] They also competed with the Byzantine Empire (and sometimes Norman adventurers) for control of the island of Sicily and southern Italy during this period.

The Fatimids possessed a powerful *ghulam* slave army and formidable navy and are remembered for their religious tolerance towards non-Shia Muslims, Jews and Coptic Christians and their pragmatic approach to statecraft (government positions were based on merit and open to all religions). The result of these policies was a secure and prosperous caliphate with strong economic ties to Christian Europe and a vested interest in maintaining a balance of power with its neighbours, chief among them the resurgent Byzantine Empire and a weakened Abbasid Caliphate under the control of the Shia Buyid dynasty (932–1055). Originally from Persia, the Buyids and their famous Daylami warriors became a major players in Mesopotamia in the tenth century and used that influence to push their way into Abbasid politics, acting as sort of mayors of the palace over weak Sunni caliphs.[36] The Fatimids supported the Buyid regime in Baghdad, recognizing the utility of maintaining the caliph's role as the spiritual leader of Sunni Islam while simultaneously patronizing the Buyids and other local emirs who kept the once-powerful caliphate politically and militarily divided. However, the arrival of the Seljuk Turks and their removal of the Buyids as the power behind the caliphate altered the balance of power in the region. Despite the Fatimids' tolerant views, the newly converted Sunni Seljuks regarded the Egyptian Shia dynasty as followers of a heretical form of Islam and opposed them on religious grounds. And as the Seljuks gained political and military prominence over the Abbasid court, the Sunni-Shia split provided a convenient rallying point for Sunni Muslims, Arab and *Mawali* alike, to the Seljuk banner. So strong was this antipathy that future sultans regarded the Fatimids as a greater threat to the *Dar al-Islam* than their long-time Christian foe, the Byzantine Empire. The question remains whether the Fatimids, wary of the growing threat of the emerging Seljuk sultanate on their north-eastern border, sought to readdress this balance of power in the second half of the eleventh century through invigorated diplomatic ties with their old enemy Byzantium in an attempt to hold the Seljuk Turks at bay.[37] There is some evidence of a Fatimid embassy sent to Byzantine territory in 1069, but whether this embassy influenced a Byzantine expedition against the Seljuk Turks is impossible to know for certain.

Warriors from the Steppes: The Coming of the Turkic Peoples

The Seljuk Turks that swept down into south-west Asia in the mid-tenth century to wrestle the Abbasid Caliphate from Buyid control were the latest migration of Turkic peoples from the steppes of Central Asia. The first state to bear the name Turk was founded in 552 CE, opening a 400-year period of pre-Islamic Turkic state formation in Central Asia. Historians have labelled this pre-Islamic Turkic period of state building the first Turk Empire (552–630), the second Turk Empire (682–745), and their successors in the east, the Uighurs (744–840), and in the west, the Khazars (630–965). All of these peoples shared a similar language (Turkish is in the Altaic language group) and similar customs and fighting styles. These early Turkic states have been described as 'trade-tribute empires' because they both extracted tribute from their weaker sedentary neighbours, but also engaged directly in trade along the Eurasian trading or silk routes.[38] The establishment of these Turkic states corresponds roughly to the rise of the Sui (589–618) and Tang (618–907) dynasties in China and the Islamic expansion in south-west and Central Asia under the successors of Muhammad, the Umayyad (661–750) and early Abbasid (750–1258) caliphates, and represents a significant movement in Eurasian history, the establishment of Turkic peoples in Central Asia as a buffer and conduit between east and west Asia.

Like other steppe peoples, the pre-Islamic Turks lived in a socially stratified society. At the top of this society was the ruler or *khagan* (sometimes *kaghan*), who ruled by heavenly mandate. The *khagan* had to maintain control over the sacred Mount Otuken in the Orkhon Valley in central Mongolia and performed religious rites at this location. In this way, the *khagan* served as a type of shaman to his people. Surrounded by horse and yak tails, flags and drums as his symbols of rulership, the *khagan* commanded the army and, through the power of his personality, maintained order among his people while forcing enemies to pay tribute. Like in all courage cultures, the *khagan's* power was derived from his ability to ensure the welfare of his retainers and subjects through the distribution of the spoils of war and tribute from subject peoples. Success as a leader depended on his ability to mobilize and redistribute resources.[39] Failure meant an internal challenge to his leadership, civil war, and perhaps the disintegration of the Turkic confederation. As was common to steppe empires, the Turkic states were laterally organized, with power often shared between brothers passing from elder brother to younger brother until all of the brothers had died.[40] This power-sharing system created stability and unity between siblings, but often produced conflict when the succession passed to cousins in the next generation. Ultimately, succession was guaranteed only through the use of force.[41] These succession problems account for the often rapid rise and disintegration of steppe empires.[42]

Below the *khagan* were the ruling elite or *begs*, made up of the ruling clan and a hierarchy of other noble clans, and the *kara bodum* or common people.[43] As was common in all steppe cultures, militarily there was no distinction between male members in society. Every male was an *er* or 'man' and every man was considered implicitly a warrior. Young men earned their warrior name (*er ati*) either through success in battle or in the hunt. Veterans were considered elite men (*er bashi*) and were given command in battle.[44] Practically born in the saddle and raised to be effective mounted hunters and herders, these warriors were inured to the hardships of the Eurasian steppes, facing extremes in weather and lacking the luxuries, rich food and soft mattresses of sedentary living. This harsh lifestyle forged warriors with strong minds and bodies, capable of almost superhuman endurance on horseback.

After the second Turk Empire collapsed in 745, the Turkic Uighurs organized a state in the east centred in what is now Mongolia. Heavily influenced by contacts with Persia, the Uighur Empire (744–840) built a capital at Ordubalik on the Orkhon River (near where later the Mongols would build their capital of Karakorum) and created an empire that dominated the Eurasian silk roads and was a major power equal in status to the Tang dynasty.[45] But the destruction of the Uighur khaganate in 840 by the Kirghiz forced Turkic tribes westward, and over the next few centuries, Mongolia slowly became peopled with tribes that would later become the Mongols, giving the region its present name. Turkic tribes migrated as far west as the Caspian and Black Sea regions, displacing or absorbing indigenous Iranian and other smaller populations.[46]

Meanwhile, from the beginning of the eighth century, Central Asia was contending with the expansion of Islamic rule from the south-west, converting peoples along the way. Between 705 and 715, the Arab general Qutayba ibn Muslim campaigned in Transoxiana, bringing what is now modern Uzbekistan and south-west Kazakhstan into the *Dar al-Islam*. The Islamization of Central Asia intensified after the Abbasid triumph over the Tang Chinese at the battle of Talas River in 751. Islam now penetrated

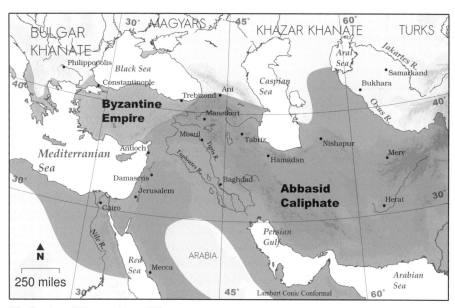

The Empires of Western Asia, c. 800.

the cultures of this region, including many Turkic peoples and three eastern Indo-European populations: the Khwarazmians of Transoxiana, the Sogdians around Bukhara, Samarkand, and Shash; and the Tokharians in the east in what was ancient Bactria (modern southern Tajikistan and northern Afghanistan).[47]

Although Islam pressed successfully into Central Asia, father west, in the area north of the Black and Caspian Seas, Islam did not have as much success converting Turkic and other steppe peoples. Vying for power in this region were the Turkic Khazars and the Bulgarian confederation, already at war with Byzantium. The Khazars, from their homeland north of the Caspian Sea, ruled over perhaps twenty subject peoples and were organized as a dual-khaganate, with two rulers sharing power. Surprisingly, the Khazar ruling elite adopted Judaism as their religion in the late eighth or early ninth century. By the late tenth century, the Khazars were conquered by the Slavic Rus in alliance with Oghuz Turks, a confederation of clans from which the victors at Manzikert, the Seljuk Turks, would claim descent.[48]

Historians identify the Turkish influx into the Islamic world taking place in three stages during the medieval period. The first phase began in the ninth century when Turkic nomads, captured in border raids, were converted to Islam and used as slave-soldiers (*ghulams* or *mamluks*) in Baghdad and elsewhere where their services were required. But these first slave-soldiers did not create a lasting Turkic impact in the Middle East. A second, more significant phase began in the tenth century when a minor Turkic clan, the Seljuks, converted to Sunni Islam and migrated from Transoxiana into Iran to seek their fortune. The Seljuks would quickly rise to prominence in the Abbasid court, taking only a few decades to bridge the distance from palace guard to caliph-makers in Baghdad. Using their influence in Baghdad as a springboard, the Seljuk Turks would go on to become the most powerful Islamic empire builders of their day, expanding Islam into Byzantine territory in Armenia and Anatolia, challenging the Catholic crusaders in the Levant, and paving the way for the third and final phase of Turkish migration into the region, the rise of the Ottoman Turks in the fourteenth century.[49]

Into the *Dar al-Islam*: The Conversion and Rise of the Seljuk Turks

Tradition holds that the original leader and apical ancestor of the Seljuk Turks, Seljuk himself, converted to Islam late in his long life in 985 at Jand (modern Khujand) on the Jaxartes River in what is now Tajikistan.[50] He was a commander from the Kinik tribe of the Orghuz Turks. Along with his four newly converted sons, Seljuk made war against the pagan steppe peoples as part of an Islamized Turkic border population. Pagan Turks (those who practised the Central Asian cults) were not protected by Islamic law as members of the *dhimmis* and their treatment by Muslim adversaries could be very harsh. When the Iranian Muslim ruler Ismail ibn Ahmed (r.892–907) took the Turkic town of Talas in 893, he put most of the city to the sword and enslaved the rest. Only those who converted to Islam were spared.[51]

But political instability and pressure from rival tribes made border life difficult even for those Turks who did convert to Islam, and Seljuk's grandsons, Toghril Beg, Ibrahim Inal, and Chaghri Beg, led the newly named Seljuk Turks into Khurasan in 1034 where they began to raid the local Muslim population. Khurasan was under the control of a rival Turkic dynasty called the Ghaznavids (975–1187), former *ghulam* slave-soldiers for the Iranian Samanid dynasty (819–1005) who had administered the Transoxian frontier for the Abbasids for over 180 years. Under their powerful and charismatic leader Mahmud (r.997–1030), the Ghaznavids would eventually found an empire stretching from Khurasan north into Central Asia and east into India, although in the west in Iran, the rise of the Seljuks would cut short Ghaznavid hegemony.

On 23 May 1040, these two Turkic powers fought at the battle of Dandanqan near Merv, a battle described by a modern historian as 'a victory of Seljuk desperation over Ghaznavid exhaustion.'[52] After Dandanqan, the Seljuks became masters of Khurasan, and used this territory to extend their control westward over Iran and beyond. As per steppe society custom, the three brothers separated to establish their own regimes. Chaghri set out west to conquer the lands east of the Tigris, while his brother Ibrahim Inal established himself in north-west Iran. In 1045, Ibrahim began raiding into Christian Armenia and Georgian territory, attacking Manzikert, Kars, Theodosiopolis (later called Erzurum) and Trebizond. Meanwhile, Toghril concentrated on conquering north-eastern Iran and most of Azerbaijan, coming into conflict with Ibrahim and forcing his brother to cede the ancient Persian city of Hamadan to him.[53]

Like other Turkic and Islamic armies, the Seljuks did not excel at siege warfare. Isfahan took a year to submit to Toghril, and then only because the people were starved into submission.[54] Toghril made Isfahan his capital in 1051, and by 1054 he had expanded Seljuk influence all the way into Mesopotamia. That same year, the Abbasid caliph Al-Qaim (r.1031–1075) and the captain of his palace guard, Besasiri, summoned the Seljuk leader to Baghdad to oust the Buyid transgressors from Baghdad. But the Buyid's stranglehold over the Abbasids weakened in the early eleventh century when Mahmud's Ghaznavids conquered much of Iran in 1029. By 1055, the Buyids were

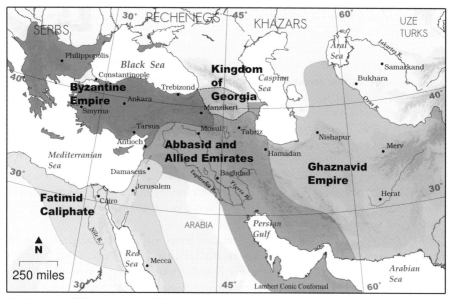

The Empires of Western Asia, c. 1025.

clinging on to power in Baghdad and Al-Qaim, seeing an opportunity to remove the Iranians, bestowed the title of 'sultan and sovereign of East and West' on Toghril and invited him to visit the Abbasid capital on his way to Mecca on pilgrimage.[55] Toghril entered Baghdad at the head of a powerful Seljuk army as the champion of the Abbasid caliph.

Storm from the Steppes: The Seljuk Art of War

The Seljuk army that escorted Toghril into Baghdad was a cavalry-based steppe army, influenced militarily by Iranian and Islamic contacts. As a steppe army, it shared many characteristics with the great nomadic armies that came before and after, such as the Scythians, Parthians, Huns, Uighurs, Tartars and Mongols. In fact, a traditional saying attributed to Genghis Khan (r.1206–1227) concerning Mongol warfare is equally relevant when considering how the Seljuk Turks approached war in the eleventh century: 'In daylight, watch with the vigilance of an old wolf, at night with the eyes of a raven. In battle, fall upon the enemy like a falcon.'[56] Seljuk warfare was typical of the eternal nomadic tactics that evolved from constant mounted raiding on the fringes of civilization and from great hunting drives on the Eurasian steppes. Stalking herds of deer taught the Seljuks how to send forward a group of silent scouts to observe the enemy while keeping out of sight, ensuring the element of surprise when the nomads struck. Herding horses from horseback required excellent equestrian skills, skills put to use when fighting enemy cavalry and infantry, allowing the nomadic warriors to outflank both wings of a confused army as one heads off a fleeing herd of wild animals on the steppes.

The Seljuk warrior relied on the mobility of his horse as his best defence, but if close combat did occur, he was well protected by panoply that mirrored the arms and armour of his civilized adversaries, with important Central Asian additions. Wealthier warriors adopted the chainmail hauberk and pointed conical helmet with chain or leather aventail or chain coif to protect his neck and shoulders. Sometimes, scale armour or leather lamellar armour was worn instead. Still, most Seljuk warriors went into combat without armour, instead wearing the kaftan-like overcoat typical of steppe nomads of all eras (these warriors were often the Turkomans, Islamized Turks who retained their nomadic ways while fighting in the service of their more civilized Seljuk brothers). Loose-fitting breaches and leather boots completed the warrior's dress.[57] For additional protection, he carried a small round convex shield, although from the late eleventh century onward, the kite shield made its appearance in Muslim armies, possibly from contacts with Norman mercenaries in service with Byzantium.

Offensively, the Seljuk warrior's primary weapon was his short composite bow, although his other weapons could include javelins, a light lance, mace, battleaxe, lasso or sabre. Javelins were utilized as short-distance missile weapons or stabbing weapons, while the light twelve-foot lance, a weapon preferred by Arabs and Iranians, was not neglected by Turkic warriors despite their love of mounted archery.[58] Maces and small battleaxes were also used by Turkic warriors from horseback and examples of these types of weapons go back to the origins of steppe cultures and are commonly seen in the archaeological record.[59] Small equestrian battleaxes were also used by Turkic warriors. While not typically associated with warfare, the steppe lasso was a very effective weapon when used to capture an enemy horse or rider or a victim on foot. Long a tool used by herders, lassos could be a rope alone or a rope attached to a pole.[60]

Although history does not record definitively the precise date when the curved sabre made its appearance in Islamic warfare, it is believed the weapon had its origins in Turkic Central Asia and was widely used in the Islamic world after the Seljuk conquests. By the early twelfth century, the curved sabre (Turkish *kilij* and the later Persian *shamshir*) was the most popular sword type in use in the Islamic Near East, although straight swords continued to be used.[61] With a blade length of between twenty-five and thirty inches and a rounded grip made of wood or ivory, the curved *kilij* proved to be an excellent equestrian sword. This sword type would also make its way to Christian Hungary by way of the Magyars, and a variation of this weapon, the *karabela*, would continue to be used for centuries by Polish cavalry.[62]

The centrepiece of a Seljuk warrior's arsenal was his short composite bow. Smaller than its Mongolian or Persian brothers, the Turkish bow was about three feet in length, strung and recurved in shape. The bow was constructed in three parts: a thin central stave of wood (often maple, cornus or mulberry because these woods absorb glue well) laminated with sinew on the back and horn on the belly. Some bows used bamboo as the wood source. Typically, the bowyer cut the wood into five sections joined together with fishtail splices some three and a half inches long. Each bow had a central section for the grip, joined to two bow arms and tipped with grooved ends where the string would attach. Horn from buffalo, long-horned cattle, or ibex was then glued to the belly of the bow.[63]

To create the characteristic recurve shape of these composite bows, the arms were then bent back and tied into an arc against the shape it would be drawn into. Gluing was done in the winter when the weather was cooler and humidity higher. Typically, drying took about two months. Next, sinew taken from the hamstrings or back tendons of cattle or deer was beaten into fibres, then soaked in glue and applied in one layer on a warm day. After the sinew was applied, the bow was tied again into an even more extreme recurved shape with a cord holding the ends together. The bow was then left for another two months to dry tied down in this way. After the bow had dried, it was unstrung, warmed and then strung in the direction in which it would be shot. The bowyer next adjusted the bow, tillering the two limbs until they curved uniformly when drawn. This involved a slow process of filing until the bow arms could bend evenly at full draw. Finally, strips of bark or thin leather were applied in diagonals to cover and waterproof the sinew, completing the construction of the bow. The bow string was usually made of silk, horsehair, or animal sinew. Warriors always carried more than one string and often different kinds of strings depending on the climate (horsehair strings were better suited for colder weather, while leather or sinew strings absorb moisture and stretch easily, losing their effectiveness).[64]

This composite construction gave the Turkish bow a powerful draw weight, while the short recurve design allowed the steppe warrior to shoot the arrow quickly, in any direction, and at great distance. Much has been written about the extraordinary draw weights of steppe war bows. The most powerful of these war bows belonged to the Mongols with an estimated 160 pound draw weight and a range of over 350 yards.[65] Turkish bows were smaller and less powerful, though still capable of impressive ranges and penetration. The mounted Seljuk warrior could draw and shoot up to twelve arrows a minute, keeping an arrow in flight as the first shaft hit its target and the third was notched on the string. Successful mounted archery was a numbers game, as most arrows were sent towards the enemy in volleys rather than the warrior carefully picking his target. When combined with the arrows of his comrades, this medieval 'firing for effect' barrage could riddle a battlefield with shafts.

The famous Catholic chronicler, William of Tyre (1130–1186), described a crusader encounter with Seljuk archery during the First Crusade (1097–1099), although he could have been writing about every Seljuk assault:

> At the first onset the Turks shot at us with such rapidity as to darken the heavens as neither rain nor hail could do, so that we suffered many casualties; and when the first had emptied their quivers and shot their bolts the second wave, in which there were yet more horsemen, came after them and began to shoot faster than could be believed.[66]

This type of coverage was often necessary, since only between one and fifty and one and a hundred arrows would be a kill shot and a single arrow strike was most often only temporarily debilitating to horse or rider. The range of a war bow was around two-hundred yards, while the effective killing distance was between fifty and sixty yards.[67] Steppe warriors were also adept at shooting their arrows at steep angles (forty-five degrees) in order to have the arrows rain down on a target, an effective tactic against massed enemies.[68]

Unlike their western European counterparts who steadied the arrow and pulled the string of the bow back with their fingers in what has been termed the 'Mediterranean draw', steppe warriors utilized a thumb release. This type of draw pinched the bowstring between the first finger and the thumb and the release was often assisted by a thumb ring made of leather, bone, ivory, metal or stone. This type of draw and release is often called the 'Mongolian draw' or the 'Mongolian release', although it was practised long before the rise of the Mongols.[69] Seljuk arrows were usually about twenty-eight inches long and carried in multiple quivers containing up to thirty specialized arrows apiece: light arrows with small, sharp points for use at long ranges, heavier shafts with large, broad-heads for use at close quarters, armour-piercing arrows, arrows equipped with whistling heads for signalling and incendiary arrows for setting things on fire.[70] Arrowheads were usually socketed, with the tang inserted into the wooden shaft.[71] Steppe warriors were so adept at mounted archery that they could bend and string the bow in the saddle at full gallop.[72]

The Seljuk warrior's archery skill was assisted by his equestrian equipment and riding position. The bridle, metal horse bit, saddle and stirrups were all Central Asian nomadic inventions. Steppe warriors used a frame saddle with a high pommel and cantle and rode with a short stirrup or 'forward seat,' putting the rider's weight over the horse's shoulders instead of square on its back. This riding stance was very comfortable over rough terrain and facilitated archery from horseback.[73] Originally, Turkic warriors rode sturdy steppe ponies similar in appearance to the Przewalski horse, a breed noted for its stocky build (thirteen to fourteen hands high), relatively short legs and large head. These mounts possessed a combination of excellent qualities, including courage, stamina and the ability to subsist on little food and food of a lesser quality.[74] But contacts with the Islamic world introduced Seljuk warriors to the leaner and more nimble Turkmene and Arab breeds. Turkmene horses weighed 800 to 900 lb and measured in at around fifteen hands high (similar to their modern descendents, the Akhal-Tekes of modern Turkmenistan). The Arabians would have been smaller, well under fifteen hands high and weighing between 700 and 800 lb.[75] Unlike the Christian counterparts in Western Europe, steppe warriors preferred mares over stallions as war horses. Broken and ridden hard for their first two years, these horses were then put out to pasture for the next three years to develop a herd mentality. If left untied, the horses did not stray.[76] Afterwards, they were trained for warfare. These war horses were treated as comrades-in-arms and mounts ridden in battle were never killed for food, and when old or lame, were put out to pasture to live out their last days. When a warrior died, his mount was sacrificed and buried with him so that he would have a companion for the afterlife.[77]

One of the secrets to the steppe warrior's military success was strategic surprise, and this surprise was dependent on the number and quality of his remounts. Typically, a raiding party might have three or four remounts available per man, thus allowing the warrior to cover great distances per day and still have a suitable horse for war if required.[78] Although distances covered depended on topography, one observer of Mongol prowess in the saddle noted that a steppe warrior could cover 600 miles in nine days. Maintaining this many horses was easy to do in Central Asia because of the abundant forage available on the steppes and the reliable horse breeding and procurement system nomads developed over the centuries. By the time of the great Mongol armies of the thirteenth century, tens of thousands of horses could be assembled without difficulty.[79]

When first approaching the enemy, Seljuk horse archers would hover just within bowshot of their enemy, firing in echelon and slipping away after discharging a volley. A twelfth century Catholic observer of Seljuk tactics during the Third Crusade (1189–1192) commented that the nomads were 'like flies that could be beaten off but not driven away.'[80] When the enemy offered battle, the Seljuks would retreat, twisting their torsos and firing arrows backward at their pursuers in what is often now referred to as the 'Parthian shot'.[81] Although Seljuk Turks was infamous for their archery skills from horseback, this tactic alone was seldom enough to give them victory on the battlefield. Mounted archery was used to break-up enemy formations for a follow-up shock attack with lances, sabres, maces and axes.

Seljuk commanders understood the importance of the principles of surprise, offence and manoeuvre in military operations and of seizing and maintaining the initiative, even if the strategic mission was defensive. When the enemy was located, Seljuk scouts relayed information concerning his strength, complement, position, and direction of movement to the commanding general, who in turn disseminated this information back to local commanders. Once intelligence had been gathered and the plan coordinated, the main force converged and surrounded their adversary, while other elements continued to advance and occupy the country behind the enemy's flank and rear, threatening their lines of communication. If the enemy force was small, it was simply destroyed, but if it proved formidable, then Seljuk generals used manoeuvre, terrain and their enemy's preferences to best advantage. If the enemy army was stationary, the Seljuk commander might command his main force to strike it in the rear, or turn its flank, or engage and then feign a retreat, only to pull the enemy into a pre-planned ambush using elite cavalry, killing both men and horses.[82] The Seljuks excelled in this kind of feigned retreat. Sometimes, their retreats lasted many days, designed both to wear down their enemies and draw them away from their bases and towards a larger body of steppe warriors.[83] Once their enemy tired, the Turks would wheel and strike or spring a trap.

One Byzantine commentator and chronicler of the First Crusade, Princess Anna Komnene (the daughter of Emperor Alexios I Komnenos) described her father's respect for Seljuk tactics:

He [Alexios Komnenos] knew from long experience that the Turkish battle-line differs from that of other peoples…but their right and left wings and their centre formed separate groups with the ranks cut off, as it were, from one another; whenever an attack was made on right or left, the centre leapt into action and all the rest of the army behind, in a whirlwind onslaught that threw into confusion the accepted tradition of battle. As for weapons they use in war, unlike the Kelts [Franks] they do not fight with lances, but completely surround the enemy and shoot him with arrows; they also defend themselves with arrows from a distance. In hot pursuit the Turk makes prisoners by using his bow; in flight he overwhelms his pursuer with the same weapon and when he shoots, the arrow in its course strikes either rider or horse, fired with such a tremendous force that it passes clean through the body. So skilled are the Turkish archers.[84]

In the thirteenth century, the Italian merchant Marco Polo also described steppe warrior tactics in his passage about a people he referred to as the Tartars, although in all likelihood they were Central Asian Turkoman warriors.[85] These warriors employed the same practices as Seljuk cavalry in the eleventh century:

When these Tartars come to engage in battle, they never mix with the enemy, but keep hovering about him, discharging their arrows first from one side and then from the other, occasionally pretending to fly, and during their flight shooting arrows backwards at their pursuers, killing men and horses, as if they were combating face to face. In this sort of warfare the adversary imagines he has gained a victory, when in fact he has lost the battle; for the Tartars, observing the mischief they have done him, wheel about, and make them prisoners in spite of their utmost exertions. Their horses are so well broken-in to quick changes of movement, that upon the signal given they instantly turn in every direction; and by these rapid manoeuvres many victories have been obtained.[86]

Most of the tactics above worked well because the predominantly mounted Seljuk army was faster and more manoeuvrable than the mixed cavalry and infantry-based armies of its civilized foes, whether they were Arab, Byzantine or later, Catholic crusader. With speed on his side, the Seljuk commander's primary objective was to harass an enemy and force him to fight on the march. Once on the move, the Seljuk commander would target the rear of the marching enemy column where the enemy was most vulnerable with the hope of whittling away at the enemy's strength by killing men and, just as importantly, horses (the effectiveness of Byzantine and later crusader armies was based on quality cavalry forces).[87] In the mountainous and valleys of Anatolia and Armenia, rearguards were often at the mercy of this tactic, especially since the soldiers who made up this contingent could be harassed or cut off from the rest of the column in the rough terrain. Numerous eyewitness accounts from both the Second Crusade (1145–1149) and Third Crusade (1189–1192) tell of Seljuk attacks on Catholic rearguards as they attempted to cross Anatolia for the Holy Land. As a result twelfth century crusader commanders paid careful attention to the organization and leadership of the rearguard.[88] Interestingly, this same tactical advice concerning the rearguard is present in tenth century Byzantine manuals that recommend large contingents of foot archers in the rear 'to ward off the onslaughts of Arab and Turks.'[89] This advice was usually followed by Byzantine generals, and when it was not, the consequences could be tragic as the lack of sufficient light infantry bowmen to fend off Seljuk horse archers at the battle of Manzikert in 1071 illustrates.

Seljuk Turkish tactics, like the tactics of steppe warriors before and after, adhered to the primary military maxim that an army should attempt to exploit every advantage over its enemy before committing to combat. For Seljuk commanders, this meant using the time-honoured tactics of surprise, fire, and manoeuvre to seize and maintain the initiative against their enemies. Accustomed to the martial proclivities of nomadic peoples along their northern and eastern frontiers, Byzantine military theorists and *strategoi* in the field since the time of Justinian created doctrines to meet and defeat the various cavalry-based armies originating from the Eurasian grasslands. These sound military practices led to the revival of the Eastern Roman army and the expansion of Byzantine territories in the tenth and early eleventh centuries, but a series of weak emperors, fiscal challenges, and resurgent enemies in the eleventh century weakened the Eastern Roman army and put the empire's strategic position in jeopardy.

Chapter 5

Byzantine and Seljuk Campaigns in Anatolia and the Battle of Manzikert

Problems with Byzantine Military Structures and Strategy in the Eleventh Century

The Byzantine Empire faced numerous strategic and military structural problems in the decades after the death of Basil II in 1025, problems brought about by the successful expansionist strategy that began in the mid-tenth century under Romanus II, Nikephoros II Phokas, John I Tzimiskes, and their capable commanders. Under these men the Balkan frontier was expanded and secured and imperial troops once again garrisoned the important fortress cities of eastern Anatolia and Armenia. One consequence of this success was the creation of new command structures known as ducates (governed by a duke) or katepanates (governed by a katepano), much smaller military districts than the traditional themes developed from the late seventh to ninth centuries. These ducates and katepanates created a protective curtain between the inner regions of the Byzantine Empire and the frontier zones, but also resulted in the thematic militia being neglected. These smaller military districts were ideal for addressing local threats or mobilizing for large expeditionary offensives, but were not as responsive to major raiding or invasions aimed at the heart of the empire like that which would appear in the late 1040s with the attacks on the eastern frontiers by the Seljuk Turks.[1] This decentralization of command into smaller districts around the periphery meant that local commanders no longer were strong enough on their own to meet a large-scale incursion. Now, an emperor or his commanding general was required to organize the troops from different districts and mount a successful defence. Unfortunately for Byzantium, emperors and generals of the calibre of those who expanded the empire were in short supply after the death of the 'Bulgar-slayer' and later emperors turned once again to alliances and diplomacy, rather than large military expenditures, to secure the imperial borders.

This movement away from large standing armies worked well along the northern Danubian frontier. Expanded trade, cultural exchanges and the threat of military action kept the peace in this region, allowing emperors to reduce permanent garrisons. Without large standing armies directly under imperial control, emperors began to rely more and more on full-time regionally recruited *tagmata* and vassals and the soldiers of allied foreign rulers for military assistance. Also, foreign mercenary groups, especially the well-trained and outfitted western knights from France, Germany and Norman

Italy, as well as Varangians from Scandinavia and Rus lands, played an increasingly prominent role in Byzantine military planning, with these soldiers usually serving under their own commanders.[2]

After Basil II the Byzantine Empire was plagued by a string of militarily incompetent emperors and empresses who fostered court intrigue, civil war and both provincial and military rebellion, severely weakening the empire's security on numerous fronts. In 1038, Michael IV (r.1034–1041) sent the brilliant general George Maniakes to reconquer Sicily from the Muslims with an army supplemented with both Norman and Varangian Guard mercenaries (among them the Varangian captain and future Scandinavian king Harald III Hardrada).[3] The Byzantines captured the important city of Syracuse, but in a move reminiscent of the relationship between Justinian and Belisarios, Michael imprisoned his commander on suspicion of disloyalty. Arabs retook the city of Syracuse, while the Normans fighting in the service of Byzantium rebelled and began conquering southern Italy, forging new states for themselves that would eventually consist of the southern third of Italy and most of Sicily by the end of the eleventh century.[4] Byzantine rulers would continue to spend both blood and treasure attempting to reclaim Italy, a region of immense strategic, economic and emotional significance to the Eastern Roman Empire since the time of Justinian. After the deposition and blinding of the short-reigned Michael V by the mobs of Constantinople, the new emperor, Constantine IX Monomachos (r.1042–1055), faced a military revolt led by George Maniakes, restored to command and now katepano of Italy. George's men proclaimed him emperor and he crossed the Adriatic and marched on Constantinople. He probably would have seized the throne had he not been mortally wounded in 1043 in a battle fighting imperial forces near Thessalonika in northern Greece.[5]

Under Constantine imperial finances were lavished on building projects and court largess, so much so that in 1050 he was forced to mint gold coinage (*nomismata*) that was only three-quarters pure. His debasement of the currency lowered the value of most military pay, further sowing the seeds of rebellion. To make matters worse, Constantine opened his eastern provinces to dreadful raiding when, in 1053, he decommissioned some 50,000 thematic troops manning the Armenian frontier to save money.[6] Within two years, the gravest Muslim threat to Byzantium in centuries, the Seljuk Turks, would raid unopposed into Byzantine territory through those very lands.[7]

Seljuk Raiding in Armenia and Eastern Anatolia, 1048–1063

Toghril Beg (r.1055–1063) entered Baghdad in 1055 escorted by his powerful Seljuk army and assumed control of the Abbasid court, becoming de facto ruler of Islamic Persia and Mesopotamia. His new domain brushed up against the eastern frontiers of Byzantine-controlled Armenia and eastern Anatolia, retaken from the Arabs in the mid-tenth century. But as we have seen Byzantine frontier military capabilities had eroded since the death of Basil II in 1025 at the very time the Seljuks were emerging on the scene in south-western Asia. The first Turkic raids into Armenia and eastern Anatolia began as early as 1029, but intensified in the 1040s after the Seljuk victory over the Ghaznavids at Dandanqan. The bulk of these warriors were Turkomans, a term that emerged at this time for the Islamized Turks who retained their nomadic ways and continued to raid and plunder in the manner of steppe warriors, differentiating them from their more civilized converted Turkic brothers who settled on the land or who ruled from the cities.

Both Toghril and his brother Chaghri used the Turkomans to supplement their armies and their presence was instrumental in the victories that created the first Seljuk empires. Toghril did not allow the Turkomans raiding privileges in Muslim territories he was consolidating into his empire and also denied them the right to bring their own women with them, a practice designed to keep the nomads from putting down roots. To Toghril the Turkomans were a valuable ally in times of war, but he feared their wild ways could undermine his growing empire. For this reason the Turkomans were allowed to wander to the edges of empire, capable of being summoned back to assist the Seljuk leaders against the rival Buyid and Fatimid dynasties or rebelling emirs within their own territories.[8] However, not all of the Turkomans were under the control of Toghril and his kin, and it is doubtful the Seljuk ruler could have stopped all the raids even if he wanted to. Perhaps as a way of gaining more influence over the majority of the Turkomans, Seljuk leaders began to lead these raids personally beginning in 1048, probably to placate the steppe nomads by allowing them periodic large-scale 'official' plundering campaigns in return for continued service to the future sultanate.[9]

Unable to raid Muslim Persia and Mesopotamia, the Turkomans pushed north-westwards into Azerbaijan between Hamadan and Tabriz, a region whose topography and weather was similar to the steppes. From bases there, the Turkomans attacked the Byzantine frontier. In the eleventh century there were no organized linear defences to hold the Seljuk marauders at bay, no chains of forts connected by patrols to discourage raiding, only the point defence of walled towns, fortress-monasteries, and the fortified mansions of local lords.[10] This point defence strategy made holding these frontier fortifications crucial to the security of the region and Byzantine generals invested enormous time and manpower in defending, taking, and sometimes retaking, these important walled cities and monasteries.

Unlike their civilized opponents, Turkoman raiders sought only booty, never trying to occupy Armenian and Byzantine cities or create their own political administrations in the territories they overran.[11] However, although the Turkomans did not occupy these Christian regions, their raiding could be devastating. In 1048, Toghril's half-brother Ibrahim Inal took a large Turkoman army north from Azerbaijan and then west along the traditional invasion route to the Araxes River Valley and then to the region of Theodosiopolis. From here, the Seljuk army overran the important regional trading city of Arzen, near Amida (modern Diyarbakir in south-eastern Turkey), which guarded the trade route from Anatolia to upper Mesopotamia. According to the eleventh century Armenian cleric and historian Aristakes of Lastivert:

> Like famished dogs, bands of infidels hurled themselves on our city, surrounding it and pushed inside, massacring the men and mowing everything down like reapers in the field, making the city a desert....
>
> A pitiful and harrowing sight was to be seen. All the city, the market stalls, the lands, the inns, were filled with the bodies. But who could count the number of those who perished in the flames? They burned priests whom they seized in the churches and massacred those whom they found outside....

Such was the unhappy history, oh happy and famous city, renowned throughout the world. Lift your eyes and look to your sons taken into slavery, your infants smashed without pity against the stones, your youths given to the flames, your venerable ancients thrown down in public places, your virgins, raised gently and in comfort, dishonoured and marched off on foot into slavery....[12]

Another historian, the Armenian Matthew of Edessa (d.1144), wrote that 150,000 people were massacred in Arzen and that forty camels were required to carry off the city's treasure. Additionally, 5,000 cattle were taken in the spoils. The Armenian chroniclers indicate the local Byzantine troops were able to catch up to the raiders on their return to Azerbaijan, but the Turkomans were able to force passage and escape.[13] So severe was the raid on Arzen that it ceased to be a city. Those who survived fled to the nearby city of Theodosiopolis, and began to call it by the name of their old home, Arzn ar-Rum ('Arzn of the Romans'). The term Rum comes from the Arabic world for Rome, a name adopted because the lands in Anatolia were long considered Roman (i.e. Byzantine) by Muslim armies. Over time, this name became Erzurum, the modern name of this important modern Turkish city.[14] Over the next twenty years numerous other Armenian and Byzantine cities would share the fate of Arzen, illustrating the scorched-earth raiding policy of the Seljuks in the mid–eleventh century.

Despite the depredations of Turkoman raiding along the Byzantine frontier, Toghril and the Eastern Roman court maintained good diplomatic relations, mostly out of

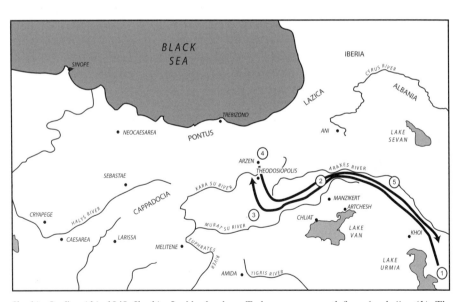

Ibrahim Inal's raid in 1048. Ibrahim Inal leads a large Turkoman army north from Azerbaijan (1). The raiders then head west along the Araxes valley (2), before turning north again towards Theodosiopolis (3). The Turkomen then overrun and destroy the city of Arzen (4), putting much of the population to the sword before returning home (5). A Byzantine force attempts to intercept the raiders, but is brushed aside by Inal's force. Arzen ceases to exist, as the surviving populace flee to nearby Theodosiopolis.

strategic necessity in the eyes of the Greeks. Constantinople had a new, and what it perceived as more immediate, problem along its northern Balkan frontier with renewed Pecheneg attacks, forcing the Byzantine Emperor Constantine IX to redeploy his eastern troops in 1050 and again in 1053.[15] This action simultaneously weakened the defences of the region most vulnerable to Turkoman raiding while also requiring him to negotiate a peace with Toghril for fear that raiding would expand to invasion and occupation by the official troops of the future Seljuk Sultanate. This truce with Byzantium also served Toghril who was engaged in struggles closer to home with the Buyid dynasty still in power in Baghdad at this time.

But in 1054, Toghril personally led a large Seljuk force into Armenia, probably to consolidate his hold on vassals there on the frontier, some of whom were tilting towards alliances with Byzantium, while also providing his Turkoman allies with an opportunity for plunder. A year later, these same Turkomans would be needed in his campaigns in Iraq against the Buyids and accompany him into the Abbasid capital. Toghril ordered his army into four columns, sending three north to ravage the centre and north of Armenia while he led an army against the region north of Lake Van. Here, he took Perkri and Artchesh north of the lake, before turning west and riding sixty miles to invest the strategically crucial fortress city of Manzikert (modern Malazgirt in eastern Turkey) located on the Murat Su River, an important headwater of the Euphrates River.[16]

Our understanding of the events of the 1054 siege of Manzikert comes from Matthew of Edessa who describes Toghril's army as 'numerous as the sands of the sea' and the attack against the city's walls as 'like a serpent consumed with malice.'[17] Unfortunately, we are not left with a detailed account of the month-long siege (specifically numbers and disposition of troops), although Matthew does mention the defence of the city by its Byzantine *strategos*, the half-Armenian and half-Georgian Basil Apokapes. When Toghril sieged the city and began to dig a mine under the defensive walls, Basil set a counter-mine and captured the Seljuk sappers, including the Muslim commander, Toghril's father-in-law. In a calculated move to inspire his own troops and enrage his enemy, Basil marched his prisoners to the ramparts and massacred them all in sight of the besieging Seljuk army.[18]

Angered by the killings on the wall, Toghril ordered a large catapult siege engine brought to Manzikert from the city of Baghesh (modern Bitlis), a distance of nearly fifty miles. The catapult was left there by Basil II some thirty years earlier. Once assembled, the converted Turkish war machine drove the defenders from the walls. In response, a Christian priest inside Manzikert organized the construction of his own catapult that, according to Aristakes, damaged the front of the Seljuk siege engine on its first shot.[19] Toghril ordered a revetment built to protect the engine, and the attack continued after the catapult was repaired.[20]

Unable to destroy the now well-protected siege engine with a direct attack, Basil asked for a volunteer from his garrison to embark on a sabotage mission against the Seljuk stone thrower. The contemporary sources tell us that a 'Frank' responded to the call, a generic term often used in this period for a European mercenary, although it is possible the soldier was a Norman in the employment of Basil. The Frank was outfitted as a messenger in surcoat and armour and mounted on a fast horse with a letter attached to the point of his spear. However, inside his surcoat were three clay or glass pots filled with an incendiary liquid, perhaps a version of Greek Fire. To continue the ruse, Basil sent the Frank outside the city walls during the noonday sun, a time when both armies were usually resting in their tents away from the heat of the day. The Seljuks did not try to intercept the messenger as he neared the siege engine and the Frank was able to quickly circle the machine three times, hurling his incendiary pots and setting the catapult on fire and eventually destroying it. Amazingly, the Frank escaped back to the safety of city walls, his mission accomplished. This event has been scrutinized by modern historians who wonder what the incendiary devices consisted of and how the grenades were ignited.[21]

With his primary stone thrower destroyed, Toghril redoubled his efforts to mine the walls, but was rebuffed at every point of attack. After a month-long siege, Toghril abandoned the effort. It should be noted that Aristakes relays the presence of a Byzantine spy or traitor in the Seljuk camp who apparently shot arrows carrying messages of the besiegers' strategy over Manzikert's walls.[22] This would help explain the effectiveness of Basil's defence. Although Manzikert was not taken in the siege of 1054, its importance to both Byzantium and the growing Seljuk Empire was demonstrated. Whoever controlled this fortress city controlled an important gateway

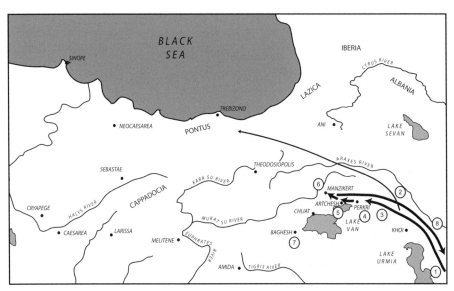

Toghril's raid in 1054: In 1054, Toghril personally leads a large Seljuk army out of Azerbaijan into Armenia (1), possibly to consolidate his frontier while providing an incentive to his Turkoman allies in the form of plunder. Toghril divides his army into four columns, ordering three to veer off to the north to raid into central and northern Armenia (2) while he takes the fourth column towards the Lake Van region (3). After capturing Perkri (4) and Artchesh (5) near Lake Van, Toghril moves west and invests the fortified city of Manzikert (6). A Seljuk mine is stopped by a Byzantine countermine that results in the capture of the Seljuk sappers and their commander, who is Toghril's father-in-law. The Byzantines execute the prisoners on the city ramparts in view of the Seljuk army. Toghril is enraged and orders a large siege engine transported from Baghesh (7) to the city walls. The engine fails to turn the tide, as do several other attempts at bringing the siege to a successful conclusion. After a month, Toghril abandons the works and returns home (8).

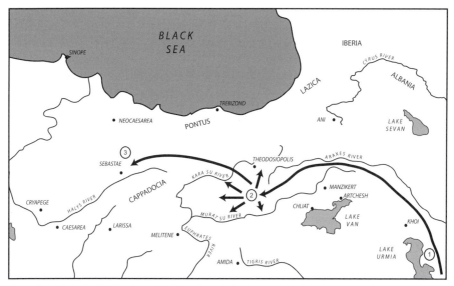

Samuh's raids in 1056-59: Around 1056, a Seljuk chieftain named Samuh raised a force of some 3,000 men and marched north and west out of Azerbaijan (1). Joined briefly by Herve Frankopoulos, a Norman commander of some repute, Samuh and his army established themselves in the upper Araxes and Murat Su valleys where they proceeded to pillage throughout the region (2). In 1059, Samuh launched a raid into the upper Halys valley, sacking the important city of Sebastae and putting much of the population to the sword (3).

into the riches of Anatolia. However, it would not be until 1071 that Manzikert would be threatened again by the Seljuks, and this time it would be the site of the pivotal battle that changed the trajectory of both Byzantine and Seljuk history.

In 1055, one year after the failed siege of Manzikert, Toghril was finally able to secure his ultimate goal and enter Baghdad in a Roman-styled triumph as sultan and the champion of the Abbasid caliph Al-Qaim. Toghril's Seljuk military might, amplified by the availability of Turkoman raiders, ended over a century of Shia Buyid domination over the caliphate. However, almost at once, the new sultan was embroiled in steppe culture succession problems with his half-brother Ibrahim Inal and relatives not content with their share of the spoils. He also faced a renewed threat by the Buyids who, backed by the coin of their fellow Shia Fatimid Caliphate, retook Baghdad for a short time in late 1058 before being expelled again by Toghril.[23] With the assistance of his three loyal nephews, the sons of his brother Chaghri, Toghril was able to finally secure his empire, but to maintain it the new sultan realized he needed to concentrate his energy in Iran, not Mesopotamia. In the land between the Tigris and Euphrates the Seljuks would have to be content with working with the existing emirs as vassals rather than exerting direct control over the region.[24] Faced with these realities, official campaigning in Armenia was suspended and Toghril consolidated his rule over Persia from his capital at Merv in Khurasan.

Even with the end of official Seljuk campaigning against the Armenian-Byzantine frontier, Turkoman raiding continued unabated beginning in 1056. To make matters worse for the Christians in Armenia, events in Constantinople encouraged nomadic penetrations. Empress Theodora's death in 1056 brought her weak candidate and successor, the sixty-something Michael VI Bringas (r.1056–1057), to the throne. Michael was immediately faced with a revolt by the Byzantine military aristocracy.[25] The rebellious *strategoi* of Armenia and eastern Anatolia elevated one of their own, Isaac Komnenos (later Emperor Isaac I, r.1057–1059) as leader of the revolt and gathered their armies to fight Michael at Nicaea, stripping the eastern provinces of their imperial soldiers for the campaign. Although ultimately successful (Michael was defeated and abdicated in favour of Isaac in 1057), the weakening of this frontier only served to entice the Turkomans deeper and deeper into Byzantine-held Armenia and eastern Anatolia.

About this same time, around 1056, a Seljuk chief named Samuh joined briefly with a decorated Norman commander named Herve Frankopoulos to ravage the region. Herve had served with distinction with George Maniakes in Sicily between 1038 and 1040. A decade later he commanded Norman mercenaries in the eastern themes, but when he was called back to fight the Pechenegs along the Danube, he was defeated. Six years later, in 1056, he demanded the high court title of *magistros* from Michael VI, but was rejected and withdrew to his military estate in Armenia along with some 300 loyal Norman soldiers. There, he intrigued with Samuh and joined in the mayhem, devastating the upper Araxes and Murat Su river valleys, but later fought against the Seljuks and local Armenians perhaps in an attempt to carve out his own fiefdom in Byzantium's deteriorating 'wild east'.[26] However, the Norman general's Armenian adventure was short lived. He was captured by Abu Nasr, the Arab Emir of Chliat (a region north-west of Lake Van) and sent back to Constantinople in chains. But as so often happens in Byzantine politics, Herve was able to court favour from the up-and-comer Isaac I and the title of *magistros* in the army of the new emperor. Herve ultimately proved an unreliable ally and, according to Matthew of Edessa, was executed by Isaac's successor, Constantine X Doukas (r.1059–1067), in 1063 after being charged with taking a bribe from Seljuks in the city of Amida and holding his army back from battling the infidel.[27] First with and then without his celebrated Norman ally, Samuh and his Turkomans stayed in Armenia for a few years, burning and pillaging the countryside with an army of perhaps as many as 3,000 men.[28] In 1059, he crossed to the upper Halys River Valley and led his Turkomans downstream to the city of Sebastea (modern Sivas in central Turkey), putting the entire city to the sword and flame in a devastating sack.[29]

Toghril died on 4 September 1063 and was succeeded in lateral steppe society fashion by his nephew Alp Arslan, a son of Chaghri. Together, Toghril (r.1037–1063) and Alp Arslan (r.1063–1072) are considered the first two sultans of the Great Seljuks of Iran (1037–1194). Ruling from Merv in Khurasan, the Great Seljuks would become the power centre of the Islamic world, eventually ruling over a vast empire stretching from Transoxiana to Armenia and down to Palestine, and from the Persian Gulf to the Caucasus. This dynasty is usually considered separately from the later Seljuk Sultanate of Rum (1077–1243) that would take hold in most of Anatolia after the Byzantine defeat at Manzikert in 1071. Together, the Great Seljuk Empire of Iran and the Seljuk Sultanate of Rum would launch a new period of Sunni Islamic reunification and reshape the map of Islam in Asia while threatening the very existence of the Byzantine

Empire, and in doing so, bring a new and determined adversary, the Catholic Crusaders, into the heart of the Islamic world.

The 'Valiant Lion' Roars: The Rise of Alp Arslan and the Seljuk Raids, 1064–1068

Turkoman raiding into Byzantine territories continued in the early 1060s, launched primarily by Turkic chieftains on their own initiative but with the usual tacit approval from their sultan. Devastating raids took place in Mesopotamia below the city of Melitene, with the cities of Edessa and Antioch targeted for annual sieges beginning in 1065. Captives from these raids were taken to the Turkish-held city of Amida and sold into slavery.[30] However, the Seljuk's political world changed with Toghril's death in 1063, leaving his nephew, Muhammad bin Da'ud Chaghri, known to history by his soubriquet Alp Arslan ('Valiant Lion') as the new leader of the Seljuk Turks. Alp Arslan (r.1063–1072) became ruler of the eastern provinces of Khurasan and Khwarizm when his father, Chaghri, died in 1058. When his uncle died in 1063, the title of sultan went to Alp Arslan in lateral steppe society fashion, although not without problems. Alp Arslan faced numerous challenges from rival claimants, including a cousin (who he killed in 1064) and an uncle (who he pardoned that same year).[31]

Alp Arslan was about thirty-three when he became sultan. Evaluations of his character depended on the source. The Armenian historian Matthew of Edessa called him a drinker of blood, while Aristakes of Lastivert believed he was an agent of the Antichrist. These dreadful descriptions of steppe princes by Christian chroniclers date back to Attila the Hun's devastating campaigns across Roman Europe in the fifth century, earning him the famous epithet 'Scourge of God'. However, the twelfth century Christian patriarch of Antioch, Michael the Syrian, described Alp Arslan as a just and able ruler. The Arab historian Ibn al-Adim wrote that he did not observe Islam's prohibition concerning the drinking of wine and that he was prone to violent outbursts. Little was written by the sultan's contemporaries concerning his appearance other than the length of his moustache required it to be tied behind his head when he went hunting. What is reflected in all accounts was that he was an excellent military commander.[32]

After securing his succession, Alp Arslan and his men crossed the Araxes River on boats and invaded Armenia in February 1064 in a resumption of official raiding. Matthew of Edessa describes the campaign in fateful terms below:

> Proud of his success, the sultan, this dragon of Persia, that year pounced upon Armenia. Instrument of divine vengeance, his wrath spread over the oriental nations, which he forced to drink the vial of his malice. The fire of death enveloped with its flames the faithful of Christ. The lands were inundated with blood, and the sword and slavery spread their ravage here.[33]

Despite Matthew of Edessa's proclamation of the sultan as an agent of divine vengeance, Alp Arslan's action was probably designed to reinforce the frontier zone and strengthen his control over the Turkomans and the Arab emirs in Azerbaijan, the same strategy utilized a decade earlier by Toghril. Alp Arslan split his army into two forces, the northern army under the sultan's command operating against rebellious Georgian

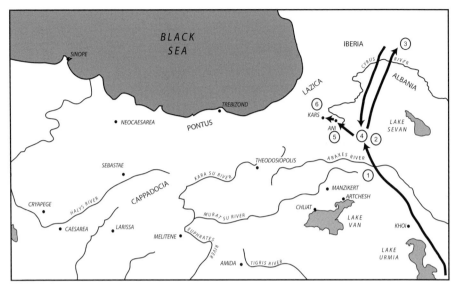

Alp Arslan's raid in 1064: In February 1064, shortly after securing his succession as sultan, Alp Arslan crosses the Araxes by boat at the head of an invading army (1), probably with the intent of securing his borders and solidifying his hold over his Turkoman subjects and his Arab emirs. He splits his force into a northern army under his personal command and a southern army under the nominal command of his ten-year-old son Malik Shah and the actual leadership of his general, Nizam al-Mulk (2). Alp Arslan's northern force strikes into the mountains to reduce the strongholds of some rebellious Georgian subjects (3) before rejoining his southern army (4) and laying siege to the fortified city of Ani (5). After successfully reducing Ani, the Seljuks move west against Kars (6), which offers no resistance and is invested by Alp Arslan's victorious troops. From 1064 to 1068, Alp Arslan would launch annual campaigns into Georgia, eventually taking the king's daughter as a bride to guarantee the alliance.

mountain strongholds, and a southern army under the titular command of his son, Malikshah (then only a boy of about ten), but under the actual command of the experienced Persian scholar and general Nizam al-Mulk (1018–1092). Nizam al-Mulk would serve as the trusted vizier to both Alp Arslan and his son Malikshah I (r.1072–1092) as one of the most influential and celebrated chief ministers in Islamic history. After reducing the northern strongholds, both armies reunited and sieged the ancient capital of Armenia, the impressive fortress city of Ani.

In the eleventh century Ani was an important lynchpin in the defence and prosperity of Christian Armenia and a city that at its height of power rivalled Constantinople, Baghdad, and Cairo in size and splendour in the medieval world. Ani was built in a naturally defensive position on a high triangular-shaped escarpment formed by the convergence of two rivers. The city was protected on the east by a ravine carved by the Akhurian River and on the west by the steep embankment formed by the Bostanlar and Tzaghkotzadzor river valleys, with both meeting in the south in the sharp point of an isosceles triangle. These cliffs ranged from 200 to 300 feet high, creating a nearly impregnable natural rampart that was also topped by a single curtain wall for added protection. A northern double-curtain wall with numerous towers formed the base of this triangular defence, running east and west from precipice to precipice, while the city's citadel occupied the southern tip of the triangle. There are no reliable numbers concerning the city's population in the mid-eleventh century, but because of favourable comparisons with the other large cities mentioned above, it was probably more than 100,000 people. Ani was also notable for its many famous churches, giving it the probably exaggerated designation of the 'City of a Thousand-and-One Churches' by Matthew of Edessa.[34]

Alp Arslan ordered his newly combined Seljuk army to invest the ancient Armenian capital, which had come under Eastern Roman control in 1045 when pro-Byzantine forces within the city's walls won influence. The primary Byzantine chronicler for this period, Michael Attaleiates (sometimes spelled Attaliates), wrote that the reason for Alp Arslan's assault on Ani was an unprovoked Byzantine attack against the Seljuk army's rearguard, an act that required the sultan's retaliation.[35] It is just as likely that Seljuk intelligence identified a lightly defended wealthy city whose internal politics were in disarray and provided an attractive target for plunder for the sultan's Turkoman allies. Alp Arslan commanded his army to attack the double curtain walls along the northern edge of Ani, the only vulnerable part of the city's defence. Here, the sultan ordered a large wooden tower built and covered with vinegar-soaked padding to protect it from enemy combustibles. Manned with archers and a siege engine of some sort (either a ballista or small catapult), the tower was pushed against the city wall. Arab chroniclers note that after this action, a tower or section of the wall collapsed, an event attributed by them to the will of Allah, but more likely due to a successful sapping of the fortification.[36] One of these Arab chroniclers, Ibn al-Jawzi, quotes an eyewitness to the events that followed:

> The [Seljuk] army entered the city, massacred its inhabitants, pillaged and burned it, leaving it in ruins and taking prisoner of all those who remained alive…. The dead bodies were so many that they blocked all the streets; one could not go anywhere without stepping over them. And the number of prisoners was not less than 50,000 souls. I was determined to enter the city and see the destruction with my own eyes. I tried to find a street in which I would not have to walk over the corpses, but that was impossible.[37]

The Byzantine commanders and garrison, most likely made up of mostly Armenians and Georgians, retreated to the citadel in the southern part of the city, only to be burned out and murdered.

Despite the eyewitness account above, Alp Arslan must have called off the Turkoman plunderers, sparing Ani from the complete destruction that followed the sack of Arzen some sixteen years earlier in 1048. He placed the city under the governorship of a local Arab emir where it recovered in the decades that followed. News of the conquest of Ani reverberated throughout the *Dar al-Islam*, more evidence of the significance of this ancient Christian capital to the Muslim world. The Abbasid caliph Al-Qaim issued a declaration praising Alp Arslan and his soldiers as *ghazi* or 'warriors for the Faith' and bestowed on the young sultan the title 'Conqueror'.[38] Alp Arslan no doubt appreciated these new endorsements from the Sunni caliph as it helped strengthen the sultan's desire to be recognized as the de facto leader of Islam, a claim challenged by the Seljuk's powerful rival, the Shia Fatimids in Cairo.

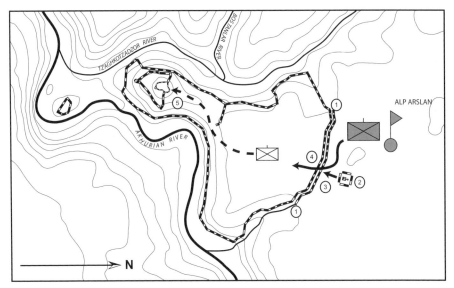

Map 5.1. The Siege of Ani, 1064 CE. Alp Arslan's Seljuk army invests the Byzantine-controlled city of Ani, deploying along the city's only vulnerable defence, the northern double-curtain wall that runs east-west from one river gorge to another (1). The sultan orders the construction of a large wooden siege tower (2), manned by archers and equipped with either a ballista or small catapult. Covered in vinegar-soaked rags to protect against enemy fire, the tower is pushed against the city walls (3). The wall is successfully breached (4), precipitating a Byzantine retreat to the citadel (5), but the Seljuk forces burn out the defenders and massacre the survivors. Alp Arslan orders a halt to the subsequent looting and places Ani under the control of a local emir.

Alp Arslan followed up his victory over Ani by taking another important Armenian city in the region, the stronghold of Kars, located forty miles west. According to Matthew of Edessa, on news of the Seljuk army's approach the mayor of Kars opened his city's gates and offered his garrison to the sultan, but escaped to Constantinople when the Turks left the area. Kars was then invested and made a Seljuk subject. Alp Arslan went on to subdue the kingdom of Georgia in annual campaigns between 1064 and 1068, taking the king's daughter as his bride to cement the alliance. With the Christian mountain kingdoms of Georgia and Armenia now under his control, Alp Arslan could have directed his armies deep into Byzantine Anatolia, but instead Seljuk attacks tended to keep to north and east of the Euphrates, although powerful local Muslim emirs, probably with the sultan's blessing, assaulted Byzantine Syria in annual campaigns.[39] Interestingly, with vulnerable Byzantine lands throughout Anatolia beckoning, Alp Arslan did not send his armies westward in a campaign of occupation at this time. His strategy seemed to be one of shoring up his north-western frontier in preparation for campaigns against a more dangerous enemy on his south-western flank, the heretical Shia Fatimids and their allies.

However, a prolonged Seljuk raid deep into Byzantine Anatolia between 1067 and 1068 was a notable exception to the sultan's border policy with Byzantium. The architect of the incursion, a renegade Seljuk nobleman named Afsinios (sometimes

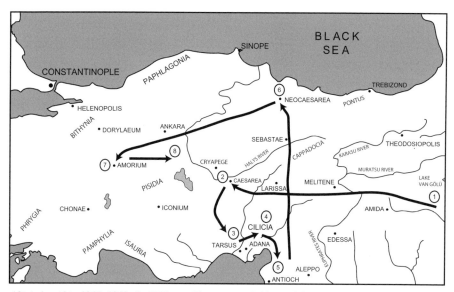

Afsinios' raid in 1067–1068: In 1067, a nobleman named Afsinios kills a member of Alp Arslan's court and flees Seljuk territory with an army (1). He heads west, sacking Caesarea (2) before looping south through the Cilician Gates (3). He proceeds to pillage throughout Cilicia (4) and the region around Antioch in Syria (5). Here, in the fall of 1068, he evades Romanus IV Diogenes' Byzantine army and strikes north, sacking Neocaesarea on the other side of the Anatolian peninsula (6). Afsinios then heads south-west to strike the city of Amorium (7) before finally returning eastward to Seljuk-held territory (8). Alp Arslan pardons Afsinios and the raider will ably serve the sultan in future campaigns.

referred to as Afsin Beg in history) killed a member of Alp Arslan's court and fled west with an army for an impressive expedition across Turkey. Afsinios sacked the Eastern Roman city of Caesarea (modern Kayseri in central Anatolia), and then wheeled south and went back through the Cilician Gates and raided first Cilicia and then the region around Antioch in north-western Syria.[40] Here, Afsinios' army escaped a Byzantine force under the capable new emperor, Romanus IV Diogenes (r.1068–1071), who was campaigning in Syria in the fall of 1068 to prop up and hopefully expand his possessions in the Levant. After evading Romanus, Afsinios turned north again and crossed nearly the breadth of Anatolia and sacked Neocaesarea (modern Niksar) near the Black Sea coast.[41] From there, Afsinios pressed south-west into the interior beyond Cappadocia to the city of Amorium in Phyrgia, a hundred miles south-west of the modern Turkish capital of Ankara, before returning east to Seljuk territory. Afsinios was pardoned by Alp Arslan for the audacity of his raid and would accompany the sultan on future campaigns as a capable lieutenant.[42]

Romanus IV Diogenes and his Early Campaigns, 1068–1070

Romanus IV Diogenes was recognized as co-emperor of the Byzantine Empire on 1 January 1068. Cappadocian by birth and in his thirties when he assumed the throne, Romanus was an experienced campaigner who distinguished himself as a *strategos* fighting against the Turkic Pechenegs when they, along with the Turkic Uzes, invaded south across the Danubian frontier and penetrated almost to Constantinople's Theodosian Walls. But when Constantine X died in 1067 his young and inexperienced son, Michael VII Doukas (r.1067–78) officially succeeded him, with his mother Eudokia Makrembolitissa appointed as regent. Seeing an opportunity to seize the throne for himself, Romanus rebelled, but was defeated and exiled. However, the devastating Seljuk expedition in central and eastern Anatolia in 1067 persuaded the patriarch of Constantinople, John Xiphilinos, that a strong military leader was needed on the throne. The patriarch and political counsellor convinced the empress, who had sworn that she would never take another husband, to recall Romanus from exile and marry him, making him Michael's co-emperor.[43]

As the first capable emperor-general since Basil II, Romanus immediately set out to strengthen the Byzantine army and shore up the frontiers. Byzantine military fortunes had declined precipitously under the reign of Constantine. The Seljuks were raiding nearly unopposed in the east, while the Pechenegs and Uzes were terrorizing the Balkans and the Normans were conquering most the Byzantium's remaining territories in southern Italy. The army that Romanus assembled for his campaign into Byzantine Syria would have been barely recognizable to the emperor-general John I Tzimiskes who commanded the skilled Byzantine army a hundred years earlier at Dorostolon. The twelfth century Byzantine historian George Kedrenos, relying on earlier accounts, describes the condition of Romanus' troops:

> The emperor, leading an army that did not befit the emperor of the Rhomaioi [Eastern Romans], but one which the times furnished, of Macedonians and Bulgars and Cappadocians and Uzes and other foreigners who happened to be about, in addition, also of Franks and Varangians, set out hastily.... These were bent over by poverty and distress and were deprived of armour. Instead of swords and other military weapons...they were bearing hunting spears and scythes... and were without war horses and other equipment.... They were cowardly and unwarlike and appeared to be unserviceable for anything brave.... These things being observed by those present, they were filled with despondency, as they reckoned how low the armies of the Rhomaioi had fallen, and by what manner and from what moneys and how long it would take to bring them back to their former condition. For the older and experienced were without horse and without armour, and the fresh detachments were without military experience and unaccustomed to the military struggles, whereas the enemy was very bold in warfare, persevering, experienced, and suitable.[44]

Despite the poor condition of his army, Romanus set off for Syria in the autumn of 1068 where he was successful in recapturing the fortress city of Hieropolis (modern Manbij) near Aleppo in northern Syria. A prudent commander, he had left a garrison at Melitene to guard his rear, but these troops failed to stop the Seljuk Turks' plundering expedition, which escaped the Byzantines and went on to sack Amorium. Romanus wintered in the region, and then returned to Constantinople in early 1069, leaving the Norman captain Robert Crispin and his mercenaries in charge of guarding the Armenian passes. Robert used this commission to rob the local tax collectors, and even though he was dismissed from his post, his men continued to terrorize the area, further weakening the Armenian frontier.[45]

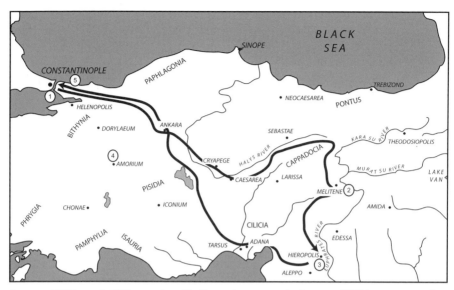

Romanus IV Diogenes', 1068 campaign: The Byzantine army under Romanus IV Diogenes sets out from Constantinople in the early fall of 1068 (1). After leaving a portion of his army as a rear guard in Melitene (2), Romanus recaptures Heliopolis in northern Syria (3). The Melitene garrison fails to check a Seljuk raid that manages to sack Amorium (4), deep in Byzantine territory. Romanus winters near Hieropolis before returning to Constantinople in early 1069 (5).

Romanus set off again in the spring of 1069 for north-eastern Anatolia with the goal of taking the strategically important Seljuk fortress city of Chliat (modern Ahlat in eastern Turkey), located on the western shore of Lake Van. A careful campaigner, Romanus left the Armenian general Philaretos Brachamios with a large force to guard his rear on the upper Euphrates while he marched east towards Chliat. However, the emperor's campaign was interrupted when a Seljuk army attacked and defeated the Byzantine rearguard, forcing Romanus to turn back and pursue the Turkish army who evaded him and went on to sack Iconium (modern Konya) in another deep Seljuk raid into Byzantine central Anatolia. Alp Arslan took advantage of Romanus' retreat by capturing Manzikert, just north of Chliat, as well as Artchesh on the northern coast of Lake Van. The sultan now controlled all three strategically important fortress cities, consolidating his control over the Lake Van area. Romanus, denied the prize of Chliat where he would have likely wintered his army in preparation for an expanded campaign the following year, marched his army back to Constantinople having achieved nothing in the campaign of 1069.[46]

The Byzantine army did campaign in the East in the first half of 1070, but Romanus was not commanding in the field. Instead, the *basileus Rhomaion* stayed in Constantinople where he devoted his energies to improving the condition of the army and keeping his court enemies at bay. On the first account he settled his soldiers' arrears in pay, purchased new military equipment, and instituted new training programmes in an attempt to reverse the neglect of previous administrations that had eroded the combat capabilities of the Byzantine army.[47] It also gave him time to recruit new

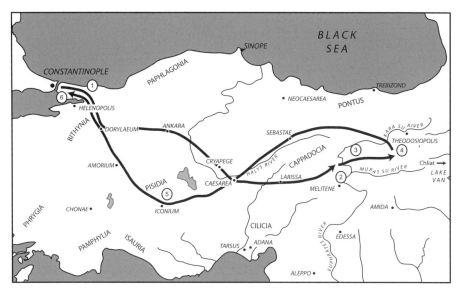

Romanus IV Diogenes', 1069 campaign: In the spring of 1069, Romanus opens a new campaign with the capture of Chliat on the north-western shore of Lake Van as his objective. Marching east from Constantinople (1), Romanus leaves a large rear guard on the upper Euphrates under the command of Philaretos Brachamios (2) before striking east towards Chliat (3). The Byzantine campaign plan goes awry as a Seljuk army defeats the Byzantine rear guard, forcing Romanus to reverse direction (4) in an attempt to cut off the enemy force. The Seljuks evade contact and sack Iconium (5), deep inside Byzantine Anatolia. Alp Arslan takes advantage of Romanus's discomfiture by consolidating his position in the Lake Van region. Romanus returns to Constantinople (6) with nothing to show for his efforts.

mercenary forces to supplement his army. The campaigning of the previous two years illustrated the need for professional soldiers to help his native forces meet the threat of the Seljuk Turks. These recruits included long-time allies like Armenians and Georgians, and those who were sometimes allies, sometimes foes like the Arabs, Bulgars, Rus, Khazars, Uze, and Pechenegs. Normans (or other Europeans often referred to as Franks), were also on the payroll.[48]

The second reason why Romanus stayed close to his capital on the Bosporus was the very real possibility of a palace *coup* in his absence. In Constantinople his rivals included a bitter court advisor named Michael Psellos, who had the ear of the young co-emperor, Michael VII, and influential members of the Doukas family itself, who resented Romanus' meteoric rise to power and were determined to bring about his destruction.[49] The leading figure in the Doukas family was John Doukas, the younger brother of Constantine X. John was given the title of caesar by his brother and would become one of the most prominent members of the Byzantine Senate and protector of his nephew, the co-emperor Michael. John Doukas' wealth derived from his estates in Thrace and Bithynia and it was from these holdings that he intrigued against Romanus before being exiled from the imperial court on the orders of the new emperor right before the 1071 campaign. The caesar's eldest son, Andronikos Doukas, was taken on the 1071 campaign, ostensibly as a general, but more likely as a hostage to guarantee that the Doukas family would not attempt to initiate a coup during the emperor's absence. Andronikos Doukas would play a pivotal role in the Byzantine loss at the battle of Manzikert when he and his contingent deserted Romanus during the engagement.

While Romanus stayed in Constantinople, he sent the Byzantine army east under the command of Manuel Komnenos, nephew of the former emperor Isaac and elder brother to the future emperor Alexios (r.1081–1118). Manuel Komnenos was faced with a difficult choice as the city of Hieropolis in Syria, recaptured from the Muslims two years earlier in 1068, was under siege again. Komnenos divided his army and sent a large part of it to relieve the besieged city, while he kept the remainder of his forces at Sebastae in central Turkey. At Sebastae, his divided army fell prey to a Seljuk attack. His army was defeated and he was captured. This loss opened central Anatolia to further Seljuk depredations. The Greek city of Chonae, located on the Lycus River in Phrygia, was attacked and sacked. Here, the sacred Eastern Orthodox shrine of the Archangel Michael was reportedly profaned and turned into a stable for Turkish horses. To make matters worse, those Greek inhabitants lucky enough to flee to the safety of the subterranean caverns commonly found in this region, all drowned when the Lycus suddenly flooded. Christian chroniclers tell us that when news of the violent sack of Chonae, desecration of the shrine, and drowning of the refugees reached Constantinople, Byzantine society interpreted the events as a sign of God's anger towards the unfaithful that lived in Orthodox Greek lands.[50] In February 1071 Romanus and Alp Arslan signed a truce, giving the Byzantine emperor additional time to rebuild his army and deal with the machinations against him in Constantinople before attempting to stabilize his Armenian frontier, while the Seljuk sultan used the peace to deal with enemies in Syria and prepare for the long-awaited campaign against the heretical Fatimids.

Byzantine and Seljuk Movements in Early 1071

In the second week of March 1071 Romanus set out from Constantinople at the head of a substantial field army that would eventually consist of around 48,000 soldiers once the Anatolian reserves joined the effort, although thousands of non-combatant camp followers that usually accompanied a medieval army on the march would have made the army appear larger.[51] This number is a modern estimate because Byzantine sources give no information on troop strength and Muslim sources range from 200,000 to 600,000 men, clearly fantastical numbers.[52] The goal of the campaign was to recapture both Manzikert and Chliat from the Seljuk Turks and reestablish control over the porous Anatolian-Armenian frontier. It is also possible that Romanus intended to use a secured Lake Van region as a base of operations to launch an attack down the Euphrates Valley deep into the heartland of the sultanate in a campaign similar to the one launched by Herakleios in the seventh century against the Sassanians.[53]

The Byzantine army that would eventually fight in the battle of Manzikert was a multi-national force built around a core of native Byzantine troops. As was normal since the time of Constantine V in the eighth century, the emperor was accompanied by his elite imperial troops, in this case imperial *tagmata* from throughout the empire, each numbering around 1,000 men. Thematic troops from Anatolia and Syria were also present, but the precise numbers are unknown and many of these men were both poorly equipped and inexperienced. These Byzantine troops were joined by the private levies

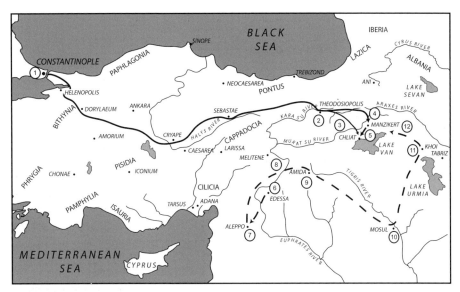

Byzantine and Seljuk movements in early 1071: Romanus IV Diogenes departs Constantinople (1) in March 1071 with what would eventually swell to a 48,000-man field army, his intent to recapture Manzikert and Chliat and establish some measure of control over the eastern Anatolian border region. The expedition's immediate goal is the base at Theodosiopolis (2), where Romanus's army rests and refits prior to striking at his targets. He sends a small contingent to Chliat (3) to secure forage and fodder. After initially striking out in the same direction, the bulk of the army turns south and crosses the Araxes River to arrive at Manzikert in late August (4). Romanus makes the fateful decision to send the bulk of his army, some 25,000 men, to Chliat (5), leaving only around 23,000 at Manzikert. Meanwhile, Alp Arslan's Seljuk army is besieging Edessa in late March 1071 (6). Romanus sends him a message, proposing terms for a renewed truce. Alp Arslan lifts his siege at Edessa and moves southwest to invest Aleppo (7). Some weeks later, Alp Arslan receives a second letter from Romanus, this one in more blustering tones. The letter, combined perhaps with intelligence of Byzantine movements, spurs Alp Arslan into action; he abandons his siege of Aleppo and strikes out for the Armenian-Anatolian border region. Crossing the Euphrates (8) proves costly in animals and results in his army being scattered. He directs his vizier to recruit reinforcements in Azerbaijan while the remainder of the army travels via Amida (9) and Mosul (10) to arrive at Khoi (11). Alp Arslan's 23,000-man army is only slightly smaller than the force remaining with Romanus at Manzikert and the Seljuk leader has the advantage of strategic surprise as he marches his forces towards Manzikert (12).

of Anatolian landholders and Armenian infantry from the frontier zones of eastern Anatolia and possibly Syria, as well as the military engineers and sappers, along with their siege equipment, required to retake Manzikert and Chliat. In addition to these traditional Byzantine contingents, Romanus had at his disposal numerous foreign troops, usually led by their own commanders. The Normans, commanded by the experienced Roussel de Bailleul, numbered perhaps 500 men. Pecheneg, Uze, and Varangian mercenaries, as well as allied or vassal states from the Balkans, rounded out the Byzantine army.[54]

Our best source for the 1071 campaign is Michael Attaleiates who served Romanus as an admiring court advisor and historian and was with the Byzantine emperor on the

Manzikert campaign. Another Byzantine source for the Manzikert campaign, John Skylitzes, lived in the second half of the eleventh century, but elements of his narrative about this event clearly derive from that of Attaleiates. Both chroniclers make note of a campaign plagued by evil omens, accidents and insurrections, beginning with the voyage across the Bosporus to Asia Minor. A grey dove landed on the imperial flagship and then came to the emperor's hand, a sign interpreted by some as an evil portent.[55] Once on shore, the army made its way immediately eastwards towards the secure Byzantine base at Theodosiopolis where the army would be resupplied for its march to the Armenian frontier. Along the way at Helenopolis in Bithynia, the central pole supporting the imperial tent snapped, sending a wave of restlessness throughout the ranks.[56] The Byzantine army continued east to Dorylaeum and then farther into the Anatolikon Theme to muster the Anatolian reserves. Here, the stable built to house the emperor's horses, wagons and personal equipment caught fire, destroying armour, bridles, and carriages and setting alight many of his finest horses and beasts of burden. Some of these animals were saved, while others were seen running madly through the camp as living torches.[57] To make matters worse, the mission to collect the Anatolian levies was unsuccessful as frequent Turkish raiding in the area had scattered the conscripts far and wide away from the urban centres to the safety of the countryside. Unable to swell his ranks as intended, Romanus pressed east, crossing the Halys River and marching on to the Byzantine base at Cryapege. Once encamped, many of the Frankish mercenaries in Romanus' service began to ravage the countryside in search of plunder. When Romanus tried to intercede, the Franks attacked the imperial guard, forcing the emperor to muster the remainder of his army to put down the Frankish contingent.[58] Finally, on the road from Sebastae to Theodosiopolis the Byzantine army witnessed the now year-old corpses of Manuel Komnenos' failed expedition against the Seljuk Turks, a sight that unnerved many in Romanus' army and was taken as a particularly bad harbinger for the coming campaign.

By now, news of another Byzantine defeat reached Romanus. In April, just a month after the Manzikert expedition left Constantinople, the capital and last stronghold in Byzantine Italy fell to the Norman adventurer Robert Guiscard. Since the time of Justinian the city of Bari had been the wealthiest and best defended city in Byzantine-held Apulia. Bari held out for thirty-two months before succumbing to the Norman land and sea blockade, ending more than five centuries of Byzantine rule in Italy.[59] The defeat of the last Byzantine stronghold in Italy laid the groundwork for the strong feudal principality of Apulia that, when combined with Norman possessions in Sicily, would blossom into a Norman kingdom by 1130.

When Romanus' army reached Theodosiopolis each soldier was handed two months' rations because, according to Attaleiates, 'they were about to march through uninhabited land which had been trampled underfoot by the foreigners.'[60] Decades of Seljuk raiding had severely depopulated the frontier region and destroyed the area's agricultural capacity, a capacity a large expedition like the Byzantine campaign of 1071 would have normally relied on to supplement its logistical needs. Because of these extra provisions, the Eastern Roman army would have been slowed by the large number of pack animals and possibly carts required to feed this army and its attendants for two months.[61] After resupplying at Theodosiopolis, Romanus continued his march east, sending first a large contingent of allied Pechenegs followed later by 500 Norman troops under Roussel de Bailleul, ahead to the region around Chliat with instructions to collect fodder and provisions and secure the region's harvest for later consumption. Romanus followed along the same route before turning south to cross the Araxes, then east again to march through the Murat Su Valley, or perhaps farther south at Taron, then towards Manzikert itself.[62] Romanus arrived in the Lake Van region in late August.

Once in the region, Romanus divided his army again, sending the larger portion of around 25,000 men with the very best troops under the command of the Byzantine general Joseph Tarchaneiotes to retake Chliat, while he moved on Manzikert with the smaller force of around 23,000 men. The Chliat expedition included most of the *tagmata* and light infantry archers, troops that would be sorely missed in the upcoming battle of Manzikert. Located on the high Armenian plateau at about 5,000 feet above sea level, the fortress of Manzikert sat on a slight rise about two and half miles east of the broad, south-flowing Murat Su River.[63] This walled city, protected by a small garrison of Seljuk and Daylami soldiers, fell almost without resistance.[64] The emperor's decision to divide the army was possibly due to an intelligence report by Byzantine spies that Alp Arslan, who was sieging Aleppo as a precursor for a campaign against the Fatimids, broke off his siege when he learned that a large Byzantine host was on the Armenian frontier. Byzantine intelligence reported that the sultan retired to the east in such haste that his army virtually disintegrated through desertion and in a dangerous river crossing of the Euphrates. In reality, Alp Arslan still had perhaps around 10,000 troops still at his disposal after the fateful river crossing, and would add to this host as he returned to the Armenian frontier.[65] Based on these reports, Romanus divided his army in order to attack both fortress cities quickly. Having captured Manzikert, Romanus retired to his camp outside the fortress city and planned to march on Chliat the following day and rendezvous with the remainder of his army. Chliat was located twenty-nine miles south of Manzikert as the crow flies, or about thirty-three miles by way of an ancient winding road that crossed a small 7,000-foot mountain range and dropped down into the plain where the walled city was located about a mile away from the shores of Lake Van.[66] It was at this time that the emperor learned of a Seljuk raiding party that had surprised Byzantine forces foraging in the area. Believing the warriors were simply Turkoman raiders who frequently attacked the borderlands, the emperor dispatched a small force under Nikephoros Bryennios, the duke of Theodosiopolis and commander of the Armies of the West, to oppose them. What Romanus did not know was that the raiders were the vanguard of Alp Arslan's relief army.[67]

Alp Arslan was not planning on a military campaign against the Byzantines in the summer of 1071. The sultan's original strategy was to secure his north-western frontier before turning his attention towards his enemies in Syria and, later, the hated Fatimids in Egypt, knowing full well that the unofficial Turkoman raiding would continue into Armenia and Anatolia in his absence. To set up his long-awaited Fatimid campaign he left his headquarters at Khurasan in 1069 to campaign east, capturing Manzikert, Chliat and Artchesh and securing a truce with the Byzantine emperor. His north-western frontier seemingly secure, Alp Arslan marched south-west to Amida and then on to Edessa where, towards the end of March 1071, he besieged the city. While setting up the siege of Edessa, Alp Arslan received a message from Romanus (who was now beginning his march from Constantinople towards Armenia) proposing a renewal of the truce and the exchange of Muslim-held Manzikert and Artchesh for Byzantine-held

Hieropolis in Syria. The sultan accepted the offer, abandoning the siege of Edessa and investing the city of Aleppo. The Arab emir of Aleppo, Mahmud bin Nasr, was a pragmatic ruler who had switched his allegiance to the powerful Shia regime in Cairo when Fatimid influence in the Levant was waxing, then back to the Sunni caliph in Baghdad with the rise of Alp Arslan. Despite being back in the Sunni fold, the emir refused a parley with the Seljuk sultan, precipitating a protracted siege in the spring of 1071 to ensure his loyalty.[68] Weeks later Alp Arslan received a second letter from Romanus repeating the offer as if the original acceptance was not received, but this time with a more threatening tone.[69] By this time Romanus was closing in on Armenia with a large Byzantine army and felt confident in his chances of success in retaking the Armenian fortresses-cities and stabilizing the frontier, especially in light of the sultan's campaigning out of theatre in Syria. Although Muslim sources are mostly silent on the role of spies and scouts in providing Alp Arslan with information on the Byzantine army's progress, it is reasonable to assume the sultan routinely utilized these resources and understood the size and complement of the Byzantine army bearing down on the Lake Van area and the threat it represented. Still camped beneath the walls of Aleppo, the sultan raised the siege and, abandoning his Fatimid expedition, marched back towards the Byzantine eastern frontier.

Preamble to Battle and Locating the Battlefield

It was on this march back towards the Lake Van region that some of Alp Arslan's army scattered and he lost a great many horses and mules crossing the Euphrates. To make up for his manpower losses, the sultan directed his vizier, Nizam al-Mulk, to press ahead and raise troops in Azerbaijan while he marched his remaining army directly towards the Armenian border by way of Amida and Mosul and then to Khoi (modern Khvoy in north-western Iran) between Lake Van and Lake Urmia, picking up another 10,000 Kurdish cavalry along the way.[70] By the time Alp Arslan reached Khoi his army consisted of around 20,000 horsemen, a little smaller in size than Romanus' Manzikert expedition. Perhaps more importantly, the Seljuk army was just over 100 miles away from the numerically superior but separated Byzantine armies and had the element of strategic surprise on its side.[71]

When Romanus learned of the Seljuk horsemen in the vicinity of his camp at Manzikert he dispatched a force under Nikephoros Bryennios to deal with what he perceived was a small raiding party sent out from Chliat. Bryennios' contingent was unable to manage the Turkish forces and sent word to the Byzantine emperor requesting reinforcements. Romanus, still unaware that the Seljuk troops in the area were the vanguard of Alp Arslan's army, first accused Bryennios of cowardice, but then sent out a relief force an hour or two later under the command of the Armenian general Vasilak Basilakes to aid him. Basilakes and his cavalry charged the Turks, dispersing the steppe warriors, but in the pursuit that followed, probably as part of a Seljuk feigned retreat, Basilakes was captured near the enemy defences.[72] To make matters worse, many of the soldiers in the relief army returned to the Byzantine camp severely wounded, their bodies and those of their horses peppered with Seljuk arrows. Bryennios himself suffered three wounds, two in his back from arrows and one in his chest from an enemy lance, although he was able to continue in his duties, probably due to the excellent armour worn by Byzantine commanders in this period. To his credit,

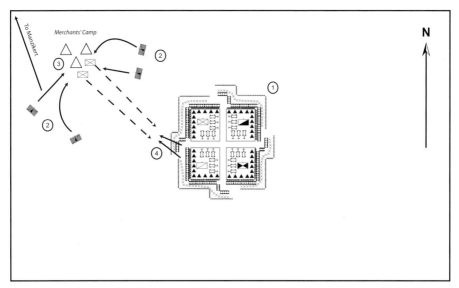

Map 5.2.1. The Seljuk attack on the Manzikert Camp, 1071 CE. Phase I: Pursuing, but failing to catch a force of Seljuk horseman that had mauled part of his Byzantine army and captured one of his commanders, Romanus IV Diogenes makes camp outside of Manzikert (1). That night, under the cover of a new moon, Seljuk raiders return (2), striking a group of Uze mercenaries that had wandered from their fortified camp to purchase goods from some nearby merchants (3). Surrounded by circling groups of enemy horse archers, the Uze dash back to camp, where they lose more men to sentries unable to distinguish them in the dark (4).

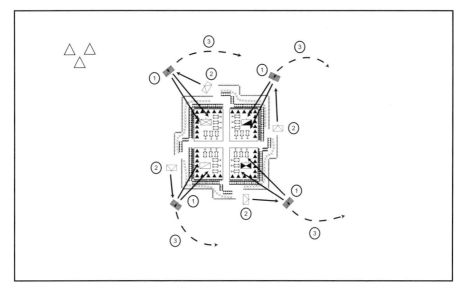

Map 5.2.2. The Seljuk attack on the Manzikert camp, 1071 CE. Phase II: The Seljuk spend the night raining arrow shafts over the camps palisades (1). The following morning, 1,000 Uze mercenaries and their commander, Tamis, defect to the Seljuks. In a move perhaps calculated to boost morale amongst his troop, Romanus orders his light infantry archers to advance from the camp and attack the Seljuks (2) who are driven off with heavy losses (3).

Romanus immediately assembled an army and mounted a counterattack, but the Seljuk horsemen had disappeared into the countryside, and he returned to camp.[73]

That night, Wednesday 24 August, there was a new moon rising over the Byzantine camp, and the Seljuk raiders took advantage of the darkness by returning to the Byzantine encampment and attacking a contingent of Uze mercenaries buying goods from merchants outside of the fortified camp. Thrown into disorder by the circling Seljuk horsemen, the Uze rushed back into the camp where some of them were probably attacked by Byzantine troops unable to distinguish the allied Uze from the attacking Seljuks. We learn from Attaleiates that the Seljuks did not attempt to enter the camp, but instead spent the night making noise and raining arrow shafts over the palisades into the Byzantine tents from the safety of the shadows. After a long sleepless night, the Byzantine army was further weakened by the desertion of 1,000 Uze mercenaries, with their commander, Tamis, to the Seljuk cause. The desertion of this contingent of Uze put the loyalty of the remaining Turkic steppe warriors in question, and without the certain participation of these significant mercenary groups (and their light cavalry capabilities), the effectiveness of the entire Byzantine army was now suspect. Romanus, perhaps seeing the morale of his men slipping, ordered his light infantry archers out of the camp where they drove the Seljuks from the vicinity, inflicting heavy casualties on the enemy horsemen.[74]

Attaleiates explains that Romanus wanted to engage the Seljuk army immediately, but understood that he needed the remainder of his army in order to be successful. The emperor still believed the majority of his forces, perhaps as many as 25,000 troops, were still encamped before Chliat and represented a significant strategic reserve for the upcoming engagement. What he did not know was that Tarchaneiotes and Roussel de Bailleul, with their Byzantine and allied troops, had scattered upon hearing of Alp Arslan's arrival in the Lake Van region. Without bothering to inform their emperor of their decision, the Byzantine and Norman generals retreated west back to the safety of Byzantine Anatolia, leaving Romanus and his smaller army to fend for themselves.[75] Still unaware of the retreat of over half his expeditionary force, Romanus sent messengers to Chliat to summon that army to him but also prepared his own smaller army to fight the Seljuks the following day, Friday 26 August.

On Thursday 25 August (the day of the Uze defection) the Abbasid caliph Al-Qaim in Baghdad sent Romanus a peace embassy, although it was obviously sent with the acquiescence of the sultan. But why would Alp Arslan desire a political solution instead of a battlefield engagement when he was well aware of Romanus' rapidly degrading strategic position? The sultan knew that even facing half the original Byzantine army in a set-piece battle was a dangerous proposition as his mounted steppe warrior army was much more comfortable fighting on the run using raids, ambushes and surprise attacks. He also understood his Byzantine adversary preferred this type of positional warfare, despite the ragtag composition of its army, and was commanded by a very capable emperor-general. Moreover, a peaceful resolution that stabilized the Armenian frontier, even temporarily, would also allow the sultan to return to his original campaign objective, a war against the Fatimids.[76]

But Romanus did not want peace. When the Seljuk embassy arrived, the Byzantine ruler placed firm conditions on the opening of discussions, specifically requiring Alp Arslan to withdraw from his present camp so the Greek army could occupy it. It is likely that this precondition was designed to be rebuffed as the emperor wanted war. What is not known is the influence of Romanus' counsellors on his final decision. These generals and advisors pressed the point that the sultan was afraid of a confrontation and was simply stalling for time and waiting for reinforcements to arrive.[77] Some of the men may have seen the merits of a decisive battle, while others may have understood a loss would ruin Romanus and reshuffle the political deck with the emperor's enemies in Constantinople, creating opportunities for advancement. However, what is certain is that by this time, Romanus and his counsellors knew his Chliat army was nowhere to be found and would likely not be a factor in the coming day's battle.

Much has been written over the centuries on the wisdom of Romanus' decision to fight Alp Arslan in a set-piece engagement with only half his army, but from the Byzantine emperor's perspective this was a sound strategy. The campaign of 1071 was very expensive and it is unlikely the emperor would be able to finance another large expedition in the near future. Also, a failed campaign would only embolden his political enemies in Constantinople, while a victory at Manzikert would provide much-needed political capital in the domestic struggles that lay ahead. On purely military merits, Romanus recognized that having the Seljuk sultan and his main army within striking distance was a rare occurrence, one that had not taken place in the first four years of his reign. A similar opportunity might not present itself again, so the emperor prepared his troops for the upcoming engagement.[78]

Both armies prepared for battle on the morning of Friday 26 August. Orthodox Mass was celebrated in the imperial pavilion, and then the cross was paraded through the camp as the troops said their prayers before putting on their kits and preparing for battle. Similar praying took place in the Muslim camp but with a greater emphasis as the battle fell on the *yaum al-juma* ('day of assembly') or weekly Islamic holy day of Friday. In fact, in support of the upcoming battle the Abbasid caliph had circulated a prayer for victory every Friday in August in all of the mosques in his domain, leading some later Muslim chroniclers to conclude, erroneously, that the sultan launched his assault on the infidel during the midday prayers on a Friday, when in fact it was the Byzantines who offered battle first by marching out of their camp and confronting the waiting Muslim army.[79] Alp Arslan prepared for battle by dressing himself in white so that his garment might serve as a shroud should he be martyred in battle. The Muslim sources state that the sultan threw aside his bow and quiver and seized his sword and mace, an action that has been interpreted as a symbolic gesture to his troops that he would remain on the battlefield until the very end.[80] In case of this outcome, he also enforced oaths from those around him that his son Malikshah would succeed him as sultan should he be killed.[81] These actions may have been his normal routine on the morning of an engagement, however they give us insight into the mindset of the Seljuk ruler, whose actions illustrate he understood the military capabilities of the Byzantines, despite their reduced strength, and the possibility of death on the battlefield.

Because of the fluid nature of the battle of Manzikert, the precise location of the battlefield is difficult to pinpoint precisely. We know the battle was fought on the gently rolling steppes within a mile or two of the walls of Manzikert to the south or south-east of the city. One source for the battle, another Nikephoros Bryennios, the grandson and namesake of the general wounded just days before the climatic engagement, states that in the closing stages of the engagement the Seljuks ambushed the Byzantine forces. The topography of the Lake Van region consists of barren foothills and mountains separated by strips of steppe lands, and since the open plain does not lend itself to this kind of surprise tactic, it is most likely these ambushes took place in rougher, hillier country. Steppe lands are present to the south and east of Manzikert, some three or four miles across, extending for ten miles on a south-west-north-east axis. Beyond these grasslands are a line of foothills, sliced through with mazes of ravines and gullies ideal for setting up ambushes. These foothills slope upwards into a small mountain range some 2,000 feet above the steppes. Modern historians believe that somewhere in this forty-plus square mile area the armies of Romanus and Alp Arslan met face-to-face early in the afternoon on that fateful Friday.[82]

The Battle of Manzikert

Romanus marched his army of around 22,000 men out from its fortified camp near the walls of Manzikert south towards Alp Arslan's position on the steppes. Here, a Seljuk and allied army of similar strength was arrayed in three divisions (centre, left and right) in a long continuous crescent made up of steppe cavalry (the sources do not tell us whether this formation was initially concave or convex in shape) stretching from east to west. Alp Arslan commanded his troops from a nearby hill probably located south of the initial formations just on the edge of the rough terrain. To meet their frontage, the Byzantine emperor ordered his army to deploy some distance from the Seljuk line with infantry in the centre formation several ranks deep and cavalry on the wings. Nikephoros Bryennios commanded the left division consisting of about 5,000 troops, and as commander of the Armies of the West, would lead troops from Byzantium's European territories. The right division would also have consisted of about 5,000 troops and was commanded by the Cappadocian governor and strategos Theodore Alyates, whose soldiers were primarily from Armenia and Anatolia. Romanus controlled the centre division made up of about 5,000 troops. The emperor would have been protected by a contingent of his Varangian Guard perhaps 500 strong. These Rus warriors were only part of the whole Varangian Guard as many of these units would have remained in Constantinople to protect the young-co-ruler Michael. Other guard units, including the elite *Scholai Tagmata*, would have been present in some numbers to protect the emperor, although the sources do indicate that many of the best troops were allocated for the Chliat expedition, so how many of these imperial *tagmata* were present in Romanus' division is unknown. Armenian heavy infantry and a substantial contingent of European mercenaries rounded out the centre. A large contingent of 2,000 Uze and Turkish steppe cavalry allies provided a light screen on the left and right wings and probably for the trailing reserves.[83]

The Byzantine emperor was arraying his multinational army without the benefit of all of the elements of a balanced-combined arms army present. Most of the Byzantine infantry archers, with their heavier and longer range bows, were with the missing Chliat army. Offering battle against Seljuk and allied horse archers without these missile troops meant the Byzantine army could not return fire and keep the steppe warriors at a comfortable distance. Romanus' insistence to offer battle without these archers in place went against long-standing Byzantine doctrine dating back to Leo VI's *Taktika* and the absence of these specialized troops would prove to be a decisive factor in the upcoming engagement.

Behind the forward three divisions Romanus placed a substantial rearguard of 5,000 men made up of the 'levies of the nobility', the private armies of the great lords of Byzantium, commanded by Andronikos Doukas, the son of Caesar John Doukas and nephew of the late emperor. These Greek troops would probably have been protected by a screen of allied horse archers as they marched behind the main force. Historians have wondered why Romanus allowed the son of his greatest rival in Constantinople to have command of his strategic reserve. Perhaps he believed having the young general in his retinue kept a potential political hostage close by. The historian Nikephoros Bryennios the younger praises the skills of Andronikos, relating that he 'exceeded those of his age in wisdom and was surpassed by no one in courage. He was marvelouslly trained in ruses and strategems.'[84] The chronicler continues with a statement on Andronikos' feeling for Romanus, writing 'he was not very favourably disposed towards the emperor.'[85] Giving Andronikos command of his reserve would prove to be the greatest mistake of Romanus' life. Finally, with more than half his army missing the Byzantine emperor knew he would require every available soldier for the upcoming battle so he pulled his guards from the imperial camp to fight.

Once in formation, Romanus ordered his troops to march forward to engage the Seljuk lines. But the mounted Muslim steppe warriors, aware of the shock capabilities of the Christian heavy cavalry *kataphraktoi* and *klibanophoroi* and heavy infantry, steadily withdrew in a wide crescent, maintaining a safe distance between themselves and the advancing enemy. The Byzantine army advanced over what had been the sultan's camp, now abandoned, as the afternoon wore on. During this slow strategic retreat southwards, Alp Arslan did order his horse archers to harass the Byzantine flanks with arrow fire, an action that infuriated some Byzantine cavalry into ignoring Byzantine military doctrine. They broke rank and pursued the steppe archers away from the main battle line and into the southern foothills, where the Christian horsemen were killed in carefully planned ambushes in the rough terrain.[86]

Romanus and his generals were able to maintain control over the majority of their troops as they marched south, holding to the strategy that eventually the Greek host would press the retreating Seljuk crescent against the rough terrain and compel Alp Arslan into the set-piece battle Romanus wanted. But because of the long duration of the retreat, this engagement, which began in early afternoon, was quickly running into the evening, and Romanus understood that his main camp was undefended, completely vulnerable to the kind of Seljuk raid that took place just two nights before. As the two armies neared the foothills Romanus ordered the imperial standards to be reversed, the signal to his troops to begin an orderly retreat back to their own camp. Surrounded by his Varangian Guard, Romanus wheeled his horse to begin the slow countermarch back to camp near Manzikert. At this time, the Byzantine host was probably about eight miles south of the walls of Manzikert and close to the southern foothills.[87]

Turning a large army around, even a well disciplined army, was a very difficult exercise on the pre-modern battlefield, and Romanus' army was far from a well disciplined force. When performing a countermarch manoeuvre under enemy fire gaps can appear in the rank and file within formations and adjacent formations can tilt away from one another exposing flanks that can be exploited by a hovering foe. The Byzantine army's multinational composition, with its various command structures and orders given in numerous languages, added to the confusion of this seemingly simple retrograde

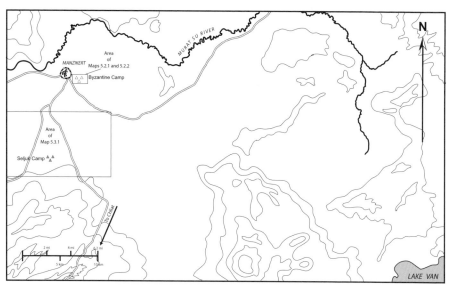

Map 5.3. Locating the Battle of Manzikert, 1071 CE.

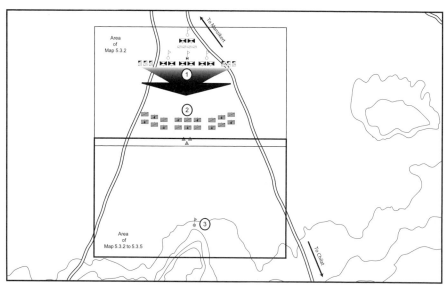

Map 5.3.1. The Battle of Manzikert, 1071 CE. Phase I: The Byzantine army marches south (1) from their camp outside Manzikert towards the Seljuk position on the steppes. The Muslim force is arrayed in three divisions in a crescent-shaped formation (2). Alp Arslan establishes his command post on slightly rising terrain to the south of his formations (3).

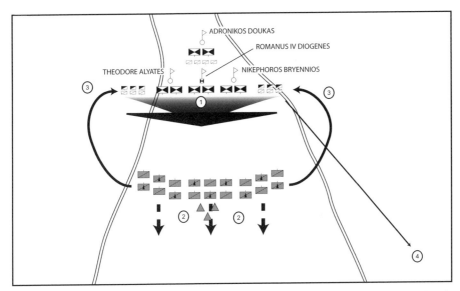

Map 5.3.2. The Battle of Manzikert, 1071 CE. Phase II: As Romanus' army advances (1), the Seljuks steadily withdraw (2), maintaining their formation and abandoning their camp to the Christians. During this retreat, Alp Arslan orders horse archers to harry the Byzantine flanks with missile fire (3), goading some of the Christian horsemen to pursue their tormentors (4) into the rough terrain where they are killed in carefully laid ambushes.

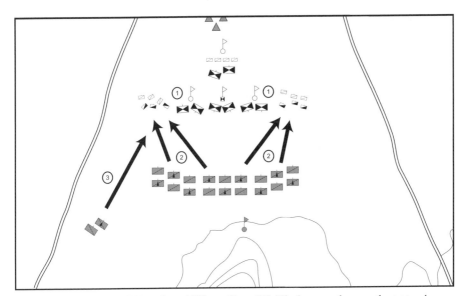

Map 5.3.3. The Battle of Manzikert, 1071 CE. Phase III: The long march across the steppes drags on towards evening. As the armies near the foothills, Romanus decides not to risk leaving his camp undefended and signals for a countermarch. The Byzantine army, a less disciplined, polyglot force, has difficulty with the manoeuvre (1). Gaps in the lines and exposed flanks are open without the support of their infantry archers who are absent with the task force sent to Chliat. Alp Arslan recognizes his opportunity and orders his army to attack the enemy wings (2). They are joined by reserve cavalry from deeper in the hills (3).

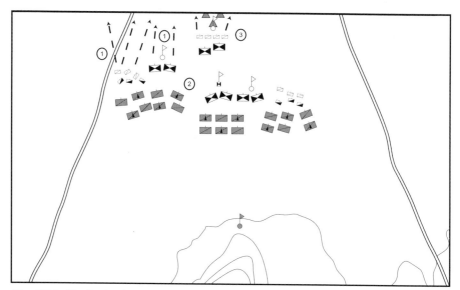

Map 5.3.4. The Battle of Manzikert, 1071 CE. Phase IV: Alyates' right wing breaks under the Seljuk attack and flees back towards the Byzantine camp outside of Manzikert (1). Seljuk forces pour into the resulting gap (2). Adronikos Doukas' reserves should fill the gap and stop the penetration, but Romanus' rival spreads the news that the emperor has been defeated. The reserves break and rout towards the camp (3).

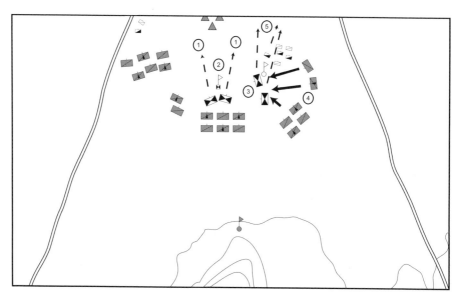

Map 5.3.5. The Battle of Manzikert, 1071 CE. Phase V: Much of the centre division routs (1) as word of the disappearance of the army's reserve spreads, though some 2,000 Turkic cavalry remain with the emperor and the Varangian guard (2). Nikephoros Bryennios attempts to support the centre with his wing (3), but is struck from the rear by Seljuk horsemen (4) that shatter the Byzantine formations, which flee the field (5).

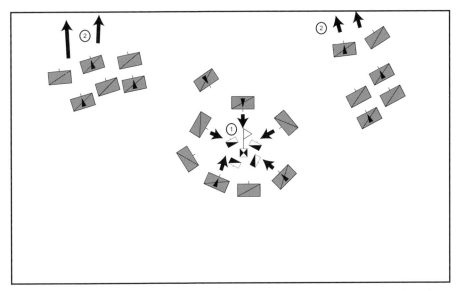

Map 5.3.6. The Battle of Manzikert, 1071 CE. Phase VI: Romanus stands his ground (1) and even signals a turn back to the south in an attempt to rally his army, but the Seljuk forces pursuing the routed Byzantine formations (2) are too strong. The Turkic cavalry that remains with the emperor suffers greatly in the ensuing action. Surrounded by his Varangian guard, Romanus himself fights until his horse is killed and finally surrenders after his sword hand is wounded. The following morning, the Byzantine emperor is brought to Alp Arslan in chains. He is forced to kiss the ground before the victor's feet and Alp Arslan steps on the emperor's neck in a final gesture of subjugation.

manoeuvre. Communication from the emperor in the centre formation took time to reach the officers on the edges of the outside formations, and orders were not always executed at the same time. Making this manoeuvre even more dangerous for the Byzantine army was the absence of significant numbers of light infantry archers who would have been used to keep the mounted steppe archers at bay as the army turned around.

Alp Arslan, watching the Byzantine army slowly turn around from his command post on a nearby hill, seized this moment to launch an aggressive attack on the Byzantine wings. The Seljuk sultan, understanding the confusion inherent in his enemy's retrograde manoeuvre, ordered all of his Seljuk and allied cavalry forward at precisely this moment. Muslim reserve cavalry rode out of the hills to join the melee. Faced with the steppe cavalry attack on the wings while the countermarch manoeuvre was under way, the Byzantine right wing under the command of Alyates broke in confusion and separated from the centre and left formations. It is also possible that Byzantine soldiers and allies in the right wing, far away from the emperor's actual location, saw the reversed signals to march back to camp at the same moment the general Seljuk assault was underway and believed the emperor had been killed in the initial attack. Many of these soldiers broke ranks and fled back towards the fortified Byzantine camp or the safety of Manzikert's walls.

More Seljuk cavalry poured into the fray, cutting across immediately behind the broken right wing. This tactic should have placed the Muslim steppe warriors in a precarious position between the broken right wing and the advancing reserves led by Andronikos Doukas, but the reserves were not there. Andronikos was, according to Michael Attaleiates, fulfilling 'the plot he had already hatched for the emperor's destruction by personally spreading the word' to his troops that Romanus was defeated.[88] From their perspective in the rear formations, these Greek reserves witnessed the swarming Seljuk attacks on the flanks of Romanus' army and the chaos in the right wing, a sight that no doubt made them nervous. Add to this tension the lies sown by Andronikos and his allied lords and the reserves lost faith and broke, running back in the direction of the camp. The dissolution of the reserve formations precipitated a general rout as the Armenian heavy infantry and European mercenaries from the centre now joined the flight. It should be noted that a sizeable contingent of perhaps as many as 2,000 Turkic allied cavalry did stay to defend the emperor and were virtually annihilated.[89] With the centre formation collapsing all around him, Romanus soon found himself surrounded by only his faithful Varangian Guard. To his credit, Nikephoros Bryennios, seeing the rapidly disintegrating centre, ordered his men on the left wing to rescue the emperor, but these troops were charged from behind by Seljuk horsemen, who shattered the Byzantine formation, forcing it to flee from the field.

The chaos of this moment of the battle is recounted by Attaleiates below:

> Outside the camp all were in flight, shouting incoherently and riding about in disorder; no one could say what was happening. Some maintained that the Emperor was still fighting with what was left of his army, and that the barbarians had been put to flight. Others claimed that he had been killed or captured. Everyone had something different to report.
>
> It was like an earthquake: the shouting, the sweat, the swift rushes of fear, the clouds of dust, and not least the hordes of Turks riding all around us. Depending on his speed, resolution and strength, each man sought safety in flight. The enemy followed in pursuit, killing some, capturing others and trampling yet others under their horses' hooves. It was a tragic sight, beyond any mourning and lamenting. What indeed could be more pitiable than to see the entire imperial army in flight, defeated and pursued by cruel and inhuman barbarians; the emperor defenceless and surrounded by more of the same; the imperial tents, symbols of military might and sovereignty, taken over by men of such a kind; the whole Roman state overturned – and knowing that the empire itself was on the verge of collapse?[90]

Whether the loss at Manzikert placed the Byzantine Empire on the 'verge of collapse' is a subject of historical debate. However, Attaleiates' passage does illustrate the confusion generated by the rout and the hopelessness of a broken Byzantine army wondering about the fate of their imperial leader.

Romanus, surrounded by his Varangian soldiers, stood his ground and even turned his men (and presumably his remaining imperial standards) to the south again in an attempt to rally those troops who remained in vicinity to his banners. But the emperor's army did not return to the battlefield. The pursuing Seljuk cavalry archers and lancers would have kept all but the largest, most disciplined infantry and cavalry formations from returning, and those contingents, if they were still in formation at this point in the battle, had various reasons for not coming to the aid of Romanus. The Greek reserves, led by the plotting Andronikos and other Anatolian nobles in league with the Doukas family, willfully abandoned their ruler before battle was joined. Of the non-Greek troops, the Armenians in the right wing were mauled in the opening stages of the battle, and those who survived held little love for their Greek allies who conquered their country centuries before and persecuted them for adhering to their non-Orthodox version of Christianity.[91] These troops, now close to their homes in the Armenian frontier, had long-standing and immediate reasons not to reengage. The other European mercenaries in Byzantine service, well trained and well compensated, did not fulfil their contractual obligations and abandoned their imperial employer in his moment of need. Sources point to friction between Romanus and his soldiers for hire stemming from the emperor's overt favouritism towards his native troops, but as the core of the centre formation, the mercenaries' poor showing was instrumental in the collapse of one-third of the imperial army. Only the Turkic steppe warriors stayed and fought at great cost in lives, and these troops were considered the most unreliable at the beginning of the engagement due to the Uze defection the day before.

Attaleiates notes that Romanus fought well until his horse was killed underneath him and he, fighting now on foot, was wounded in his sword hand and taken prisoner.[92] Presumably, his Varangian Guard stayed with him until the very end. The sources do state that he was dressed as a common soldier when he was finally captured. What is not known is whether he, like Muhammad at the battle of Uhud, consciously put on the panoply of a common soldier in an attempt to hide his identity, or whether he was forced to put on this kit after capture. Romanus and the survivors spent that late August night among the dead and dying on the field of battle and the Byzantine emperor was given no special treatment. The next morning, Saturday 27 August, Romanus was brought before Alp Arslan in chains and flung at the feet of sultan sitting on his throne. At first the Seljuk ruler refused to believe the exhausted captive was the Byzantine emperor, as the two men had never met face to face. But Romanus was identified by former Seljuk ambassadors to the Byzantine court and the previously captured Armenian general Vasilak Basilakes. Now knowing the Byzantine ruler was on his knees in chains before him, Alp Arslan rose from his throne and ordered Romanus to kiss the ground before him and then placed his foot on the neck of his imperial prisoner in a ritual of complete subjugation.

Debacle at Manzikert: Romanus' Political and Military Failures

The Byzantine loss at the battle of Manzikert was precipitated both by a political failure of Romanus to secure the cooperation of his own officers and allies before and during the engagement and a military failure brought about by his inferior generalship. A victim of his own political and military circumstances, Romanus was hamstrung by a powerful enemy in the Doukas family undermining his influence in Constantinople and among important thematic governors. Still, he managed to shore up the empire's military readiness by settling his soldiers' arrears in pay, purchasing new equipment, and instituting new training programmes designed to resurrect the impressive Byzantine fighting force present in the early eleventh century under Basil II. Unfortunately, these measures did not create battle-ready Greek forces overnight, and Romanus was required to rely on foreign mercenaries to supplement his native armies in his campaigns. Although described by his contemporaries as a devout and resolute leader, Romanus was unable to secure the political loyalty of his own generals, and this failure led to the evaporation of over half his fighting force before the battle even began when Tarchaneiotes and Roussel de Bailleul abandoned the expedition. The presence of these troops at Manzikert would have given Romanus an impressive numerical advantage, as well as returning valuable *tagmata* and the light infantry archers to the battlefield. In fact, Romanus' willingness to offer battle against a mounted steppe enemy without his archers went against his training and centuries of Byzantine experience fighting these types of warriors. The emperor also placed the entire Manzikert expedition in jeopardy by not knowing the position and movements of his enemy when he entered the Lake Van region. Here, the emperor's spies and scouts were unable to locate and evaluate the enemy, leading to the mauling of Byzantine forces two days before the main battle and the capture of the Armenian general Vasilak Basilakes. Basilakes' presence on the battlefield two days later may have compelled the Armenian forces into a better showing and altered the engagement's outcome. This lack of operational security continued on the day of the battle when he let the afternoon sun slip away towards dusk as his army was pulled miles away from the protection of its camp and towards an ambush. This demonstrated poor situational awareness and a blatant disregard for the military capabilities of his mounted foe. Manzikert was, at its heart, a battle of Byzantine heavy cavalry versus Muslim light horse. Due to the prolonged duration of the battle, the lighter and leaner Turkish mounts had a distinct advantage over the heavier and more muscular Byzantine mounts ridden by the *kataphraktoi* and *klibanophoroi* as these horses were never meant to make extended marches in full kit. Larger, fleshier horses tire easier than leaner ones, and lose more fluid from their tissues under physical duress. Ideally, these horses would be dressed for war and used on the battlefield before the weight of barding and rider wore the horse down. At Manzikert, these heavier war horses were under arms in the heat of an August day from at least mid-morning until the battle began before dusk. The Seljuk mounts, on the other hand, would have been light-framed breeds from Turkoman and hot-blooded strains accustomed to constant skirmishing and better able to deal with the fatigue of the day's harassing actions against the slow-marching Byzantine lines.[93] Finally, Romanus showed poor political and military judgment in placing the young Andronikos Doukas as the commander of the reserve units, falsely believing the brilliant commander would place the prospect of a Byzantine victory against the dangerous Seljuk Empire above the political aspirations of himself and his family.

Contemporaries or near contemporaries of the battle emphasize the loss at Manzikert as a catastrophe for the Byzantine Empire, while some modern historians have reinforced this perception.[94] Seen purely as a military defeat, the battle of Manzikert did not produce the crippling effect on the Byzantine Empire described above by Attaleiates during the darkest moments of the fight. Byzantine casualties were, despite Greek and Muslim accounts to the contrary, relatively light because most of the Byzantine host was either not present before the battle began (the Chliat army), deserted during the engagement (Andronikos' reserves, Armenian heavy infantry, and the European mercenaries), or withdrew under duress before the final collapse (Bryennios' left wing). One modern estimate places overall losses in dead and wounded at no more than 10 per cent of those troops present at the beginning of the engagement.[95] If Romanus opened that battle with Alp Arslan with around 22,000 combat troops total (a figure that subtracts the defecting Uze contingent, but adds to the field army troops normally stationed as camp guards), this 10 per cent estimate places casualties at around 2,200 men, a very modest number and far from the annihilation of a Byzantine army often attributed to this battle. Even at 20 per cent casualties (4,400 men), Manzikert was not a devastating engagement. Contributing to this low casualty figure was the fact that the engagement did not begin until nearly dusk and most of the fighting and dying took place near the centre division where Romanus and his Varangian Guard, as well as the Uze auxiliaries, were staying and fighting. This concentration of Seljuk combat power on the centre division as darkness fell meant that most of the fleeing Byzantine and allied troops from the other divisions were able to make their escape into the safety of Manzikert fortress or farther afield towards friendlier territory by separate routes and at different rates. Those few Byzantine soldiers near the emperor's pavilion and baggage train were not as lucky as these riches were a primary target of the Seljuk warriors, and it is outside of this camp where many of the other imperial casualties took place. The treasure taken from the Byzantine camp was enormous; so much so, Muslim sources indicate that it was beyond the Seljuk army's ability to immediately haul away.[96] The loss of a substantial part of the imperial treasury to the Seljuks would weaken an already frail Byzantine economy, while simultaneously enriching and emboldening Alp Arslan, and, more ominously, his recalcitrant Turkoman allies.

The Byzantine defeat at Manzikert was not the great military disaster recorded by Christian and Muslim sources. It was, however, a great political disaster. Over eight hundred years had passed since a Roman emperor had been captured in battle, dating back to Valerian's defeat at the hands of the Sassanian emperor Shapur I in 260.[97] Romanus' defeat and capture sent a shockwave throughout Christendom and the *Dar al-Islam*, challenging the notion that the Byzantine Empire was, in the words of one prominent modern historian, 'a permanent, stable and unshakable element of the political universe of the era.'[98] After Manzikert, the Islamic world saw the power and prestige of the Eastern Roman Empire and its *basileus Rhomaion* in an entirely new light. Byzantium was now viewed by its enemies as a vulnerable state unable to defend itself on multiple fronts, whose wealth and lands were there for the taking. But more damaging than the actual battlefield loss at Manzikert was the ensuing civil war and subsequent challenges to Byzantine hegemony on the edges of empire, draining men and resources empire-wide. These challenges weakened the eastern frontier and opened central and eastern Anatolia up for a permanent Seljuk invasion and conquest in the decade ahead.

Conclusion

In Manzikert's Wake – The Seljuk Invasion of Anatolia and the Origins of the Levantine Crusades

The Deaths of Romanus IV Diogenes and Alp Arslan

After placing his foot on the neck of the prone Byzantine emperor, Alp Arslan helped Romanus to his feet and asked him to sit next to him as an equal, reassuring him that he would be treated as a guest in the highest tradition of Islamic hospitality. For the next week Romanus remained a guest in the Seljuk pavilion as the two rulers worked out the conditions of his release. Alp Arslan demanded the surrender of Manzikert, Antioch, Edessa and Hieropolis, and the hand of one of the Byzantine ruler's daughters for one of his own sons. The sultan also requested a ransom of ten million nomismata, but when Romanus explained that this sum was impossible to come up with due to the expense of the recent military expeditions, the sultan agreed to a million and a half nomismata gold pieces and an annual tribute of 360,000 nomismata.[1] The ransom and tribute decided, Alp Arslan released Romanus knowing full well that for his conditions to be met, Romanus needed to return quickly to Constantinople and resume his imperial duties. One week after the defeat at Manzikert, Romanus left the Seljuk camp with Alp Arslan on the first leg of his journey, then escorted by two emirs and one hundred armed ghulams prepared to take him back to Constantinople. This Muslim escort proved unnecessary when Romanus met up with the remnants of this defeated army, and the emperor dismissed the guard and rode with his men to Dokeia (modern Tokat) in Paphlagonia where he learned that his enemies in Constantinople had deposed him when news of the Manzikert defeat reached the imperial capital.[2]

Romanus' nemesis, Caesar John Doukas, returned from exile in Bithynia on hearing the news of the Byzantine loss and, with the support of the palace Varangian Guard, proclaimed his weak-willed nephew Michael VII as sole emperor. Michael's mother, the regent Eudokia Makrembolitissa, was arrested and exiled to a convent she founded at the mouth of the Hellespont. Michael VII Doukas was quickly crowned in Hagia Sophia on 24 October 1071.[3] With his new power base secured in Constantinople, John next turned to deal with the now deposed Romanus and his tattered veterans taking refuge in Dokeia – the first stages of a civil war. John sent both of his sons to deal with Romanus. The caesar's youngest son, Constantine, defeated Romanus at Dokeia in the

Armeniakon Theme, forcing him to retreat with his remaining troops first to the fortress of Tyropoion in Cappadocia and then to Adana in Cilicia. There, Romanus was confronted by Andronikos Doukas, the young general who betrayed him at Manzikert, who defeated the deposed emperor a second time. Exhausted and demoralized, Romanus was forced to surrender to Andronikos by the garrison at Adana under the condition that no harm would come to him, and, in return, he would renounce all claims to the throne and retire to a monastery. Andronikos agreed to these conditions and, while waiting for the arrangement to be ratified by the new emperor, Michael VII Doukas, in Constantinople, mounted his monk-garbed prisoner on a mule in humiliation and paraded him from Adana to Kotyaion (modern Kutahya in western Turkey), a nearly 500-mile journey through the countryside.[4] However, Andronikos reneged on his word and sent men to cruelly put out the eyes of the ex-emperor with a hot iron, then sent him into exile on the Island of Proti (part of the Princes' Island chain) in the Sea of Marmara. Left without an attendant or any medical attention, Romanus' wounds became infected and he died later in the summer of 1072.[5]

To make matters worse, the Byzantine losses at Bari and Manzikert in 1071 emboldened the enemies of Byzantium to challenge the empire's resolve in the Balkans and Anatolia. A serious uprising in Bulgaria in 1072 required Byzantine military attention. Michael VII ordered Nikephoros Bryennios, now in the service of the Doukas family, to restore control, but at a heavy cost in men and material. In 1075, Pope Gregory VII sent his legates to crown Demetrius Zvonimir king of Croatia, pulling this kingdom into the Catholic orbit. Two years later, in 1077, Michael of Zeta received a papal coronation, further loosening Byzantium's grip in this region. Add to these developments Pecheneg and Magyar raiding, and Basil II's achievement of a secure and friendly Balkan region was beginning to unravel.[6]

In Anatolia, a military insurrection led by the Norman adventurer Roussel de Bailleul would alter the balance of power between the Seljuks and Byzantines. In 1073, Michael sent a Byzantine army to deal with Seljuk raiding in Cappadocia and Roussel was the commander of a mixed force of Norman and Frankish mercenary cavalry. Once again, Roussel deserted the Byzantine army before the engagement with the Turks, who routed the Greek army near Caesarea. Roussel then set up an independent Norman state in the Armeniakon Theme in north-central Asia Minor with 300–400 of his loyal men in a pattern similar to that used by Robert Guiscard in southern Italy after the Byzantine defeat at Bari. Enraged by this action, Michael sent an army commanded by his uncle Caesar John and the veteran strategos Nikephoros Botaneiates to deal with the rising Norman threat, but this Greek army was soundly defeated and John was captured. Roussel retaliated by marching across Bithynia to the Bosporus and burning the city of Chrysopolis across the strait from Constantinople. Roussel also proclaimed John emperor, apparently with the caesar's approval, and his boldness attracted perhaps as many as 3,000 Frankish mercenaries to his standard. Distraught, Michael turned to the Seljuk Turks who were raiding in the eastern regions of Anatolia for assistance, hiring a large mercenary force operating in Bithynia under the command of the Seljuk emir Artuk to defeat the Normans. In return for their service, Michael was willing to cede territory held by the Seljuks to them permanently, greatly strengthening the steppe warriors' hold on Anatolia. Artuk surprised Roussel at Metabole, defeating and capturing the Norman general and freeing John. But a ransom was raised by Roussel's wife and the Norman adventurer resumed his activities.[7] In 1074, Michael sent the young general and future emperor, Alexios Komnenos, to hunt down and bring Roussel back to Constantinople in chains. Alexios was able to restore some imperial authority in the region, but could not return home to the capital by land because of the hostile Turkoman presence in the area, returning instead from the Black Sea port of Heracleia (modern Eregli) to Constantinople by sea.[8] Roussel's revolt and attempt to create his own Norman domain within the boundaries of Byzantium would leave a lasting impression on young Alexios Komnenos, who would be emperor twenty years later at the time of the First Crusade and would remember well his dealings with Norman adventurers wanting to carve their own principalities in the east.[9]

In south-east Anatolia the Armenians, secure in their Taurus Mountains strongholds, violently threw off centuries of Byzantine rule and established various small fiefdoms in the region further south in Cilicia and northern Syria. However, one former Byzantine general, the Armenian Philaretos Brachamios who had protected Romanus' lines of communication before the Manzikert campaign, consolidated these fledgling Armenian holdings into a sizeable state encompassing his base at Melitene and Edessa in Upper Mesopotamia, Tarsus in Cilicia, and Antioch in northern Syria. The core of his army was a contingent of 8,000 Franks supplemented by Armenian and Seljuk mercenaries. A pragmatic politician, Brachamios did not hesitate to call on the services of local Seljuk emirs to assist him with disobedient Armenian princes and is even rumored to have converted to Islam.[10] This new Armenian state effectively ended Byzantine control over a large area of south-eastern Anatolia, although some of these cities continued to recognize nominal Byzantine authority or that of the Arab emirs of Syria while paying annual tribute to the victorious Seljuk Turks.

The new emperor, Michael VII, did not honour the treaty Romanus signed with Alp Arslan for the late emperor's release, causing tension between the Great Seljuk Empire and Byzantium. Beginning in 1073, Turkoman raiders resumed their raiding into Anatolia from the north-east, but on this occasion Alp Arslan was unable to exert any influence on the marauders as he was killed in the late fall of 1072. After Manzikert, the sultan returned to the homeland of the Seljuk Turks, apparently to quell a rebellion encouraged by a former vassal in Transoxiana in what is now Turkestan. After crossing the Oxus River, Alp Arslan laid siege to a rebel fortress stubbornly defended by Yusuf al-Harani. Unable to take the fortress by force, Alp Arslan was able to convince Yusuf to open his gates by promising no harm would come to him and that he would retain his title and holdings. Yusuf was captured by the sultan's bodyguard and brought before the Seljuk leader, ostensibly to be killed for his treasonous behavior. Yusuf was able to escape from his captors and fall upon Alp Arslan with a hidden dagger, severely wounding the sultan before the Seljuk bodyguard killed him. Alp Arslan died four days later on 24 November at the age of forty-one. The sultan's body was taken back to the Seljuk capital of Merv by his son and successor, Malikshah, and his trustworthy vizier Nizam al-Mulk, to be buried in the land of his steppe warrior ancestors.[11] The 'Valiant Lion' had ruled over the Great Seljuk Empire of Iran for nearly a decade, during which time he had consolidated the conquests of his predecessors Chaghri and Toghril, humbled the Byzantine Empire on the field of battle, and captured and released its *basileus*.

When Malikshah (r.1072–1092) succeeded his father as sultan he was still a minor and under the guardianship of Nizam al-Mulk. Malikshah's twenty-year reign would witness the expansion of the Great Seljuk Empire through the annexation of vassal Marwanid Emirate in south-eastern Anatolia and the Karakhanid Empire in Central Asia. By the end of Malikshah's reign his empire stretched from Arabia to the edge of India and included nearly all of the Muslim territories in Asia.[12] However, the Great Seljuk Empire was not the primary Turkish aggressor in Anatolia during the remainder of the 1070s. This distinction fell on the nominally affiliated Turkoman raiders who, during this time, invaded Asia Minor and began to finally set up small states. One of these states was founded in the north-west extremity of the peninsula in Nicaea and controlled by a long-time rival of Alp Arslan, Suleyman ibn Qutulmish. Suleyman and the Turkoman emir Artuk had positioned themselves as powerful political players and sometimes allies of Byzantium in its upcoming civil war.[13]

The Byzantine Civil War and the Rise of the Sultanate of Rum

In 1077, two Byzantine generals rebelled nearly simultaneously against the reign of Michael VII. Nikephoros Bryennios, who had fought with distinction at Manzikert and put down the Bulgarian revolt in 1072, becoming governor of Dyrrachium. When he learned that the emperor's eunuch counsellor had placed his name on a list for assassination, Bryennios raised the banner of revolt in November 1077 and marched on his native city of Adrianople where he was proclaimed emperor. Gathering the western armies, a week later he and his troops were camped beneath the Theodosian Walls of Constantinople.[14] The second general, Nikephoros Botaneiates, *strategos* of the Anatolikon Theme, capitalized on provincial dissatisfaction and the emperor's inability to halt the Seljuk raiding and migration into Asia Minor, raising the standard of rebellion in the east and marching on the Byzantine capital. When Michael learned of Botaneiates' treachery, he hired Suleyman ibn Qutulmish and his Seljuk troops to halt the advance of the rebel army, forcing Botaneiates and his men off the major highways and to travel only at night. Suleyman eventually overtook the Byzantine host, but Botaneiates was able to bribe the Seljuk general into abandoning Michael and supporting him. Suleyman's defection assisted Botaneiates greatly as he was short of troops. Turkish horsemen escorted the Greek army to Constantinople. Attaleiates tells us that Seljuk warriors were left to garrison numerous cities in Botaneiates' wake, including Nicaea, Chalcedon, Nicomedia, Cyzicus and Chrysopolis.[15]

With two pretenders to the Byzantine throne outside of Constantinople's walls, the citizens of the capital showed their own displeasure with Michael's rule by rioting in every corner of the city and looting and burning government buildings. Michael abdicated and Botaneiates who, as an accomplished general and veteran politician in his mid-seventies, had more support than his rival, entered the city in triumph on 24 March 1078. Bryennios refused to accept the title of caesar in the settlement and continued his rebellion. Once again, Alexios Komnenos was called to serve his emperor, this time the newly crowned Nikephoros III Botaneiates (r.1078–1081), who sent him to deal with Bryennios. But Alexios was unable to muster a suitable army for the task and was forced to rely on 2,000 Seljuk horsemen provided by Suleyman, who was already in the area sacking the Byzantine city of Chrysopolis.[16] Bryennios was eventually hunted down and blinded, but was also granted new honours and his lands back by the new emperor in a bizarre Byzantine act of reconciliation.

The reign of Nikephoros III marked the end of Byzantine Anatolia as the primary source of military manpower and horses. Loss of access to horse breeding lands in Phrygia, Cappadocia and Armenia hurt the cavalry-intensive Byzantine army, who required consistent access to quality horses to sustain their cavalry corps.[17] The Seljuk occupation of Asia Minor also removed the Byzantine Empire's principal source of tax revenues while also severing major trade routes between Constantinople and the riches of the east, all of which weakened the empire's economic vitality.[18] Finally, the loss of large portions of Anatolia took away a primary source of grain for Byzantium's remaining cities.

Military rebellions continued in the Byzantine provinces. In 1078 the newly crowned Nikephoros III sent Alexios into the Balkans to put down yet another revolt, this time led by the general Nikephoros Basilakes, who had succeeded Bryennios as the governor of Dyrrachium. Two years later, in late 1080, another military rebellion broke out in western Anatolia in Nicaea, this time led by another Nikephoros, Nikephoros Melissenos. Melissenos proclaimed himself rival emperor and made an alliance with Suleyman that brought Seljuk warriors to his cause. This time, however, Alexios did not do his emperor's bidding as he was making his own way to the purple. A brilliant general, Alexios was also a cunning politician who had made peace with the powerful Doukas family by marrying the daughter of Andronikos Doukas. Fortunately, Melissenos was Alexios' brother-in-law and the two came to an agreement where Melissenos would support Alexios as the new emperor in exchange for the title caesar and command of the armies of the west. Alexios also had the support of the German commander of Constantinople's garrison, who let Alexios and his army into the capital. After three days of violence, the elderly Nikephoros III abdicated and Alexios was crowned *basileus Rhomaion* on Easter Sunday (4 April) 1081.[19]

The reign of Alexios I Komnenos (r.1081–1118) begins a period of Byzantine military, economic and territorial recovery known to history as the 'Komnenian Restoration'. But

The Byzantine Empire at the accession of Alexios I Komnenos, 1081.

the Byzantine Empire Alexios presided over at the beginning of his rule was much smaller than it was a decade earlier in the immediate wake of the battle of Manzikert, and the new emperor faced enemies old and new on his frontiers. The Pechenegs were raiding in the Balkans again, and the Norman adventurer Robert Guiscard, emboldened by his successes in Italy, was now making inroads into Byzantine territories and planning the conquest of Constantinople itself, even defeating Alexios at Dyrrachium in 1081.[20] Seljuk successes in Anatolia had shrunk Byzantine possessions, but imperial strongholds still existed at the beginning of the new emperor's reign. Strategically important cities and partial regions were still in Byzantine hands, including the Black Sea port of Heracleia, and parts of Paphlagonia, Cappadocia, and Trebizond.[21] However, Alexios was forced to pull Byzantine troops from these regions to meet the growing threats in the west, thereby enabling the Turks to advance further in these regions. Closer to Constantinople, Alexios was forced to deal with the growing threat of the Seljuk ruler Suleyman ibn Qutulmish, who used the numerous Byzantine civil wars in this period to consolidate his control over an ever-increasing part of the peninsula while also playing the part of an indirect 'king-maker' by loaning his troops to both pretender and emperor as he saw fit. Suleyman had been building his credentials since the death of Alp Arslan in 1073, capturing Aleppo a year later and receiving from the Abbasid caliph a robe of honour and a *manshur* or patent confirming his sovereignty in Asia Minor. About this same time Byzantine and Muslim records begin to assign the title of sultan to Suleyman, who was carving his own Seljuk Sultanate of Rum (1077–1243), named in honour of its location on hallowed Roman territory. Suleyman took the city of Nicaea in Bithynia as his first capital.[22] By 1079 the Seljuks had reached and occupied the western coast of Asia Minor, an area known since the Archaic Period (c.800–c.500BCE) as Ionia. The revolt of Nikephoros Melissenos and his subsequent alliance with the new sultan delivered more central and western Byzantine cities to the Seljuks in return for military assistance, allowing the Turkish steppe warriors peaceful entrance into the traditional heartland of the Byzantine Empire.[23] Years later, Alexios' daughter Anna Komnene (1083–1154), born just two years after he became emperor, describes in vivid detail the proximity of the Seljuk Turks to the Byzantine capital

> …the godless Turks were in sight, living in the Propontis [Sea of Marmara] area, and Suleyman, who commanded all the east, was actually encamped in the vicinity of Nicaea. His sultanate was in that city (we would call it his palace). The whole countryside of Bithynia and Thynia was unceasingly exposed to Suleyman's foragers; marauding parties on horseback and on foot were raiding as far as the town called Damalis on the Bosporus itself; they carried off much booty and all but tried to leap over the very sea. The Byzantines saw them living absolutely unafraid and unmolested in the little villages on the coast and in sacred buildings. The sight filled them with horror. They had no idea what to do.[24]

But despite Princess Anna's dire description of Seljuk depredations near the Byzantine capital, the Seljuk conquest of the north-western Anatolia was not permanent, and Byzantium's overall strategic position would slowly improve beginning in 1085 with the deaths of Guiscard and Suleyman. Guiscard died of fever trying to restore land lost to Byzantine counterattacks on the islands of Corfu and Kefalonia, creating confusion in

Norman Italy and suspending briefly Norman ambitions in the east, while Suleyman died campaigning in his eastern frontiers after capturing the important city of Antioch in Syria.[25]

On news of Suleyman's death, his emirs began to carve independent domains out of his territories, although order would eventually be restored and the Seljuk Sultanate of Rum would continue until the Mongol conquests of 1243. One of Suleyman's numerous successors, Tzachas, established a powerful maritime emirate centred in the Ionian coastal city of Smyrna. Once a prisoner in the court of Nikephoros III Botaneiates, Tzachas understood Byzantium's ultimate pressure point was the city of Constantinople itself, and allied with the Pechenegs to invest the capital. During the winter of 1090–1091, Tzachas used his fleet to blockade Constantinople by sea while the Pechenegs sieged the city by land. Alexios, using the age-old Byzantine strategy of playing one barbarian people off the other, purchased the services of another Turkic people called the Cumans (Kipchaks) to help him against the Pechenegs. Like the Pecheneg and Uze tribes before them, the Cumans had recently migrated through the Ukrainian Steppes into the Balkans where this horde of 40,000 steppe warriors joined up with an Alexios-led Byzantine army and, on 29 April 1091, annihilated the Pecheneg host at the foot of Mount Levunion in eastern Thrace, effectively ending the Pecheneg menace for ever.[26] His nomadic allies defeated on land, Tzachas was forced to withdraw his fleet. Alexios seized this opportunity to conclude a peace treaty with the emir of Smyrna's son-in-law, the emir of Nicaea, Abul Kasim, and afterwards with his successor, the new Sultan of Rum, Kilij Arslan (r.1092–1107), isolating Tzachas and also resurrecting another Byzantine foreign policy of playing Muslim emirs against one another. The son of Suleyman, Kilij Arslan's absence in Anatolian affairs was due to being a hostage in the court of Malikshah. Malikshah's death in 1092 freed the prince to return to his father's sultanate where he would have the unfortunate distinction of reigning during the time of the First Crusade and the loss of Seljuk power in Anatolia.[27]

During the early 1090s Alexios launched successful counterattacks to recover Epirus and Albania from the Normans and northern and western coastal regions of Anatolia from the Seljuk Turks. The emperor eventually prevailed by wearing down his Norman adversaries and avoiding costly set-piece battles like that at Dyrrachium.[28] Alexios bribed one of Kilij Arslan's officials to recover Sinope (the capital of Paphlagonia) and neighbouring coastal regions, and in 1092, he used Byzantine naval power to defeat the Seljuk navy off the coast of Cius in Bithynia. Alexios rebuilt the ancient Hellenistic city of Cibetos in Phrygia to command the regions of the Gulf of Nicomedia. He went on to retake the important region of Cyzicus long the coast of the Sea of Marmara, and farther south, defeated Tzachas and his maritime emirate on the Ionian coast between 1093 and 1094.[29] At the same time, Alexios was taking steps to shore up the Balkan frontiers against Serbian raiding while also dealing with a revolt of the Cumans, his former allies, who were marauding through imperial lands under the leadership of a Byzantine pretender who claimed to be the son of Romanus IV Diogenes. The Cumans raided across the mountains and into eastern Thrace to the walls of Adrianople where the pretender was killed and the steppe warriors were defeated by imperial troops.[30] But despite these numerous military successes against the enemies of Byzantium in the first half of the decade, Alexios decided to ask for aid from one of the primary sponsors of his Norman adversaries, the Roman Catholic pontiff, Urban II (p.1088–1099), an act that precipitated the Levantine Crusades.

Alexios I Komnenos and the Origins of the Levantine Crusades

As early as 1090, Alexios had taken reconciliatory measures towards the papacy in order to secure western support for his wars against the Seljuk Turks. Relations between Rome and Constantinople had soured in 1054 when the papal legate and patriarch of Constantinople excommunicated one another, initiating the Great Schism. However, Byzantine strategic circumstances in the wake of Manzikert necessitated a new approach to East-West relations. In 1073 Michael VII sent ambassadors to Pope Gregory VII (p.1073–1085) in an attempt to normalize relations, and a year later the pope issued an encyclical addressed to all of Christendom warning that the Seljuk Turks were nearly at the walls of Constantinople and encouraging Christians to go east and assist their Byzantine brothers.[31] Gregory did not help relations between the papacy and Constantinople when he excommunicated Michael's successors, Nikephoros III and Alexios, regarding them as usurpers. However, Urban II's accession to the apostolic chair brought the lifting of Alexios' excommunication and the easing of tensions between the two great Christian churches. Alexios sent ambassadors to appear before Pope Urban II at the Council of Piacenza in northern Italy in early March 1095 to ask for the papacy's assistance against the Seljuk Turks.[32] The content of the letter presented to the pope has not survived, and we are left wondering why Alexios and his advisors were so eager to court the papacy at a time when the Byzantine Empire's strategic position was relatively stable. It is possible, even probable, that Alexios was seeking military aid from Urban in order to launch a sustained offensive against the Seljuk Turks to retake more of Anatolia and perhaps even the Levant south to the Holy city of Jerusalem, in Seljuk hands since 1077 and lost to Christendom during the Rashidun Caliphate in 638. Perhaps Alexios wanted to seize a moment when his Seljuk enemy was divided in Anatolia and his European provinces were relatively stable. An alliance with the papacy would help rein in the Norman threat on his western frontier, and perhaps even convince these same Norman adventurers to join his effort as mercenaries in another Byzantine expedition similar to the ones earlier in the eleventh century. Still, it is unlikely Alexios was asking for the enormous Roman Catholic hosts of soldiers and pilgrims that began gathering outside the walls of Constantinople between October 1096 and April 1097.[33]

Urban II used the letter and embassy sent by Alexios to Piacenza as a *casus belli* for war against the Seljuk Turks and as an opportunity to expand Catholic power and papal influence in the east at the expense of both Byzantium and the Muslim infidel. Urban travelled north to central France where he chaired the Council of Clermont and called into existence the First Crusade on a chilly afternoon on 27 November 1095. This 'call to arms' was heard by an estimated 300 to 400 people, although later tradition maintained a huge crowd gathered in the field outside of Clermont to hear the pope's sermon.[34] Urban's impassioned address urged his Catholic subjects to pursue two intertwined goals: the liberation of the Orthodox churches by bringing western military support to the besieged Byzantine Empire; and the reconquest of the Holy Land and the liberation of Jerusalem for Christendom.[35] Urban's exhortation for the Catholic faithful to 'take the cross' (literally sowing a cross on the crusader's breast as a symbol of the vow) served as a catalyst for the conquest and occupation of the Levant and an age of crusades that would last two hundred years and for ever reshape the relationship between Islam and the Christian West.

The Latin crusaders arrived in Constantinople in four distinct groups and travelled along three major trans-European arteries, once well-groomed Roman roads now serving as dilapidated pilgrimage routes to Byzantium, or directly by ship from southern Italy. When assembled in April 1097, this host consisted of some 60,000 soldiers and pilgrims. The northern French contingent was led by Robert of Normandy (the eldest son of William I, the victor at Hastings in 1066 and first Norman king of England), while Raymond of Toulouse commanded the southern French crusaders. Godfrey of Bouillon was the leader of the crusaders from Germany. The Norman adventurer, Bohemond of Taranto, eldest son of Robert Guiscard, led the Italian Normans. Urban did not accompany the crusaders, although his legate was present on the march as his ambassador. The Catholic leaders of this First Crusade would lead by committee and would consist of crusaders from every corner of Catholic Europe.[36]

When each of the leaders of the First Crusade arrived in Constantinople, Alexios invited him into the city to have an individual audience with him. The Byzantine emperor did not allowed the bulk of the crusaders entrance into the city, fearing what an army of tens of thousands of foreign soldiers would do to his capital. But Alexios also knew the power Constantinople held in the imaginations of the Catholic soldiers and pilgrims gathered outside his walls, and used the splendours of what was Christendom's largest and most impressive city to his political advantage. Shrewdly, Alexios was able to extract oaths of allegiance from many of the crusader princes as they arrived in his city. These pledges had two components – a promise that any territory recovered would be handed over to the emperor's representative, and a second pledge that probably was an oath of fealty to the emperor, which historians are less certain about the details.[37] What is certain is that both pledges were ultimately broken as the crusaders carved out Latin Principalities in the Levant. Once the oaths were extracted, Alexios ferried each of the four armies across the Bosporus to an assembly area in north-west Anatolia to make certain the entire crusader host was not directly threatening his city's walls or could be used by a Byzantine rival against him. This action today seems prescient as a future crusader army would, in fact, take advantage of internal dissent within Byzantium and successfully siege Constantinople in 1204, setting up a near six-decade long occupation of the city and the Aegean region in the guise of the Latin Kingdom of Constantinople (1204–1261) until the Greeks, from their base in Nicaea, retook the capital in 1261. The emperor who retook Constantinople, Michael VIII Palaiologos (r.1259–1282) was the founder of the last Byzantine dynasty, the Palaiologoi, who would rule a greatly weakened Eastern Roman Empire until 1453. And although Alexios did not promise a large-scale participation in the upcoming Roman Catholic expedition, his assistance to the crusaders was essential to the crusaders' ultimate success in carving out Latin principalities in the Holy Land. The emperor offered critical intelligence on the Seljuk enemy and how to supply an army in difficult terrain of Anatolia. Later, Alexios would instruct the crusaders on how to exploit the political and religious divisions in the Islamic world.[38]

With assistance from Alexios, the Catholic crusaders were able to successfully cross Anatolia and defeat a Seljuk army led by Kilij Arslan at the battle of Dorylaeum in the summer of 1097, clearing the way for further crusader conquests. The Seljuk-held Antioch fell after a seven-and-a-half-month siege, followed by the Armenian Christian city of Edessa in early 1098. The Latin armies continued south to Jerusalem, which was

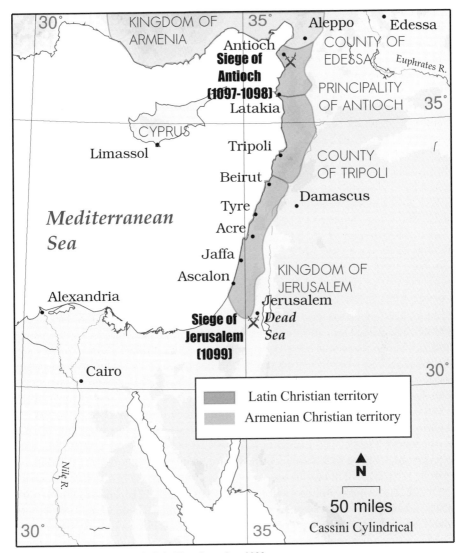

The Crusader states at the end of the First Crusade, c.1099.

captured after a five-week siege and infamously bloody storm in the summer of 1099. By the early twelfth century, the crusaders had carved out feudal possessions in the Levant consisting of the Kingdom of Jerusalem, the County of Tripoli in Lebanon, the Principality of Antioch, and the County of Edessa in Armenia. Historians consider the First Crusade the most successful of the Catholic expeditions in the nearly two-hundred year history of the Levantine Crusades, and an argument can be made that the existence of the crusader states focused Muslim attention towards this foreign occupation of what the Islamic world considered a vital part of *Dar al-Islam*. Alexios used the First Crusade and the chaos it created in the region to continue to consolidate

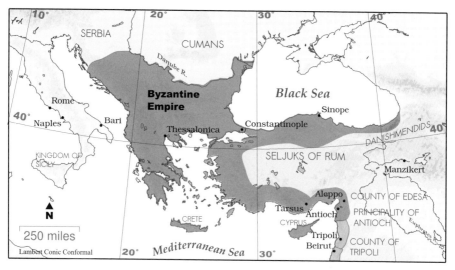

Byzantium and the Crusader states at the death of Alexios I, c. 1118.

Byzantium's strategic position in Anatolia. By the time of his death in 1118, Alexios was able to make serious inroads into Seljuk territories throughout Anatolia, reintegrating all of the land to the west of a line passing north-to-south through Sinope, Ankara, and Amorium back into the Byzantine Empire, while also controlling the Black Sea coast east to the province of Trebizond and the southern coastline east to the now Catholic crusader-held duchy of Antioch.

But even with these successes the Seljuk Sultanate of Rum continued to control the majority of the peninsula's interior from the central plateau eastwards into Upper Mesopotamia. The Seljuk Sultanate of Rum (1077–1243) was not the only Turkish state in Anatolia. These other principalities included the Saltukids of Erzurum (c.1071–1202, centred in the former city of Theodosiopolis), the Artukids of Diyarbakr (c.1102–1231, formerly Amida), and the Danishmendids of Cappadocia (1103–1178), small Turkoman states that adopted the Persian-Arabic model of decentralized rule and whose political orientation was east towards Iran rather than west towards Byzantium. The Danishmendids would be folded into the Sultanate of Rum in 1178, but the other Turkish states would survive until the Mongol invasions of the early thirteenth century sent new waves of Turks into Anatolia to press up once again against the receding Byzantine frontiers. These Turks would be organized by the leader of the Osmanlis Turks, one Osman Ghazi (later Osman I, r.1299–1326), founder of what would become the Ottoman Turks. Ottoman power would grow steadily in strength in north-western Anatolia, and then spread eastwards at the expense of rival Muslim states, finally fulfilling the final Turkification and Islamization of the peninsula often credited as a consequence of the Byzantine loss at Manzikert. Ottoman campaigning deep into the Balkans in the fourteenth century would expand the sultanate further, subduing the Bulgarians and greatly reducing the power of the Serbians. Finally, the powerful walls of Constantinople would be breached by Ottoman cannon fire and taken by storm on 29 May 1453, ending eleven hundred years of Byzantine civilization.

Notes

Introduction: Byzantium, Islam and Catholic Europe – The Battle of Manzikert as Historical Nexus

1. Edward Gibbon, *The Decline and Fall of the Roman Empire, Vol. 6* (New York: Gallery Press, 1979), 243.
2. Charles Oman, *A History of the Art of War: The Middle Ages from the Fourth Century to the Fourteenth Century* (London: Methuen, 1898), 220.
3. Hans Delbruck, *History of the Art of War, Vol. III: Medieval Warfare*, trans. Walter J. Renfroe, Jr (Westport, CT: Greenwood Press, 1980), 198.
4. Steven Runciman, *A History of the Crusades, Volume I: The First Crusade and the Foundations of the Kingdom of Jerusalem* (Cambridge and New York: Cambridge University Press, 1951), 64.
5. George Ostrogorsky, *History of the Byzantine State*, trans. Joan Hussey (New Brunswick, New Jersey: Rutgers University Press, 1969), 344.
6. John Norwich, *Byzantium: The Apogee* (New York: Alfred A. Knopf, 2006), 357.
7. Delbruck, *History of the Art of War, Vol. III*, 198.
8. For detailed studies of the transition from Byzantine to Islamic Anatolia, see Claude Cahen, *Pre-Ottoman Turkey* (London, 1968) and Speros Vryonis, Jr, *The Decline of Medieval Hellenism in Asia Minor and the Process of Islamization from the Eleventh through the Fifteenth Century* (Berkeley and Los Angeles: University of California Press, 1971). Vyronis has also published numerous excellent articles on the battle of Manzikert. See also Jean-Claude Cheynet, 'Mantzikert: Un desastre militaire?' *Byzantion* 50 (1980), 410–438.
9. Runciman, *A History of the Crusades, Volume I*, 64. Alfred Friendly's popular account of the battle of Manzikert incorporates this reference in its title, *The Dreadful Day: the Battle of Manzikert, 1071* (London: Hutchinson, 1981).
10. For an excellent compilation of Muslim sources translated into English about the battle of Manzikert, see Carole Hillenbrand, *Turkish Myth and Muslim Symbol: The Battle of Manzikert* (Edinburgh: University of Edinburgh Press, 2007).

Chapter 1: Byzantium Warfare from Justinian to Herakleios

1. John Haldon, *The Byzantine Wars* (Stroud, Gloucestershire: The History Press, 2008), 21.
2. Ibid.
3. Ibid., 21–22.
4. The fate of the triumvir Marcus Licinius Crassus (c.112–53 BCE) at Carrhae in 53 BCE dramatically demonstrated the inadequacy of the Roman infantry-based tactical system for dealing with Parthian cavalry on its own terrain. Later Roman emperors like Trajan would adopt Persian-inspired cavalry as part of their army's tactical mix.

5. For an outstanding treatment of the *cataphractii/clibanarii* controversy, see the 'Cataphracts and Clibanarii of the Ancient World' from the *All Empires: Online History Community* website, http://www.allempires.com/article/index.php?q=cataphracts (accessed 10 January 2010).

6. Haldon, *The Byzantine Wars*, 23.

7. Ibid., 24.

8. This quotation is from page 53 of George T. Dennis' fine text and translation of *The Anonymous Byzantine Treatise on Strategy* in his *Three Byzantine Military Treatises* (Washington DC: Dumbarton Oaks Texts, 2008). See chapters 15 and 16 for more information on Byzantine tactics and armament during the Justinian era. Also see David Nicolle, *Romano-Byzantine Armies, 4th–9th Centuries* (London: Osprey, 1992), 10–11.

9. Dennis, *Three Byzantine Military Treatises*, 53.

10. Ian Heath, *Armies of the Dark Ages 600–1066*, 2nd Edition (Worthing, England: Wargames Research Group, 1980), 64.

11. Archer Jones, *The Art of War in the Western World* (Urbana and Chicago: University of Illinois Press, 1987), 96.

12. Haldon, *The Byzantine Wars*, 26–27.

13. Jones, *The Art of War in the Western World*, 97.

14. Haldon, *The Byzantine Wars*, 27.

15. For a magnificent short treatment of various tactics employed by commanders on battlefields throughout history, please see 'The seven classical maneuvers of warfare' in David G. Chandler's *The Art of Warfare on Land* (New York: Penguin Books, 1974), 14–18.

16. Robert Browning, *Justinian and Theodora* (London: Thames and Hudson, 1987), 43.

17. Warren Treadgold, *Byzantium and Its Army, 284–1081* (Stanford, CA: Stanford University Press, 1995), 15. See also Haldon, *The Byzantine Wars*, 28.

18. Haldon, *The Byzantine Wars*, 28.

19. Procopius, *History of the Wars: The Persian War*, I.13.

20. See Haldon, *The Byzantine Wars*, 29–30, for a description of the Byzantine defensive lines and how the Eastern Roman army was arrayed at Dara.

21. Procopius, *The Persian War*, I.13.

22. The Persians continued to use a Hellenistic weapon system, the war elephant, as part of their art of war. In battle the elephant was normally crewed by three men; a driver (*mahout*) on the animal's neck and a pikeman and archer in the turret. Although slow and vulnerable to enemy missile attack, the war elephant's main advantages in combat was its size and the terror it inspired in troops and enemy horses not accustomed to fighting the pachyderm.

23. Ammianus Marcellinus, *The Later Roman Empire*, XXIV.6. This translation comes from the Walter Hamilton translation (New York: Penguin Books, 1986).

24. Ammianus, XXV.1. This translation comes from the J.C. Rolfe translation (Loeb Classical Library, 1940).

25. Kavah Farrokh, *Shadows in the Desert: Ancient Persia at War* (Oxford: Osprey, 2009), 231.

26. The issue of when the stirrup was introduced into Sassanian warfare is hotly debated. For more on this issue see Kavah Farrokh's *Shadows in the Desert*, 224.

27. Ibid., 182.

28. Procopius refers to Baresmanes as 'the one-eyed' (*The Persian War*, I.13).

29. Ibid.

30. Ibid.

31. Ibid.

32. Ibid., I.14.

33. Ibid.

34. Ibid.

35. Ibid.

36. Farrokh, *Shadows in the Desert*, 227.
37. Ibid., I.14.
38. Ibid., I.22.
39. Procopius, *History of the Wars: The Vandalic War*, III.11. See also A.H.M. Jones' *The Later Roman Empire, 284–602*, Volume One (Norman, OK: University of Oklahoma Press, 1964), 273. For a very good treatment of the battles of Ad Decimum and Tricameron see J.F.C. Fuller's *A Military History of the Western World, Volume I, From the Earliest Times to the Battle of Lepanto* (New York: Funk and Wagnalls, 1954–1957), 307–316.
40. Procopius, *The Vandalic War*, III.11.
41. Fuller, *A Military History of the Western World, Volume I*, 310–311.
42. Procopius, *The Vandalic War*, III.17.
43. Ibid.
44. Ibid., III.18.
45. Ibid., III.19.
46. Ibid., III.21. The walls of Carthage were some of the most formidable in the classical world. The civilization of Carthage was able to withstand numerous sieges of its capital city. However, the city was eventually taken during a prolonged siege between 149 and 146 BCE, culminating in the end of the Third Punic War and the dismantling of Carthaginian civilization.
47. Ibid., IV.1.
48. Ibid., IV.2.
49. Ibid., IV.3.
50. Ibid.
51. Ibid.
52. Ibid.
53. Ibid.
54. Ibid., IV.4.
55. Treadgold, *Byzantium and Its Army*, 15–16.
56. For a detailed explanation of what Procopius referred to as Justinian's plague, see his *History of the Wars: The Persian War*, II.22–23.
57. For an outstanding modern treatment of this plague, see William Rosen's *Justinian's Flea: Plague, Empire and the Birth of Europe* (New York: Viking, 2007).
58. Belisarios would be called into service again by Justinian in 554 to serve in Italy and again in 559 to meet a Slavic and Bulgar threat to Constantinople.
59. See Chapter Eleven of J.F.C. Fuller's *A Military History of the Western World, Volume I* for a detailed account of the battle of Taginae.
60. Haldon, *The Byzantine Wars*, 35.
61. Charles Oman suggests in *A History of the Art of War in the Middle Ages, Volume One: 378–1278 AD* (New York: Methuen, 1924, 34) that the reason why the Byzantine archers were left unmolested by Gothic cavalry and infantry was due to some sort of ditch protection. Delbruck believes (*History of the Art of War, Vol. II: The Barbarian Invasions*, 358) that the archers may have been on higher ground, inaccessible to Gothic cavalry attacks.
62. Procopius, *The Gothic War*, VIII.31. Also, see Haldon, *The Byzantine Wars*, 35.
63. Procopius, *The Gothic War*, VIII.29.
64. Ibid.
65. Ibid.
66. Procopius, *The Gothic War*, VIII.32.
67. Ibid.
68. Ibid.
69. Ibid.

70. Procopius, *The Gothic War*, VIII.35.

71. Haldon, *The Byzantine Wars*, 39. For a thoughtful discussion on troop strengths at Casilinus, see Hans Delbruck, *History of the Art of War, Vol. II: The Barbarian Invasions* (Westport, CT: Greenwood Press, 1982), 369–374. Delbruck maintains that the account of Casilinus by Agathias is suspect because of the fantastical numbers given for the Frankish expeditionary force (75,000). Delbruck does believe that Narses' forces were larger (18,000 men) because his battle line over reached the Franks on both flanks. The estimation of 15,000 Franks is my own.

72. Jones, *The Art of War in the Western World*, 98.

73. Philippe Contamine, *War in the Middle Ages*, trans. Michael Jones (Oxford and New York: Basil Blackwell, 1984), 178; Kelly DeVries, *Medieval Military Technology* (Peterborough, Ontario: Broadview Press, 1992), 56–62.

74. See the translation of Agathias in Bernard S. Bachrach's 'Procopius, Agathias and the Frankish Military' in *Speculum*, 45 (1970), 435–41.

75. Ibid., 436–437.

76. Ann Hyland, *The Medieval Warhorse from Byzantium to the Crusades* (London: Grange Books, 1994), 30.

77. Erik Hildinger, *Warriors of the Steppe: A Military History of Central Asia, 500 B.C. to 1700 A.D.* (New York: Sarpedon, 1997), 19.

78. For a detailed discussion on the introduction of the stirrup into Western European warfare, see Kelly DeVries' *Medieval Military Technology* (Peterborough, Ontario: Broadview Press, 1992), 95–110.

79. Haldon, *The Byzantine Wars*, 39–40.

80. Hans Delbruck, *History of the Art of War, Vol. II: The Barbarian Invasions*, 21, 31, 41–43.

81. Philippe Contamine, *War in the Middle Ages*, trans. Michael Jones (Oxford and New York: Basil Blackwell, 1984), 11. Archer Jones, *The Art of War in the Western World*, 64.

82. Hans Delbruck, *History of the Art of War, Vol. II: The Barbarian Invasions*, 373.

83. Charles Diehl, *The Cambridge Medieval History*, vol. II, 23. This famous description of devastated Italy after the Gothic War is often quoted. Fuller uses it in his analysis of the aftermath of twenty years of campaigning (vol. I, 328) as does Geoffrey Regan in his short, but excellent treatment of Taginae in his *The Guinness Book of Decisive Battles: Fifty Battles that Changed the World from Salamis to the Gulf War* (New York, 1992), 40.

84. Haldon, *The Byzantine Wars*, 52–53.

85. This information is taken from the introduction to George T. Dennis' translation of Maurice's *Strategikon: Handbook of Byzantine Military Strategy*, trans. by George T. Dennis (Philadelphia: University of Pennsylvania Press, 1984), xi.

86. Haldon, *The Byzantine Wars*, 52–53.

87. Dennis, *Maurice's Strategikon*, introduction, xi.

88. Ibid., introduction, xii.

89. Ibid.

90. Dennis states the *banda* consisted of around 300 men (*Maurice's Strategikon*, introduction, xiii), Treadgold maintains the *banda* was around 400 men (*Byzantium and Its Army*, 94).

91. *Maurice's Strategikon*, introduction, xiii.

92. Hugh Kennedy, *The Great Arab Conquests* (Philadelphia: Da Capo Press, 2007), 69.

93. For a thorough discussion on Herakleios' adoption of the title *basileus* see George Ostrogorsky, *History of the Byzantine State*, trans. Joan Hussey (New Brunswick, New Jersey: Rutgers University Press, 1969), 106–107.

94. Walter E. Kaegi, *Herakleios: Emperor of Byzantium* (Cambridge: Cambridge University Press, 2003), 125.

95. Kennedy, *The Great Arab Conquests*, 69.

96. Richard A. Gabriel and Donald W. Boose, Jr, *The Great Battles of Antiquity: A Strategic*

Guide to Great Battles that Shaped the Development of War (Westport, Connecticut: Greenwood Press, 1994), 644. Most of these 200,000 loses took place before the Persian expeditions of Herakleios in 624.

97. Kennedy, *The Great Arab Conquests*, 71.

Chapter 2: Islamic Warfare from Muhammad to the Rashidun Caliphate

1. The Quraysh (sometimes Quraish) were not nomads, but city dwellers in Mecca who looked after the sacred area of the city (*haram*) and organized trading caravans from Mecca to Yemen in the south and Syria in the north, developing an impressive network of contacts throughout western Arabia. Hugh Kennedy, *The Great Arab Conquests* (Philadelphia: Da Capo Press, 2007), 44.
2. Ibid., 38.
3. Ibid., 39. Leadership within Bedouin tribes was both elective and hereditary. Tribesmen would offer their services to the most able, or luckiest, members of the ruling kin. Sheiks were chosen for their ability as both war leaders and negotiators, but were also required to provide protection and booty for their followers.
4. Maxime Rodinson, *Muhammad*, trans. Anne Carter (New York: New Press, 2002), 163.
5. Richard Gabriel, *Muhammad: Islam's First Great General* (Norman, OK: University of Oklahoma Press, 2007), 82. Please see Gabriel's book for an excellent account of Muhammad's campaigns and evaluation of his military acumen.
6. Ibid., 87.
7. Ibid., 89.
8. Paul K. Davis, *100 Decisive Battles from Ancient Times to the Present* (New York: Oxford University Press, 2001), 97.
9. Gabriel, *Muhammad*, 92.
10. Ibid., 96.
11. Ibid.
12. Hugh Kennedy, *The Armies of the Caliphs* (New York: Routledge, 2001), 168–178. Please see chapter seven of Hugh Kennedy's, *The Armies of the Caliphs*, for a detailed explanation of the arms and armour of early Islamic armies.
13. Kennedy, *The Armies of the Caliphs*, 177.
14. Gabriel, *Muhammad*, 99.
15. Ibn Ishaq, *The Life of Muhammad: A Translation of Ibn Iraq's Life of Muhammad*, trans. Alfred Guillaume, (Oxford: Oxford University Press, 1967), 299.
16. Gabriel, *Muhammad*, 99.
17. Ibn Ishaq, 300.
18. Gabriel, *Muhammad*, 100.
19. Ibid., 100–101.
20. Rodinson, *Muhammad*, 167.
21. Gabriel, *Muhammad*, 101.
22. Ibid., XIX.
23. Ibid., 99.
24. Ibn Ishaq, 371. Ibn Ishaq tells us that 700 of the 3,000 Meccans wore chainmail at the battle of Uhud.
25. Rodinson, *Muhammad*, 179.
26. Ibid.
27. Ibn Ishaq, 373.
28. Ibid., 374.
29. Gabriel, *Muhammad*, 118.
30. Ibid., 120.
31. Ibid.

32. Ibn Ishaq, 387.

33. Rodinson, *Muhammad*, 181.

34. Gabriel, *Muhammad*, 122.

35. Ibid., 130–131

36. Ibn Ishaq, 452.

37. Gabriel, *Muhammad*, 132–133.

38. Ibid., 135–136.

39. Ibid., 137. Gabriel estimates that the Meccans only had enough food and fodder to feed the Meccan army's camels and horses for two or three weeks.

40. Ibid.

41. Rodinson, *Muhammad*, 210.

42. Gabriel, *Muhammad*, 138–40.

43. Ibn Ishaq, 461. Gabriel surmises that since there is no evidence of Beni Qurayzah treachery during the battle of the Ditch, they were massacred to remove a rival to Muhammad's authority in Medina and to send a message to the tribes of Arabia (Gabriel, 142).

44. Ibn Ishaq, 459.

45. Fred McGraw Donner, *The Early Islamic Conquests* (Princeton: Princeton University Press, 1981), 62.

46. John Glubb, *The Life and Times of Muhammad* (New York: Cooper Square Press, 2001), 307.

47. See chapter ten of Gabriel's *Muhammad: Islam's First Great General* for a detailed explanation of the conquest of Mecca and also Gabriel's argument that Abu Safyan intrigued with Muhammad to bring Mecca into the Islamic fold.

48. Montgomery W. Watt, *Muhammad at Medina* (London: Oxford University Press, 1956), 67.

49. Gabriel, *Muhammad*, 176.

50. Ibid., 200–201.

51. Elias Shoufani, *Al-Riddah and the Muslim Conquest of Arabia* (Toronto: University of Toronto Press, 1973), 43–47.

52. Philip K. Hitti, *History of the Arabs* (Hampshire, UK: Palgrave Macmillan, 2002), 40.

53. Shoufani, 118.

54. Kennedy, *Great Arab Conquests*, 56.

55. Diyarbakri, as quoted in Shoufani, *Ali-Riddah and the Muslim Conquest of Arabia*, 119.

56. Kennedy, *The Armies of the* Caliphs, 4.

57. David Nicolle, *The Armies of Islam, 7th–11th Centuries* (London: Osprey, 1982), 10.

58. Ibid.

59. Ibid., 11.

60. David Nicolle, *Yarmuk 636 AD: The Muslim Conquest of Syria* (London: Osprey, 1994), 43.

61. Ibrahim Akram, *The Sword of Allah: Khalid bin al-Waleed, His Life and Campaigns* (New Delhi: Adam Publishers, 2009), 7.

62. Nicolle, *Yarmuk*, 62.

63. Walter E. Kaegi, *Byzantium and the Early Islamic Conquests* (Cambridge: Cambridge University Press, 1992), 119.

64. The contemporary Muslim historian Ibn Khaldun estimates that 400,000 Byzantines fought at Yarmuk (page 126), while Ibn Ishaq estimates 100,000 Eastern Romans took the field against 24,000 Muslims in *The History of al-Tabari, Volume. III: The Children of Israel*, trans. William Brinner (Albany, NY: State University New York Press, 1991), 75. One modern estimate by Pakistani Lt General Akram places Byzantine troop strength at 200,000 men (*The Sword of Allah*, 409). Nicolle (*Yarmuk 636 AD: The Muslim Conquest of Syria*, 65) and both Kennedy (*The Great Islamic Conquests*, 82) and Kaegi (*Byzantium and*

the Early Islamic Conquests, 131) estimate between 15,000 and 20,000 men. John Haldon believes around 20,000 Eastern Romans were at Yarmuk (*The Byzantine Wars*, Stroud, Gloucestershire: The History Press, 2008, 60).

65. Muslim tactics at Yarmuk indicate they were probably outnumbered by Byzantine forces. I place the Byzantine army at around 25,000 men, larger than the Islamic host of no more than 20,000 troops.

66. Emperor Herakleios relied heavily on Armenians as generals and administrators in this period (Kaegi, *Byzantium and the Early Islamic Conquests*, 99).

67. Kennedy, *The Great Islamic Conquests*, 73.

68. Nicolle, *Yarmuk*, 65.

69. Contemporary Islamic sources are consistent in their estimates of Muslim forces being inferior in numbers to the Byzantines. Ibn Ishaq places the Muslim forces at 24,000 troops (*al-Tabari*, Vol. 3, page 75) and Ibn Khaldun at 30,000 troops. Modern historians stay in this same range. Haldon states fewer than 20,000 (60), Nicolle, 25,000 maximum (43), while Akram states 40,000 maximum (417). Kennedy quotes Islamic sources at 24,000 troops and believes it is possible that the two armies were 'not very different in size' (*The Great Islamic Conquests*, 73).

70. Nicolle, *Yarmuk*, 65–66.

71. Akram, *The Sword of Allah*, 414–415. Also see Kaegi, *Byzantium and the Early Islamic Conquests*, 114.

72. Nicolle, *Yarmuk*, 65–66.

73. Ibid., 66.

74. Ibid., 67. Also see Akram, *The Sword of Allah* (417) for a breakdown of the Khalid's thirty-six infantry and three cavalry regiments using his troop strength estimate. Akram believes the entire Muslim force consisted of 40,000 troops (not 20,000 troops as I have indicated), and divides the thirty-six regiments into units of between 800 and 900 men each, three cavalry regiments of 2,000 horse each and a mobile Guard or reserve of 4,000 men kept in reserve by the Khalid. I have halved Akram's numbers for my estimation of regiment strengths.

75. Nicolle, *Yarmuk*, 65.

76. Nicolle, *Yarmuk*, 69 and Akram, *The Sword of Allah*, 424.

77. Nicolle, *Yarmuk*, 69. The Muslim historian al-Tabari writes that Gargis (George) converted to Islam while meeting with Khalid before the battle of Yarmuk. He later was killed fighting for the faithful against his former troops. (Akram, *The Sword of Allah*, 423.)

78. Akram, *The Sword of Allah*, 425.

79. Akram, *The Sword of Allah*, 425–429. Also see Nicolle, *Yarmuk*, 69, 72.

80. Al-Waqidi, as quoted in Akram, *The Sword of Allah*, 431.

81. Nicolle, *Yarmuk*, 72.

82. Kaegi, *Byzantium and the Early Islamic Conquests*, 121. Nicolle surmises that the Byzantines may have been attempting on the complex 'mixed formation' manoeuvres described in Maurice's *Strategikon*. If this operation failed on the fourth day at Yarmuk, it could have led to a gap between the horse and foot that may have led to the Byzantine cavalry being separated from their infantry support (Nicolle, *Yarmuk*, 73).

83. Nicolle, *Yarmuk*, 73.

84. Ibid., 76.

85. Al-Waqidi, as quoted in Akram, *The Sword of Allah*, 435.

86. Ibid.

87. Akram, *The Sword of Allah*, 438.

88. Nicolle, *Yarmuk*, 76.

89. Ibid., 77. Also see Akram, *The Sword of Allah*, 440–441.

90. Al-Waqidi, as quoted in Akram, *The Sword of Allah*, 441.

91. Ibid.
92. Akram, *The Sword of Allah*, 442.
93. Ibid.
94. The hammer and anvil tactic is a relatively simple manoeuvre to conceive but difficult to execute. It involves an infantry force engaging an enemy infantry force to hold it in place (anvil) as allied heavy or light cavalry manoeuvres around the enemy infantry and attacks it from behind (hammer), sandwiching the enemy infantry force between the infantry and cavalry units.
95. John Haldon, *The Byzantine Wars* (Stroud, Gloucestershire: The History Press, 2008), 62. Also see Nicolle, *Yarmuk*, 77, 80–81. For the most vivid account of the flight of the Byzantines and the Muslim pursuit, see Akram, *The Sword of Allah*, 447–453.
96. Nicolle, *Yarmuk*, 81. Nicolle also discusses that Vahan may have survived the battle of Yarmuk to become a monk at St Catherine's Monastery in the Sinia.
97. Nicolle, *Yarmuk*, 79–80. Also see Akram, *The Sword of Allah*, 442–443.
98. Haldon, *The Byzantine Wars*, 63.
99. Ibid.
100. Kennedy, *The Great Islamic Conquests*, 106.
101. Ibid.
102. Ibid., 108
103. Kaveh Farrokh, *Shadows in the Desert: Ancient Persia at War* (Oxford: Osprey, 2009), 268. Farrokh estimates that the Sassanian force outnumbered the Muslims three to one. The figure of 18,000 to 36,000 Persian troops comes from multiplying the estimated Muslim force quoted in Kennedy by three.
104. Kaveh Farrokh, *Sassanian Elite Cavalry, 224–642* (Oxford: Osprey, 2005), 24–25.
105. Kennedy, *The Great Islamic Conquests*, 113.
106. Al-Tabari, *The History of al-Tabari, Volume XII: The Battle of al-Qadisiyyah and the Conquest of Syria and Palestine*, trans. Yohanan Friedmann (Albany, NY: State University of New York, 1992), 82.
107. Ibid., 83. Al-Tabari describes the Muslim deployment as being in three divisions, but does not mention where the infantry and cavalry were stationed. This author has placed the Muslim infantry and cavalry in two lines, with the infantry screening the cavalry as per normal Arab doctrine in this period.
108. Farrokh, *Shadows in the Desert*, 268.
109. Al-Tabari, *The History of al-Tabari: The Battle of al-Qadisiyyah and the Conquest of Syria and Palestine*, 95.
110. Farrokh, *Shadows in the Desert*, 268.
111. Ibid. Also see al-Tabari, *The History of al-Tabari: The Battle of al-Qadisiyyah and the Conquest of Syria and Palestine*, 97.
112. Al-Tabari, *The History of al-Tabari: The Battle of al-Qadisiyyah and the Conquest of Syria and Palestine*, 122–123.
113. Ibid., 123–124.
114. Farrokh, *Shadows in the Desert*, 269.
115. Gabriel, *Muhammad*, 213.

Chapter 3: Byzantine Warfare in an Age of Crisis and Recovery

1. George Ostrogorsky, *History of the Byzantine State*, trans. Joan Hussey (New Brunswick, New Jersey: Rutgers University Press, 1969), 123–124.
2. Stephen Turnbull, *The Walls of Constantinople, AD 324–1453* (Oxford: Osprey, 2004), 8. See Turnbull for a well illustrated treatment of the construction and history of the walls of Constantinople.
3. Hugh Kennedy, *The Great Arab Conquests* (Philadelphia: Da Capo Press, 2007), 329.

4. Kelly DeVries, *Medieval Military Technology* (Peterborough, Ontario: Broadview, 1992), 140–141. Also see Stephen Turnbull's *The Walls of Constantinople*), 41–43.
5. Kennedy, *The Great Arab Conquests*, 330.
6. Cyril Mango and Roger Scott, eds., *The Chronicle of Theophanes the Confessor: Byzantine And Near Eastern History, AD 284-813* (Oxford: Clarendon Press, 2006), 545.
7. Ibid., 331.
8. This quote by Theophanes the Confessor is taken from Kennedy's translation in *The Great Arab Conquests*, 331.
9. Romilly Jenkins, *Byzantium: The Imperial Centuries A.D. 610–1071* (New York: Random House, 1966), 63.
10. Ibid.
11. Ibid. 63–64.
12. Kennedy, *The Great Arab Conquests*, 332.
13. Warren Treadgold, 'The Struggle for Survival (641–780 AD)' in *The Oxford History of Byzantium*, ed. Cyril Mango (Oxford: Oxford University Press, 2002), 131.
14. Ibid.
15. John Haldon, *The Byzantine Wars* (Stroud, Gloucestershire: The History Press, 2008), 65–66.
16. David Nicolle, *The Great Islamic Conquests, AD 632-750* (Oxford: Osprey, 2009), 52.
17. Haldon, *The Byzantine Wars*, 68.
18. Warren Treadgold, *Byzantium and Its Army, 284–1081* (Stanford, CA: Stanford University Press, 1995), 24–25.
19. Ibid., 29.
20. Ostrogorsky, *History of the Byzantine State*, 251.
21. Dennis states the *bandum* consisted of around 300 men (*Maurice's Strategikon*, introduction, xiii). Treadgold maintains the *bandum* was around 400 men (*Byzantium and Its Army*, 94).
22. Haldon, *The Byzantine Wars*, 71–72.
23. See chapter two, 'Numbers,' in Treadgold's *Byzantium and Its Army, 284–1081*, for an excellent treatment of the fluctuations in troop totals from Diocletian's reign through the debacle at Manzikert.
24. Haldon, *The Byzantine Wars*, 70–71.
25. Ostrogorsky, *History of the Byzantine State*, 126.
26. Ibid., 127. This quotation by Theophanes is taken from Ostrogorsky's text.
27. Ibid., 191.
28. Ibid., 195–196.
29. Anonymous Vatican Narration, 'About the Emperor Nicephorus and How He Left His Bones in Bulgaria' from *Scriptor Incertus*. English translation found at http://en.wikisource.org/wiki/Scriptor_Incertus (accessed 30 March 2010).
30. Haldon, *The Byzantine Wars*, 75–76.
31. Anonymous Vatican Narration, 'About the Emperor Nicephorus and How He Left His Bones in Bulgaria.'
32. Ostrogorsky, *History of the Byzantine State*, 193.
33. Anonymous Vatican Narration, 'About the Emperor Nicephorus and How He Left His Bones in Bulgaria.'
34. Ibid.
35. Ibid.
36. Ostrogorsky, *History of the Byzantine State*, 196.
37. Ibid. Also see Haldon, *The Byzantine Wars*, 78.
38. For a brief account of the battle of Versinikia see Haldon, *The Byzantine Wars*, 79–81.
39. Ostrogorsky, *History of the Byzantine State*, 262–263.

40. For a concise treatment of the battle of Anchialus see Haldon, *The Byzantine Wars*, 90–93.

41. Steven Runciman, *The Emperor Romanus Lecapenus and His Reign: A Study in Tenth Century Byzantium* (Cambridge: Cambridge University Press, 1988), 85.

42. Ostrogorsky, *History of the Byzantine State*, 265–267.

43. Ostrogorsky, *History of the Byzantine State*, 277.

44. Mark Whittow, *The Making of Byzantium, 600–1025*, (Berkeley: University of California Press, 1996), 315.

45. Ibid., 315.

46. Ibid., 344.

47. Haldon, *The Byzantine Wars*, 142–143.

48. Timothy Dawson, *Byzantine Infantryman: Eastern Roman Empire, c.900–1204* (Oxford: Osprey, 2007), 6–7.

49. Ibid., 24–25. David Nicolle believes that the *solenarion* was identical to the Islamic *majra* or *nawak*. *Medieval Warfare Source Book Volume 2: Christian Europe and Its Neighbours*, (London: Arms and Armour, 1996), 74. Also see Ian Heath's *Byzantine Armies, 886*–1118 (London: Osprey, 1997), 10.

50. Heath, *Byzantine Armies, 886–1118*, 34.

51. Ibid., 10.

52. Ibid., 31–32.

53. Haldon, *The Byzantine Wars*, 143. Also see Timothy Dawson, *Byzantine Cavalryman, c.900–1204* (Oxford: Osprey, 2009), 34.

54. Heath, *Byzantine Armies*, 31–32. For an excellent treatment of Byzantine arms and armour from this period, also see Timothy Dawson's *Byzantine Infantryman*, 19–26.

55. Heath, *Byzantine Armies, 886–1118*, 36.

56. Dawson, *Byzantine Cavalryman*, 34, 36–37.

57. Heath, *Byzantine Armies, 886–1118*, 36.

58. Dawson, *Byzantine Cavalryman*, 34.

59. Ann Hyland, *The Medieval Warhorse from Byzantium to the Crusades* (London: Grange Books, 1994), 18.

60. Haldon, *The Byzantine Wars*, 144.

61. Warren Treadgold, *A Concise History of Byzantium* (New York: Palgrave, 2001), 141–142.

62. John Marsden, *Harald Hardrada: The Warrior's Way* (Stroud, Gloucestershire: Sutton Publishing Limited, 2007), 34.

63. Robin Milner-Gulland, *The Russians: The People of Europe* (London: Wiley-Blackwell, 2000), 52.

64. DeVries, *Medieval Military Technology*, 60. Also see Paddy Griffith, *The Viking Art of War* (London: Greenhill, 1995), 168–171.

65. Philippe Contamine, *War in the Middle Ages*, trans. Michael Jones, (Oxford: Basil Blackwell, 1984), 28.

66. Griffith, *The Viking Art of War*, 173–176.

67. Ian Heath, *The Vikings*, (London: Osprey, 1985), 51.

68. Heath, *Byzantine Armies, 886–1118*, 37–38.

69. Griffith, *The Viking Art of War*, 164–166 and 178–180. Also see Heath, *The Vikings*, 51.

70. Griffith, *The Viking Art of War*, 163–164.

71. Ibid., 188–196. Griffith goes into some detail giving examples of how Vikings used offensive and defensive formation in warfare.

72. Haldon quotes 30,000 Byzantine soldiers present at Dorostolon (*The Byzantine Wars*, 149), while Treadgold believes the army was 40,000 men (*A Concise History of Byzantium*, 143).

73. Warren Treadgold, *Byzantine State and Society* (Stanford: Stanford University Press, 1997), 509. See Haldon, *The Byzantine Wars*, 151, for a discussion on the exaggerated numbers for Rus and allied troops at Dorostolon.

74. Haldon, *The Byzantine Wars*, 151.
75. Alice-Mary Talbot and Denis F. Sullivan, trans., *The History of Leo the Deacon* (Washington DC: Dumbarton Oaks Texts, 2005), 185.
76. Ibid., 185–186.
77. Ibid., 187–188.
78. Ibid., 193.
79. Ibid., 194–195.
80. Haldon, *The Byzantine Wars*, 154–155.
81. Talbot and Sullivan, trans., *The History of Leo the Deacon*, 196.
82. Ibid.
83. Haldon, *The Byzantine Wars*, 156.
84. Ibid., 157.
85. Talbot and Sullivan, trans., *The History of Leo the Deacon*, 200.
86. Treadgold, *Byzantium and Its Army*, 36.
87. Ostrogorsky, *History of the Byzantine State*, 304.
88. Treadgold, *Byzantium and Its Army*, 115. Also see Heath's *Byzantine Armies, 886–1118*, 16.
89. Heath, *Byzantine Armies, 886–1118*, 15–16.
90. Treadgold, *Byzantium and Its Army*, 37.
91. For a fine brief treatment of the battle of Kleidion, see Haldon, *The Byzantine Wars*, 161–162.
92. Ostrogorsky, *History of the Byzantine State*, 310.
93. Treadgold, *Byzantium and Its Army*, 39.

Chapter 4: Islamic Warfare from the Umayyads to the Coming of the Seljuk Turks

1. For a discussion on the size and population of the Umayyad Caliphate in the early eighth century, see Khalid Yahya Blankinship's *The End of the Jihad State: The Reign of Hisham ibn Abd al-Malik and the Collapse of the Umayyads* (Albany, NY: State University New York Press, 1994), 37–38.
2. David Nicolle, *Medieval Warfare Source Book Volume 2: Christian Europe and Its Neighbours* (London: Arms and Armour, 1996), 24.
3. Hugh Kennedy, *The Armies of the Caliphs* (New York: Routledge, 2001), 31.
4. Nicolle, *Medieval Warfare Source Book*, 24.
5. Hugh Kennedy, *The Great Arab Conquests* (Philadelphia: Da Capo Press, 2007), 225–226.
6. Svat Soucek, *A History of Inner Asia* (Cambridge: Cambridge University, 2000), 67–69.
7. Kennedy, *The Great Arab Conquests*, 306.
8. Ibid., 217.
9. Ibid., 223–224. For an excellent treatment of the Islamic conquest of the Maghreb, see chapter six of Kennedy's, *The Great Arab Conquests*.
10. Ian Heath, *Armies of the Dark Ages 600–1066*, 2nd Edition. (Worthing, England: Wargames Research Group, 1980), 32.
11. Katherine Scherman, *The Birth of France: Warriors, Bishops, and Long-Haired Kings* (New York: Random House, 1987), 250.
12. Terry L. Gore, *Neglected Heroes: Leadership and War in the Early Medieval Period* (Westport, CT: Greenwood Press, 1995), 31. Victor Davis Hanson places the Muslim force at between 20,000 and 30,000 troops in *Carnage and Culture*, (New York: Doubleday, 2001), 141.
13. David Nicolle, *Armies of Islam 7th–11th Centuries* (London: Osprey, 1989), 12.
14. Kelly DeVries' *Medieval Military Technology* (Peterborough, Ontario: Broadview Press, 1992), 98.
15. Gore, *Neglected Heroes*, 33.

16. Heath, *Armies of the Dark Ages 600–1066*, 41.
17. Hanson, *Carnage and Culture*, 143.
18. Heath, *Armies of the Dark Ages 600–1066*, 84–85.
19. See Part One of DeVries' *Medieval Military Technology* for an outstanding discussion of the stirrup controversy.
20. Gore, *Neglected Heroes*, 31.
21. Gore, *Neglected Heroes*, 32.
22. Because the battle site is located between the cities of Tours and Poitiers, this battle in October 732 is called either the battle of Tours or the battle of Poitiers, depending on the source.
23. Gore, *Neglected Heroes*, 34.
24. Ibid., 35.
25. David Nicolle, *Poitiers AD 732* (Oxford: Osprey, 2008), 65, 69. Nicolle maintains the Franks successfully executed a flanking movement, using the terrain to mask their approach, and attacked the Muslim camp, mortally wounding Abdul Rahman.
26. This quotation by Isidorus Pacensis is found in Gore's *Neglected Heroes*, 35.
27. Hanson, *Carnage and Culture*, 140–141.
28. Gore, *Neglected Heroes*, 36.
29. David Nicolle, *The Armies of Islam, 7th–11th Centuries* (London: Osprey, 1982), 12–13, 20.
30. Ibid., 14.
31. Carter Vaughn Findley, *The Turks in World History* (Oxford: Oxford University Press, 2005), 45. Findley believed the purchase of slaves by Sogdian merchants to guard their homes while they were away may have served as a model for slave military recruitment in later Islamic and especially Turkic societies.
32. Ibid., 15.
33. Ibid., 21–22.
34. Ibid., 20–21.
35. Edward N. Luttwak, *The Grand Strategy of the Byzantine Empire* (Cambridge: The Belknap Press of Harvard University Press, 2009), 218.
36. Rene Grousset, *The Empire of the Steppes: A History of Central Asia*, trans. Naomi Walford (New Brunswick, NJ: Rutgers University Press, 1970), 150.
37. For more on the Fatimid embassy to Byzantium see A. Hamdani, 'Byzantine-Fatimid Relations Before the Battle of Manzikert', *Byzantine Studies* II/2 (1974), 169–179.
38. Findley, *The Turks in World History*, 37.
39. Ibid., 44.
40. Thomas J. Barfield, *The Perilous Frontier: Nomadic Empires and China, 221 BC to AD 1757* (Cambridge, MA: Blackwell, 1989), 134.
41. Ibid., 133.
42. Findley, *The Turks in World History*, 45.
43. Ibid.
44. Peter B. Golden, 'Wolves, Dogs and Qipchaq Religion', *Acta Orientalia Academiae Scientiarum Hungaricae* 50, nos. 1–3 (1997): 88–93.
45. Barfield, *The Perilous Frontier*, 157–160.
46. Findley, *The Turks in World History*, 48–50.
47. Ibid., 50.
48. Ibid., 50–51.
49. Ibid., 66–67.
50. John Freely, *Storm on Horseback: The Seljuk Warriors of Turkey* (London: I.B Tauris, 2008), 9. This and other Seljuk traditions derive from the *Malik-nama*, a work composed in the mid-eleventh century and since lost.
51. Grousset, *The Empire of the Steppes*, 142. Also see Findley, *The Turks in World History*, 68.

52. This phrase comes from Professor Findley's book *The Turks in World History*, 68.
53. Freely, *Storm on Horseback*, 10.
54. Grousset, *The Empire of the Steppes*, 151.
55. Freely, *Storm on Horseback*, 10.
56. Grousset, *The Empire of the Steppes*, 224.
57. Antony Karasulas, *Mounted Archers of the Steppe 600 BC–AD 1300* (Oxford: Osprey, 2004), 29–30.
58. David Nicolle, *Saladin and the Saracens* (London: Osprey, 1986), 40.
59. Karasulas, *Mounted Archers of the Steppe 600 BC–AD 1300*, 29.
60. Ibid.
61. Nicolle, *Saladin and the Saracens*, 40.
62. Leonid Tarassuk and Claude Blair, eds., *The Complete Encyclopedia of Arms and Weapons* (New York: Simon and Schuster, 1982), 290–291, 297
63. Horn has excellent compressibility (about 4 per cent before yielding to applied forces, or roughly thirteen kilograms per square millimetre. Wood usually yields at 1 per cent compression. Karasulas, *Mounted Archers of the Steppe 600 BC–AD 1300*, 20).
64. Ibid., 18–21. Also see Erik Hildinger, *Warriors of the Steppe: A Military History of Central Asia, 500 B.C. to 1700 A.D.* (New York: Sarpedon, 1997), 21–22.
65. James Chambers, *The Devil's Horsemen: The Mongol Invasion of Europe* (New York: Atheneum, 1985), 56–57.
66. William of Tyre, *A History of Deeds Done Beyond the Sea*, trans. E.A. Babcock and A.C. Krey (New York: Columbia University, 1943). Quoted in R.C. Smail's *Crusading Warfare* (Cambridge: Cambridge University Press, 1956), 74.
67. Karasulas, *Mounted Archers of the Steppe 600 BC–AD 1300*, 22–23. Amazing ranges have been attributed to specialized flight bows. In 1225, the Mongolian archer Esukhei fired an arrow 586 yards. This feat was recorded on the Genghis Khan Stone.
68. Hildinger, *Warriors of the Steppe*, 27.
69. Karasulas, *Mounted Archers of the Steppe 600 BC–AD 1300*, 24.
70. Chambers, *The Devil's Horsemen*, 57.
71. Karasulas, *Mounted Archers of the Steppe 600 BC–AD 1300*, 23.
72. Chambers, *The Devil's Horsemen*, 57. The author makes this claim about the Mongols, but all steppe warriors could string a bow at full gallop.
73. Karasulas, *Mounted Archers of the Steppe 600 BC–AD 1300*, 46. Also see Hildinger, *Warriors of the Steppe*, 20. Metal horse bits were apparently developed by the Scythians, while the frame saddle is believed to have been invented by the Sarmatians around 300 BCE, where it spread across the Eurasian steppes from Hungary to Hungary. The Avars are usually credited with introducing this saddle to the West.
74. Hildinger, *Warriors of the Steppe*, 16.
75. Ann Hyland, *The Medieval Warhorse from Byzantium to the Crusades* (London: Grange Books, 1994), 114.
76. Stephen Turnbull, *Mongol* Warrior, *1200–1350* (Oxford: Osprey, 2003), 16.
77. Chambers, *The Devil's Horsemen*, 58.
78. Karasulas, *Mounted Archers of the Steppe 600 BC–AD 1300*, 44–45.
79. Turnbull, *Mongol* Warrior, *1200–1350*, 17.
80. *Itinerarium peregrinorum et gesta regis Ricardi*, in *Chronicles and Memorials of the reign of Richard I*, ed. W. Stubbs, (London: Rolls Series, 1864), 50.
81. The Parthian shot was named after the Parthians who perfected this mounted tactic against the Romans at the battle of Carrhae in 53 BC.
82. Andrew Ayton, 'Arms, Armour and Horses' in *Medieval Warfare: A History*, ed. Maurice Keen (New York and London: Oxford University Press, 1999), 192–193.

83. R.C. Smail, *Crusading Warfare, 1097–1193.* 2nd Edition (New York: Cambridge University Press, 1995), 78–79.

84. Anna Komnenos, *The Alexiad*, trans. E.R.A. Sewter, (New York: Viking Press, 1979), XV.3.

85. Freely, *Storm on Horseback*, 11.

86. Found in Hildinger, *Warriors of the Steppe: A Military History of Central Asia, 500 B.C. to 1700 A.D.* , 143–144. Taken from the Marsden translation of Marco Polo's *The Travels of Marco Polo the Venetian*, ed. Thomas Wright (New York: Orion Press, 1958), 136.

87. Smail, *Crusading Warfare, 1097–1193*, 81.

88. Ibid., 80.

89. George T. Dennis, *The Anonymous Byzantine Treatise on Strategy* in his *Three Byzantine Military Treatises* (Washington DC: Dumbarton Oaks Texts, 2008), 281.

Chapter 5: Byzantine and Seljuk Campaigns in Anatolia and the Battle of Manzikert

1. John Haldon, *The Byzantine Wars* (Stroud, Gloucestershire: The History Press, 2008), 164.

2. Ibid., 165.

3. For a detailed account of the life and times of Harald Hardrada, please see John Marsden's *Harald Hardada': The Warrior's Way* (Thrupp, Stroud, Gloucestershire: Sutton Publishing, 2007).

4. Warren Treadgold, *A Concise History of Byzantium* (New York: Palgrave, 2001), 167.

5. Ibid.

6. Ibid., 167–168.

7. Ibid., 169.

8. Alfred Friendly, *The Dreadful Day: The Battle of Manzikert* 1071, (London: Hutchinson, 1981), 131–132.

9. Ibid., 132.

10. Edward N. Luttwak, *The Grand Strategy of the Byzantine* Empire (Cambridge: Belknap Press, 2009), 221.

11. Friendly, *The Dreadful Day*, 132.

12. Aristakes of Lastivert. This English translation is taken from page 134 of Friendly's *The Dreadful Day: The Battle of Manzikert 1071*.

13. Friendly, *The Dreadful Day*, 134–135.

14. Ibid., 134.

15. Ibid., 135.

16. Ibid., 136.

17. These two quotes from Matthew of Edessa are taken from Friendly's *The Dreadful Day*, 136.

18. Ibid., 137.

19. Ibid.

20. Ibid.

21. Ibid., 137–138.

22. Ibid., 138–139.

23. J.A Boyle and Stanley Grossman, eds., *The Cambridge History of Iran: The Saljuq and Mongol Periods, Volume 5* (Cambridge: Cambridge University Press, 1968), 303.

24. Friendly, *The Dreadful Day*, 139–140.

25. Treadgold, *A Concise History of Byzantium*, 169.

26. Friendly, *The Dreadful Day*, 141.

27. Kazhdan, Alexander, ed., *The Oxford Dictionary of Byzantium* (Oxford: Oxford University Press, 1991), 922. Also see David Nicolle's *The Normans* (London: Osprey, 1987), 46.

28. Friendly, *The Dreadful Day*, 141.

29. Warren Treadgold, *Byzantium and Its Army, 284–1081* (Stanford, CA: Stanford University Press, 1995), 217. Also see Friendly, *The Dreadful Day*, 141.

30. Ibid., 142.

31. Rene Grousset, *The Empire of the Steppes: A History of Central Asia*, trans. Naomi Walford (New Brunswick, NJ: Rutgers University Press, 1970), 152.

32. John Norwich, *Byzantium: The Apogee* (New York: Alfred A. Knopf, 2006), 342. For Ibn al-Adim's story concerning Alp Arslan's drunken rage, see Friendly, *The Dreadful Day*, 142–143.

33. This quotation from Matthew of Edessa is found in Speros Vryonis, Jr, *The Decline of Medieval Hellenism in Asia Minor and the Process of Islamization from the Eleventh through the Fifteenth Century* (Los Angeles: University of California Press, 1971), 94–95.

34. Norwich, *Byzantium: The Apogee*, 342. For a detailed and informative account of the history of the ancient Armenian capital city and fortress of Ani, please see the website VirtualANI at http://www.virtualani.org/ (accessed 19 July 2010).

35. This account of the eleventh century Byzantine historian Michael Attaleiates comes from Friendly, *The Dreadful Day*, 144.

36. Ibid., 146.

37. This account from Ibn al-Jawzi is taken from John Norwich's *Byzantium: The Apogee*, 342–343.

38. John Freely, *Storm on Horseback: The Seljuk Warriors of Turkey* (London: I.B Tauris, 2008), 12.

39. Friendly, *The Dreadful Day*, 147.

40. Treadgold, *Byzantium and Its Army*, 217.

41. The city of Neocaesarea/Niksar was retaken by Byzantine forces in 1068, lost to the Seljuks after the debacle at Manzikert in 1071, and then returned to Eastern Roman control in 1073.

42. Friendly, *The Dreadful Day*, 148.

43. George Ostrogorsky, *History of the Byzantine State*, trans. Joan Hussey (New Brunswick, New Jersey: Rutgers University Press, 1969), 344.

44. This quotation from George Kedrenos is found in Speros Vryonis, Jr, *The Decline of Medieval Hellenism in Asia Minor and the Process of Islamization from the Eleventh through the Fifteenth Century*, 90–91.

45. Freely, *Storm on Horseback*, 13.

46. Ibid., 14.

47. Norwich, *Byzantium: The Apogee*, 345–346.

48. Vryonis, *The Decline of Medieval Hellenism*, 75. Also see Freely, *Storm on Horseback*, 14.

49. Norwich, *Byzantium: The Apogee*, 345.

50. Vryonis, *The Decline of Medieval Hellenism*, 96.

51. Haldon maintains a number of around 40,000 troops (Haldon, *The Byzantine Wars*, 172), while Norwich believes the Byzantine army consisted of between 60,000 and 70,000 men (Norwich, *Byzantium: The Apogee*, 346). I estimate nearly 50,000 men for the eventual Manzikert field army before Romanus split the army.

52. Norwich, *Byzantium: The Apogee*, 346.

53. Paul Markham, 'The Battle of Manzikert: Military Disaster or Political Failure?' (2005) DeReMilitari.org, http://www.deremilitari.org/resources/articles/markham.htm (accessed 14 September 2010).

54. Haldon, *The Byzantine Wars*, 171–172.

55. Attaleiates, *Michaelis Attaleiates Historia*, ed. Immanuel Bekkar, (Corpus Scriptorum Historiae Byzantinae, Bonn, 1853), 143.

56. Attaleiates, 144.

57. Ibid., 145.

58. Ibid., 146–147.
59. Norwich, *Byzantium: The Apogee*, 354–355.
60. Attaleiates, 148.
61. Haldon, *The Byzantine Wars*, 172.
62. Ibid., 172–173.
63. Friendly, *The Dreadful Day*, 178–179.
64. Attaleiates, 151–153.
65. Markham, 'The Battle of Manzikert'.
66. Friendly, *The Dreadful Day*, 180.
67. Vryonis, *The Decline of Medieval Hellenism*, 98.
68. S. Zakkar, *The Emirate of Aleppo 1004–1094* (Beirut, 1971), 177.
69. Norwich, *Byzantium: The Apogee*, 347.
70. Ibid.
71. Haldon, *The Byzantine Wars*, 172.
72. Attaleiates, 154.
73. Ibid., 155–156.
74. Ibid., 157.
75. Ibid., 158.
76. Norwich, *Byzantium: The Apogee*, 349–350.
77. Vryonis, *The Decline of Medieval Hellenism*, 100.
78. Ibid.
79. Friendly, *The Dreadful Day*, 187–188.
80. Ibid., 188.
81. Norwich, *Byzantium: The Apogee*, 349.
82. Ibid., 351. Also see Friendly, *The Dreadful Day*, 178–180.
83. Markham, 'The Battle of Manzikert'.
84. This quotation by the historian Nikephoros Bryennios concerning Andronikos Doukas' military prowess is taken from Alfred Friendly's *The Dreadful Day*, 189.
85. This quotation by the historian Nikephoros Bryennios concerning Andronikos Doukas' dislike of Romanus IV Diogenes is taken from Alfred Friendly's *The Dreadful Day*, 189.
86. Ibid., Book I, XVII.
87. Friendly, *The Dreadful Day*, 188.
88. Attaleiates, 161.
89. Markham, 'The Battle of Manzikert'. Markham places the total number of Turkish auxiliaries at between 2,000 and 3,000. I agree with this number, but I believe the defection of the Uze mercenaries before the battle reduced this number by a third.
90. Attaleiates, 162–163.
91. Michael the Syrian, *Chronicles, Volume III*, French translation by J.B. Chabot, (Paris, 1905), 169.
92. Attaleiates, 162.
93. Ann Hyland, *The Medieval Warhorse from Byzantium to the Crusades* (London: Grange Books, 1994), 53. See endnote number 289 for Hyland's explanation of physical capabilities of fleshy and lean horses.
94. Numerous modern historians have reinforced the perception that the Byzantine army was destroyed at Manzikert. Ostrogorsky writes that 'the numerically superior, but heterogeneous and undisciplined, Byzantine army was annihilated by the forces of Alp Arslan' (*History of the Byzantine State*, 344). Norwich writes that 'the battle of Manzikert was the greatest disaster suffered by the Empire of Byzantium in the seven and a half centuries of its existence' (*Byzantium: The Apogee*, 357). Friendly, in the introduction of his treatment of Manzikert, is equally certain, writing 'we can move from speculation to

certainty,... the reality is that Manzikert, entailing the annihilation of the Byzantine army and the loss of Asia Minor, was profoundly decisive' (Friendly, *The Dreadful Day,* 19).

95. Haldon, *The Byzantine Wars,* 180.
96. Claude Cahen, '*La campagne de Manzikert d'apres les sources musulmanes,*' *Byzantion,* IX (1934), 638.
97. Norwich, *Byzantium: The Apogee,* 357.
98. Haldon, *The Byzantine Wars,* 181.

Conclusion: In Manzikert's Wake – The Seljuk Invasion of Anatolia and the Origins of the Levantine Crusades

1.   Alfred Friendly, *The Dreadful Day: The Battle of Manzikert* 1071 (London: Hutchinson, 1981), 196. Also see John Norwich, *Byzantium: The Apogee* (New York: Alfred A. Knopf, 2006), 354.
2.   John Freely, *Storm on Horseback: The Seljuk Warriors of Turkey* (London: I.B Tauris, 2008), 18.
3.   George Ostrogorsky, *History of the Byzantine State,* trans. Joan Hussey, (New Brunswick, New Jersey: Rutgers University Press, 1969), 345.
4.   Norwich, *Byzantium: The Apogee,* 356.
5.   For a detailed account of the capture and blinding of Romanus see Attaleiates, *Michaelis Attaleiates Historia,* ed. Immanuel Bekkar (Corpus Scriptorum Historiae Byzantinae, Bonn, 1853), 168–175.
6.   Norwich, *Byzantium: The Apogee,* 358–359.
7.   Attaleiates, 188, 190.
8.   Friendly, *The Dreadful Day,* 207–208. Also see Norwich, *Byzantium: The Apogee,* 359–360.
9.   Steven Runciman, *A History of the Crusades, Volume I: The First Crusade and the Foundations of the Kingdom of Jerusalem* (Cambridge and New York: Cambridge University Press, 1951), 67.
10. Matthew of Edessa, *Chronicles,* French translation by Eduard Dulaurier, (Paris, 1858), 173–176.
11. Friendly, *The Dreadful Day,* 202–203.
12. Freely, *Storm on Horseback,* 21.
13. Attaleiates, 239–240.
14. Norwich, *Byzantium: The Apogee,* 360.
15. Attaleiates, 263–268.
16. Nikephoros Bryennios, *Historia,* ed. A. Meineke (Corpus Scriptorum Historiae Byzantinae, Bonn, 1836), 130.
17. Ann Hyland, *The Medieval Warhorse from Byzantium to the Crusades* (London: Grange Books, 1994), 18.
18. Bryennios, 129.
19. Ostrogorsky, *History of the Byzantine State,* 349–350.
20. See Brian Todd Carey, Joshua B. Allfree and John Cairns', *Warfare in the Medieval World* (Barnsley, South Yorkshire: Pen and Sword Books, 2006, 81–84), for an account of this battle.
21. Speros Vryonis, Jr, *The Decline of Medieval Hellenism in Asia Minor and the Process of Islamization from the Eleventh through the Fifteenth Century* (Los Angelis: University of California Press, 1971), 114.
22. John Freely, *Storm on Horseback: The Seljuk Warriors of Turkey* (London: I.B Tauris, 2008), 23–24.
23. Bryennios, 158.
24. Anna Komnenos, *The Alexiad,* trans. E.R.A. Sewter (New York: Viking Press, 1979), III.11.

25. Vryonis, *The Decline of Medieval Hellenism,* 114–115.
26. John Norwich, *Byzantium: The Decline and Fall* (New York: Alfred A. Knopf, 1995), 27.
27. Ostrogorsky, *History of the Byzantine State*, 360–361.
28. John Haldon, *The Byzantine Wars* (Stroud, Gloucestershire: The History Press, 2008), 192.
29. Vryonis, *The Decline of Medieval Hellenism,* 119.
30. Ostrogorsky, *History of the Byzantine State*, 361.
31. H.E.J. Cowdrey, 'The Gregorian Papacy, Byzantium and the First Crusade', *Byzantinische Forschungen*, 13 (1988), 145–169.
32. Ostrogorsky, *History of the Byzantine State*, 362. Also see Runciman, *A History of the Crusades, Volume I*, 104.
33. Thomas Asbridge, *The First Crusade: A New History* (Oxford: Oxford University Press, 2004), 103.
34. Jonathan Riley-Smith, *The First Crusaders, 1095–1131* (Cambridge: Cambridge University Press, 1997), 53–58.
35. Asbridge, *The First Crusade*, 33.
36. Ibid., 89–95.
37. Ibid., 109–111.
38. Ibid., 112–113.

Glossary of Important Personalities

Abd al-Malik Marwan (r.685–705): Caliph during the Umayyad Caliphate. After successfully putting down a series of internal rebellions, he pushed westwards across North Africa, taking Byzantine Carthage in 698 in a combined Arab land and sea assault. Byzantine resistance crumbled after a second Arab victory at Utica. The Muslims would later found the city of Tunis in this region and use its harbours to establish a powerful Islamic maritime presence in the western Mediterranean.

Abdul Rahman al-Ghafiqi: The Arab emir of Spain. In 732 he crossed the western Pyrenees and invaded Aquitaine on a raiding expedition, the first from this direction. He then moved north and invested Orleans. The Frankish major of the palace, Charles Martel, intercepted and defeated the Muslim force at Tours. Abdul Rahman was killed in the action.

Abu Bakr (r.632–634): First caliph of the Rashidun Caliphate and father-in-law of Muhammad. He successfully prosecuted the Riddah War, centralizing Islamic authority over Arabia, and laid the foundation for subsequent expansion of Islam in the Levant, Mesopotamia, North Africa and Persia.

Abu Safyan: A leading member of the Meccan Quraysh tribe and opponent of Muhammad in battles of Uhud (625) and the Ditch (627) in the early Islamic wars. Abu Safyan negotiated a settlement with the Prophet that allowed the Islamic army to enter Mecca without bloodshed in 628. He later converted to Islam and fought at the battle of Yarmuk. He lost both of his eyes in combat. He is the father of Muawaiyah, the founder of the Umayyad Caliphate.

Abu Talib: Muhammad's uncle and protector, he was a powerful member of the Hashim clan who protected Muhammad from the age of eight until his death in 619. Abu Talib's protection was especially important in the early years of Islam when the faith was vulnerable to Quraysh persecution. After Abu Talib's death, the Quraysh stepped up their attacks, leading to open warfare between the Muslims and Meccans.

Afsinios: Renegade Seljuk nobleman and capable lieutenant to Alp Arslan. After killing a member of Alp Arslan's court, Afsinios fled west with an army, sacking cities across Byzantine Anatolia between 1067 and 1068 before returning east to Seljuk territory. He was pardoned by Alp Arslan for the audacity of his raid and would accompany the sultan on future campaigns.

Al-Qaim (r.1031–1075): Caliph during the Abbasid Caliphate. Al-Qaim ruled during a period of great transformation in the Abbasid world. His court was dominated by Shia Buyid Emirate, severely weakening his political power. In 1055, he allied with the Seljuk leader Toghril Beg, bestowing the title of 'sultan and sovereign of East and West' and making the Seljuks the de facto rulers of Abbasid territories.

Alexios I Komnenos (r.1081–1118): Byzantine emperor and founder of the Komnenian dynasty. Alexios inherited a collapsing Byzantine empire weakened by a decade of civil war and Turkish depredations after the Byzantine loss at the battle of Manzikert in 1071 and Norman incursions into the western Balkans. He successfully halted Byzantine decline and began a period of political, military and economic revival known as the Komnenian Recovery. His appeal to Pope Urban II in 1095 is often considered to be the *casus belli* for the Levantine Crusades.

Alp Arslan (r.1063–1072): Second sultan of the Great Seljuks of Iran. The nephew of Toghril, Muhammad bin Da'ud Chaghri, known to history by his soubriquet Alp Arslan ('Valiant Lion'). By 1064, he had consolidated his power in Persia and Mesopotamia and successfully added Armenia and Georgia to his territories. Over the next few years he made war against the local Arab emirs and invaded the eastern provinces of the Byzantine Empire, capturing the strategically importance fortresses in the Lake Van area. With his western flank secure, he laid plans to campaign against his greatest enemy the Shia Fatimids of Egypt, but was sidetracked in 1071 when the Byzantine emperor Romanus IV Diogenes invaded the Lake Van region, resulting in the Seljuk victory at Manzikert and the capture and ransoming of Romanus. Alp Arslan was murdered by a vassal in Turkestan, having consolidated the conquests of his predecessors Chaghri and Toghril, humbled the Byzantine Empire on the field of battle, and captured and released its *basileus*.

Andronikos Doukas: Nephew of Byzantine emperor Constantine X, Andronikos and a member of a powerful Greek family at odds with Byzantine emperor Romanus IV. He commanded the rearguard of the Byzantine army at the battle of Manzikert in 1071 and did not engage with the Seljuk Turks, leaving his emperor to be captured by Alp Arslan. He later captured Romanus after his release by the sultan. In 1074, he was captured and ransomed by the Norman adventurer Roussel de Bailleul, but died of wounds suffered in the engagement in 1077.

Basil II (r.976–1025): Byzantine emperor from the Macedonian dynasty. After winning a prolonged civil war with his Anatolian aristocracy, Basil focused his efforts on the stabilization and expansion of his eastern frontier and the subjugation of the Bulgars in the Balkans, reestablishing the Danube as the northern border. For this he was given the cognomen *Boulgaroktonos* or 'Bulgar Slayer' by later historians. He married his sister to the Rus Grand Prince Vladimir I of Kiev in exchange for assistance from the Varangian Guard. Basil died in 1025 after ruling for forty-nine years. At his death the Byzantine army was the most powerful military force in the Eastern Mediterranean.

Belisarios: Byzantine general. Born in Thrace and of Greek or Thracian ancestry, Belisarios quickly rose through the ranks of Emperor Justin I's (r.518–527) royal bodyguard, becoming a capable and charismatic officer. He led troops in the eastern campaigns against Sassanian Persians, where he later returned as commanding general under Justinian (r.527–565) and defeated the Persians at Dara in 530. He would also fight in the west in North Africa and Italy against the Vandals and Ostrogoths. Justinian removed and reinstated Belisarios a number of times. He is regarded as one of the greatest generals of late antiquity.

Chaghri Beg: Seljuk ruler and brother of Toghril Beg and Ibrahim Inal and father of Alp Arslan. After the Seljuk victory over the Ghaznavids at Dandanqan in 1040, the Seljuks became masters of Khurasan, using this territory to extend their control westwards over Iran and into Mesopotamia. Toghril installed Chaghri as governor of Khurasan to prevent a Ghazni reconquest. He stabilized the border and ruled there until his death in 1058, leaving his territory to his son Alp Arslan, who became sole ruler of the Great Seljuks of Iran when Toghril died in 1063.

Charles Martel (c.688–741): Frankish Mayor of the Palace and grandfather of Charlemagne. A brilliant Christian general who only lost one battle in his career, he is best remembered for his victory over the Spanish emir Abdul Rahman al-Ghafiqi at the battle of Tours in 732. This victory secured power over his political rivals in southern France and laid the foundation for the future Carolingian dynasty.

George Maniakes: Byzantine general. In 1038, Emperor Michael IV (r.1034–1041) reconquered Sicily from the Muslims with an army supplemented with both Norman and Varangian Guard mercenaries (among them the Varangian captain and future Scandinavian king Harald III Hardrada). The Byzantines captured the important city of Syracuse, but jealous of his success, he was recalled and imprisoned by Michael. Later released, he went on to become *katepano* (a rank equivalent to duke) in Italy and campaigned against the Normans. After being recalled again by the new emperor Constantine IX (r.1042–1055), he rebelled and marched on Constantinople where he died at the moment of victory.

Herakleios (r.610–632): Byzantine emperor. A prolific campaigner, Herakleios' twenty-two-year reign witnessed numerous military campaigns against the Sassanian Persians in the east and this period is considered one of Byzantine recovery. He personally led a series of three military expedition against the Sassanians in 624, 625 and again between 627 and 628, but these campaigns weakened both the Greeks and Persians at a time when a new and more dangerous threat was emerging from Arabia, Islam. He is also noted for dropping Latin titles and the adoption of the ancient Greek title of *basileus* (later expanded to *basileus Rhomaion* or 'king of the Romans').

Ibrahim Inal: Seljuk nobleman and brother of Toghril Beg and Chaghri Beg. After the Seljuk victory over the Ghaznavids at Dandanqan in 1040, the Seljuks became masters of Khurasan, using this territory to extend their control westwards over Iran. Ibrahim established himself in north-west Iran and in 1045 began raiding into Christian Armenia, Georgian, and the eastern provinces of Byzantium, often without Toghril's permission. He is most famous for his devastating raids using Turkoman warriors and the destruction of the important trading city of Arzen in 1048.

John Doukas: Byzantine Caesar and younger brother of Emperor Constantine X. John was one of the most prominent members of the Byzantine Senate and protector of his nephew, the co-emperor Michael VII Doukas. His wealth derived from his estates in Thrace and Bithynia and it was from these holdings that he intrigued against Romanus and was exiled from the imperial court, but returned after Romanus' defeat at Manzikert in 1071 and proclaimed his nephew sole emperor.

John Tzimiskes (r.969–976): Byzantine emperor and general of Armenian descent. A brilliant commander, John's short reign witnessed the expansion of the Byzantium's borders and the strengthening of the army. Under his rule the Balkan frontier was expanded after the victory at Dorostolon in 971 and imperial troops once again garrisoned the important fortress cities of eastern Anatolia and Armenia. He campaigned in the Levant as far south as Palestine, but failed to retake Jerusalem.

Justinian (r.527–565): Byzantine emperor. A man of enormous energy, Justinian embarked on important governmental reforms and an ambitious building program in Constantinople. During his long reign his generals Belisarios and Narses reconquered Italy from the Ostrogoths and North Africa from the Vandals, while stabilizing the eastern frontier with the Sassanian Persians. By his death in 565, the Byzantine Empire was at its greatest territorial extent, but his campaigns and projects had nearly bankrupted the empire.

Khalid al-Walid: Nicknamed *Sayfullah* or 'the Sword of Allah' by his contemporaries, Khalid al-Walid is the most celebrated Muslim general of the Rashidun Caliphate, participating first against the Prophet Muhammad at the battle of Uhud in 625 before his conversion to Islam, and then afterwards as a commander in campaigns in the Riddah War and in the Levant and Mesopotamia against Byzantine and Sassanian armies. His efforts at the battle of Yarmuk in 636 were instrumental in the Muslim victory.

Kilij Arslan (r.1092–1107): Sultan of the Seljuk of Rum and son of Suleyman ibn Qutulmish. Captured in Syria by an ally of Malikshah and sent to Isfahan as a hostage, Kilij Arslan was released in 1092 and returned to Anatolia to resurrect the Sultanate of the Rum. There, he ruled during the time of the First Crusade, losing territory to crusaders and to the machinations of Alexios I Komnenos.

Chosroes II (r.590–628): Sassanian Persian king. Sometimes known as *Parvez* or 'Ever Victorious' by the Persians, Chosroes had a close relationship with Byzantium, taking refuge in Constantinople during a civil war and marrying Emperor Maurice's daughter. Maurice's assassination by a rival general precipitated a Persian invasion of Anatolia, the Levant, and Egypt, pulling these regions into the Persian orbit. Chosroes experienced military reversals when Herakleios (r.610–640) launched a prolonged campaign deep into Persian territory, forcing the Persian king to flee. He was murdered by his son Kavad II in 628.

Krum Khan (r.803–814): Khan of the Bulgars. During his reign Bulgarian territory doubled in size, expanding from the middle of the Danube eastwards to the Dnieper

River, destroying the Avar state in the process. He also pressed south against Byzantine territories in the Balkans, triggering a military expedition in 811 led personally by Emperor Nikephoros I, who was killed by Krum at the battle of Pliska. His reign is remembered as a highpoint in Bulgarian history and a low point in the history of Byzantium.

Leo V (r.813–820): Byzantine emperor of Armenian descent. As senior general, he forced his predecessor to resign, but inherited a serious situation with Krum Khan of Bulgaria depopulating Thrace and blockading Constantinople by land. After Krum's death in 814, Leo defeated the Bulgars at Mesembria and persuaded the Bulgars to sign a peace treaty, ending a decade-long war and stabilizing the frontier.

Leo VI (r.886–912): Byzantine emperor and military philosopher and second ruler of the Macedonian dynasty. His reign witnessed Byzantine defeats in the Balkans against Czar Symeon of Bulgaria and in Sicily and the Aegean against Arab Muslims. He also faced Rus incursions against Constantinople in 907. Despite his foreign policy setbacks, Leo is also remembered for initiating a renaissance in the study of military doctrine. His *Taktika* preserved those elements of Maurice's *Strategikon* that were still relevant and added new lessons learned in the ninth century from wars against the Bulgars and Islam.

Mahmud of Ghazni (r.997–1030): Most prominent ruler of the Turkic Ghaznavid dynasty. Using his base in the Afghanistan city of Ghazni Mahmud created a wealthy capital and powerful regional empire that included much of Iran, Pakistan and regions in north-west India. However, after his death in 1030, the rising Seljuk power defeated his son at the battle of Dandanqan a decade later, absorbing the Ghaznavid western territories.

Malikshah (r.1072–1092): Seljuk sultan and son of Alp Arslan. His twenty-year reign witnessed Seljuk penetrations deep into the interior of Anatolia following the Byzantine defeat at Manzikert in 1071. He also expanded Seljuk power into Syria at the expense of the Fatimids, setting up client emirates in Edessa, Aleppo and Damascus. During his reign a rival named Suleyman ibn Qutulmish broke away in 1077 and formed the Sultanate of Rum in western Anatolia, beginning the gradual breakup of the Seljuk Empire.

Maurice (r.582–602): Byzantine emperor and military philosopher. A prominent general in his youth who distinguished himself in campaigns against the Sassanian Persians, Maurice brought the war with Persia to a conclusion and married his daughter to the Persian king Chosroes II. He also campaigned in the Balkans against the Avars and in northern Italy against the Lombards. He is also remembered as the author of the *Strategikon*, an important war treatise that influenced European militaries throughout the medieval period.

Michael VII Doukas (r.1067–1078): Co-emperor with Romanus IV Diogenes and Byzantine emperor. After Romanus' capture after the Byzantine defeat at Manzikert in 1071, Caesar John Doukas placed Michael on the throne. His reign was plagued by increased Seljuk attacks into Anatolia and popular rebellions led by Roussel de Bailleul, Nikephoros Bryennios, and Nikephoros Botaneiates. He abdicated when Botaneiates' victory seemed certain.

Muawaiyah (r.661–680): First caliph of the Umayyad Caliphate and son of Abu Safyan. After winning a Muslim civil war that ended the Rashidun Caliphate and cemented the Sunni-Shia break, Muawaiyah consolidated his rule, moving his capital from Medina to Damascus in Syria. He and his son Yazid (r.680–683) reorganized Islamic provinces and adopted regional armies (*jund*), organized around fortified provincial cities. He is remembered for favouring Arab Muslims over non-Arab Muslims (*Muwali*).

Narses: Byzantine administrator and general. A Romanized Armenian by birth, Narses spent most of his professional life as a palace eunuch, rising to the position of captain of the eunuch bodyguard and Grand Chamberlain for Emperor Justinian. His involvement in suppressing the Nike riots led to wider military command. He served his emperor twice in campaigns in Italy, the second time completing the Gothic War and the conquest of Ostrogothic Italy.

Nikephoros Bryennios: Byzantine general. Considered by his contemporaries to be the best commander of his age, Bryennios served with distinction at the battle of Manzikert in 1071, commanding the left wing of the Byzantine army. Between 1072 and 1073 he served the Michael VII Doukas in Bulgaria and was later promoted to governor of Dyrrachium. When he learned he was to be murdered by his emperor he marched on Constantinople, but was rebuffed by a new claimant to the throne, Nikephoros III Botaneiates, in 1078. He was later defeated by the young general Alexios Komnenos. Blinded by the emperor, he had his lands and honours returned to him by Nikephoros III.

Nikephoros I (r.802–811): Byzantine emperor. He campaigned aggressively against the Bulgars, initiated a reorganization of the Byzantine Empire by adding new themes in the Balkans and resettling Greeks from Anatolia in Greece in a policy of re-Hellenization of the region. He refused payment of tribute to the powerful Abbasid Caliph Harun al-Rashid in Baghdad, precipitating a new war with the Arabs.

Nikephoros III Botaneiates (r.1078–1081): Byzantine general and emperor. Considered a competent general, Nikephoros had many military setbacks during his long career as a general. As a senior officer, he became adept at court politics. Excluded from the Manzikert campaign, he became *strategos* in Anatolia under Michael VII Doukas. He rebelled against his emperor in 1078, and with the help of Suleyman ibn Qutulmish and his Seljuk host, was proclaimed emperor, pushing Michael aside. His reliance on the Seljuks for military assistance helped solidify their presence in western Anatolia, leading to the rise of the Sultanate of Rum.

Nizam al-Mulk: Persian scholar and vizier of the Great Seljuk Empire of Iran. Born in Persia, he first served the Ghaznavid rulers in Khurasan, but rose to become the chief administrator of this region under the Seljuks. His political acumen helped three generations of Seljuk rulers successfully negotiate with Byzantine emperors, Abbasid caliphs, and Fatimid rulers, creating the most powerful state in the Near East. He would serve as the trusted vizier to both Alp Arslan and his son Malikshah I (r.1072–1092) until his death in 1092 as one of the most influential and celebrated chief ministers in Islamic history.

Robert Guiscard: Norman adventurer and later duke of Apulia and Calabria. A brilliant commander, Guiscard expanded Norman territories in southern Italy and Sicily, ending Byzantine influence in the region with the reduction of Bari in 1071. He contemplated seizing the Byzantine throne during the civil war of 1078. He later defeated the Byzantine emperor Alexios I Komnenos at Dyyrachium in 1081, but was unable to follow-up on this victory.

Romanus IV Diogenes (r.1068–1071): Byzantine co-emperor with Michael VII Doukas. A capable general and prominent member of the Byzantine aristocracy, Romanus married the widowed empress and shared power with her son. He spent the first years of his reign rebuilding the Byzantine military and campaigning in the east (1068–1069) to regain lost territory. However, court politics and the hatred of the rival Doukas family kept him in Constantinople in 1070. In 1071, he embarked at the head of the ill-fated Manzikert expedition, where he was defeated, captured and ransomed by Alp Arslan. Released, he was eventually hunted down by the Doukas family, blinded, and banished to a monastery. He died shortly afterwards from these wounds in 1072.

Roussel de Bailleul: Norman adventurer and mercenary general. Western European by birth, Roussel served with the Normans in Italy and entered service with Byzantium as a mercenary captain. He participated in the Manzikert campaign of 1071, but abandoned the area before the battle began. In 1073, he attempted to found his own fiefdom in central Anatolia, but ultimately was unsuccessful. He was captured in 1074 by general Alexios Komnenos and later ransomed. He was finally defeated by a Seljuk army in Byzantium's employment and executed by Michael VII Doukas in 1077.

Samuel of Bulgaria (r.997–1014): Christian czar of Bulgaria. Reigning during the rule of Byzantine emperor Basil II, Samuel struggled to maintain his country's independence from the expanding Eastern Roman Empire. He was able to gain some ground early in his reign, recapturing most of the Balkans (minus Thrace), but the Bulgar defeat at Kleidion in 1014 broke the back of Bulgarian resistance and Basil expanded north to the Danubian frontier.

Suleyman ibn Qutulmish (r.1077–1086): First sultan of the Seljuk Sultanate of Rum and father of Kilij Arslan. A life-long rival of Alp Arslan, Suleyman asserted himself into Anatolian politics after the sultan's death in 1072 as leader of Turkoman warriors often in the service of Byzantine generals vying for the throne. He used his military influence to eventually carve out a Seljuk region in north-western Anatolia, founding the Seljuk Sultanate of Rum in 1077.

Svyatoslav (r.945–972): Prince of the Kievan Rus and father of Vladimir I. An ardent campaigner, Svyatoslav carved out a large state at the expense of the Khazars, Bulgars, and numerous eastern Slavic tribes. However, he was unable to consolidate his territories during his lifetime and a lack of stable succession led to civil war at his death.

Symeon (r.893–927): Christian czar of Bulgaria. Under Symeon, the Bulgarian Empire reached its greatest territorial extent with victories over the Byzantines, Magyars and Serbs, ushering in a golden age of Bulgarian culture. His reign was a highpoint for Bulgarian culture and a low point in the territorial size and prestige of Byzantium.

Tariq ibn Ziyad: Arab general and governor serving the Umayyad Caliphate. In 711, he crossed from North Africa into Spain and initiated the conquest of the Iberian Peninsula, defeating the Visigothic king Rodrigo and becoming the first governor of *al-Andalus* or Moorish Spain.

Toghril Beg (r.1055–1063): Sultan of the Great Seljuk Sultanate of Iran and brother of Chaghri Beg and Ibrahim Inal and uncle to Alp Arslan. After the Seljuk victory over the Ghaznavids at Dandanqan in 1040, Toghril united the recently converted Turkoman warriors and conquered westwards into Persia and Mesopotamia, entering Baghdad in 1055 and freeing the Abbasid caliph from Buyid control. In return, the caliph proclaimed Toghril sultan. Over the next eight years, he expanded Seljuk holdings at the expense of Byzantium and the Shia Fatimid Caliphate.

Umar (r.634–644): Second caliph of the Rashidun Caliphate. Regarded as a fair and just ruler who oversaw the expansion of Islam into the Levant, North Africa and deep into Sassanian Persia, he established garrison cities in these regions.

Umar II (r.717–720): Caliph of the Umayyad Caliphate. Islamic tradition remembers Umar as an extremely pious ruler who lived a simple life. One of his first decisions as ruler was withdrawal from the devastating siege against Constantinople in 717, a serious blow to Muslim prestige.

Urban II (p.1088–1099): Roman Catholic pope and church reformer. Urban II was a strong advocate of the Gregorian reforms who used his position to further the rising power of the papal monarchy. To this end, he responded to a plea from the Byzantine emperor Alexios I to send military assistance by calling into existence the First Crusade on the fields of Clermont, France, in November 1095, initiating a two hundred-year period of crusading in the Levant and Africa.

Vladimir I (r.980–1015): Grand Prince of Kiev and bastard son of Svyatoslav. After his father's death in 972, he fled to Scandinavia where he gathered a Viking force and systematically took Novgorod and Kiev, killing his brother in order to secure his throne in 980. In 987, he converted to Orthodox Christianity, pulling the land of the Rus into the cultural orbit of Byzantium. That same year, he gave his sister's hand in marriage to Byzantine emperor Basil II in exchange for the assistance of 6,000 Varangian Guard.

Glossary of Military Terms

ajnad: An Arab military district in the early Islamic period.

amsar: An Arab garrisoned city in the early Islamic period.

angon: (4th–8th centuries CE) A unique, barb-headed Frankish spear of moderate length that could be used as a javelin or in close-quarter combat.

bandum (**plural** *banda*): (7th–15th centuries CE) The basic administrative and tactical unit of the Byzantine army from the seventh century. It consisted of about 400 soldiers commanded by a tribune, and later, by a count. The *banda* were about equally divided into infantry and cavalry, with the dominant weapon system being heavy cavalry (historians believe that cavalry made up 20 per cent to 40 per cent of a Byzantine army, depending on where it was created and where it was operating).

'boar's head' formation: Germanic attack formation that placed the heaviest armoured in the front ranks in a narrow-fronted shield wall designed to punch through enemy lines. This wedge formation had limited offensive manoeuvrability, but presented plenty of impact power on a small frontage.

breidox: (10th–12th centuries CE) A long-hafted Viking battleaxe. The *breidox* or 'broad axe', first seen at the end of the tenth century, took its name from the blade's distinctive crescent shape, large size (usually 12 inches along its curved edge), and five-foot haft. This long-hafted axe also became the signature weapon of the Varangian guard.

bucellarii: (4th–6th centuries CE) These units were armed retainers of Byzantine nobles who took an additional oath of fealty to the Byzantine Emperors. They usually consisted of very high quality cavalry.

comitatenses: (4th–6th centuries CE) These units of the late Roman and early Byzantine field army comprised mixed regular and barbarian regiments not specifically tied to frontier provinces. They often supported *limitanei* and *bucellarii* on campaign.

Dar al-Harb: (Arabic for 'House of War') According to traditional Islam, the realm of the world where the infidel lives.

Dar al-Islam: (Arabic for 'House of Islam') According to traditional Islam, the realm of the world where Muslims and protected people live.

Daylami: Fierce heavy infantry from the forests of northern Persia who fought with a distinctive two-pronged javelin, but also used heavy swords and battleaxes for hand-to-hand combat and bows and slings for distance warfare. These soldiers were highly praised later by Arab Muslim commanders, who actively sought to recruit them into their armies, even paying them more than Arab troops.

Derafsh-e-Kaveyan: (Persian for 'Standard of Kaveh') The great tiger-skin standard of the Persian kings, measuring over forty yards long by six yards wide. This standard was lost to the Muslims at the battle of al-Qadisiya in 636.

dir: Arabic chainmail worn by wealthier warriors during the pre-Islamic and early Islamic periods.

diwan: Muslim soldiers enrolled for life in the *diwan* and were entitled to quarters, monthly rations, and an annual cash stipend.

foederati: (4th–6th centuries CE) Barbarians allies of Rome who retained their Germanic commanders and were allowed to roam within the boundaries of the empire. Eventually, these barbarian units became indistinguishable from regular Roman and Byzantine units, who adopted Germanic arms, armour and tactics.

francisca: (4th–8th centuries CE) A finely balanced Frankish axe used both on foot and from horseback as a close-quarters weapon or thrown as a missile.

Ghulams (also see **Mamluks**): Turkish regular troops. *Ghulam* heavy cavalry were the finest in the Islamic world, marrying elements of steppe warfare (use of bow and lasso from horseback) with those of traditional mounted Islamic warfare (use of Arab lance and sword). Other *ghulams*, purchased as slave children then trained and converted to Islam, serve the Abbasid caliphs as their personal bodyguard and were seldom employed against Islam's external enemies.

hauberk: Chain-mail armour that covered the body and arms. It was constructed with tens of thousands of round metal links. This type of armour dates back to the classical period where it was used by both barbarian and civilized peoples. It became very popular in the medieval period.

heavy cavalry: Well-armoured horsemen who use shock combat as their primary way of fighting. Heavy cavalry relied on collective effort to be effective, and collective effort required discipline and training.

heavy infantry: Well-armoured foot soldiers who use shock combat as their primary way of fighting. Heavy infantry relied on collective effort to be effective, and collective effort required discipline and training.

javelineer: A term historians use for a light infantryman who wields a javelin. Commanders often used these light troops as skirmishers or to screen while friendly heavier troops deployed.

jihad: (Islamic Holy War) In the Islamic faith, the literal Arabic translation means 'to struggle in the way of God'. The 'greater *jihad*' is the personal struggle of a Muslims to maintain his or her faith. The 'lesser *jihad*' is holy war, or spreading Islam into new territories. Traditional Islam splits the world into two realms, *Dar al-Islam* or the 'House of Islam' where Muslims and protected peoples live, and *Dar al-Harb* or 'House of War' where the infidel lives. *Jihad* was often invoked by Muslim rulers to rally political or military support in much the same way the Catholic Church used the concept of crusade.

jund: (Beginning in 7th century CE) A term for non-Arab Islamic units recruited locally. The pace of Islamic conquest forced the Arabs to include more of these units into their ranks. They fought for booty more than ideology, swelling the ranks of Islamic armies in times of victory, and evaporating in times of trouble.

kataphraktoi: Byzantine heavy shock cavalry modelled after earlier Roman and Sassanian heavy cavalry. These cavalry troops employed the *kontarion*, however, some of these heavy troops also utilized short composite bows for missile combat against similarly armed steppe warriors.

kavadion: A thick-quilted gambeson worn by Byzantine and allied troops made of thick cotton wadding in a raw silk cover.

kilij: A steppe warrior-influenced equestrian sabre with a blade length of between twenty-five and thirty inches and a rounded grip made of wood or ivory. This sabre became the most popular sword type in use in the Islamic Near East, although straight swords continued to be used.

klibanophoroi: An up-armoured *kataphraktoi* reminiscent of earlier Byzantine and Sassanian *cataphractii* in the sixth century. Armour and barding was very heavy, with the rider covered in chain or lamellar armour with the additional protection of a padded overcoat. He wore an iron helmet with coif and chain mask that covered the entire face except for the eyes. Mounts were protected by an iron headpiece and chest barding made of ox-hide lamellar split at the front for ease of movement and leaving only the eyes, nostrils and lower legs unprotected from the front.

kontarion: A Byzantine infantry pike thirteen-foot long and tipped with an eighteen-inch socketed spearhead. Later Byzantine cavalry (*klibanophoroi* and *kataphraktoi*) used a shorter version, eight feet in length.

koursores: Byzantine mounted troops expected to fill the role between light cavalry archers and heavy cavalry. They engaged other medium or light cavalry or were used to run down detached or fleeing infantry. Riders wore chain or lamellar armour, carried a round shield, and were armed with short *kontarion*, composite bow, one sword and one or two maces. They usually rode smaller faster unarmored horses capable of longer endurance.

lamellar armour: A type of composite armour consisting of a shirt of laminated layers of leather sown or glued together, then fitted with iron plates. This type of armour was popular with both barbarian warriors and the soldiers of civilization.

light cavalry: Light armoured horsemen who use missile combat as their primary way of fighting. These lighter units were less armoured than their heavier counterparts, and consequently had greater tactical mobility.

light infantry: Light armoured foot soldiers who use missile combat as their primary way of fighting. These lighter units were less armoured than their heavier counterparts, and consequently had greater tactical mobility.

limitanai: (4th–6th centuries CE) These units were a militia, retired legionaries mustered to defend their homeland. In times of emergency, *limitanai* could be promoted into the field army

Mamluks (also see *ghulams*): Turkish regular troops. Mamluk heavy cavalry were the finest in the Islamic world, marrying elements of steppe warfare (use of bow and lasso from horseback) with those of traditional mounted Islamic warfare (use of Arab lance and sword). Other mamluks, purchased as slave children then trained and converted to Islam, serve the Abbasid caliphs as their personal bodyguard and were seldom employed against Islam's external enemies.

magister militum: (Latin for 'Master of the Soldiers') A commanding general of a field army in late Roman imperial and early Byzantine periods.

mirran: Title given to the supreme commander of Sassanian Persian forces.

nawak (**sometimes called a *majra***): An Islamic short composite bow modified into a dart thrower that utilized a hand-held grooved channel or tube held up against the side of the composite bow. The dart's length was between a normal arrow and the later crossbow bolt. This weapon is identical to the Byzantine *solenarion* and could be fired at great range and velocity.

numeri (**singular *numerus*)**: (2nd–6th centuries CE) A Roman term referring to irregular units from a common ethnic background employed to patrol the *limes*. It was also applied to some units of cavalry in the late Roman Empire and early Byzantine periods.

paramerion: A Byzantine sabre-hilted, slightly curved single-edged sword whose design was probably influenced by contacts with the steppe peoples.

'Parthian shot': A standard nomadic light cavalry manoeuvre where horse archers break formation and gallop toward an enemy formation firing arrows, then wheel right and retreat back, firing over their shoulders back at the enemy. The manoeuvre is named after the Parthians, though all steppe archers practised it. The 'Parthian shot' was often used in juncture with the feigned retreat, pulling enemy cavalry into pursuit, then ambushing them far from their camp.

peltastoi (**singular** *peltastos*): Byzantine infantry named after their round *pelta* shields. They were hybrid troops who acted as a bridge between light and heavy infantry and were used to either screen heavier footmen and cavalry or act as shock units. They wore lamellar armour or chainmail when available and carried round shields.

psilos: The lightest Byzantine infantry consisting of unarmoured javelineers and slingers used as skirmishers and to screen the heavier infantry and cavalry in battle.

ribat: An Arab military monastery in the early Islamic period.

Savaran: Sassanian Persian heavy cavalry protected by ring, lamellar plate or chainmail and armed with lance, swords, maces or javelins, while some carried composite bows and arrows. Reminiscent of later western European cavalry, these noble horsemen often challenged champions of an opposing army to single combat before battle.

sayf: A long straight hilted Arabic sword used in either slashing or thrusting attacks.

scramasax: A single-edged sidearm favoured by Indo-European (Germanic and Scandinavian) warriors in the classical and early medieval periods. Often called a *sax*, this utility knife could take on the dimensions of a short sword.

shield wall: (9th–11th centuries CE) A defensive infantry formation used by Anglo-Saxon and Viking warriors standing in close order, shields overlapping to form an unbroken front. This formation could also open up enough to allow warriors enough room to throw spears and javelins and wield spears, axes and swords.

skeggox: (8th century CE) An early type of Scandinavian battleaxe. The *skeggox* ('bearded axe') took its name from the asymmetrical shape of the axe blade. Viking axes usually began as dual-purpose implements used as both tools and weapons. Later, the Vikings would develop axes used exclusively for war (see *breidox*).

skutatoi (**singular** *skutatos*): The best protected and armed Byzantine infantry. Named after their large oval shield (*skuta*), this heavy infantry wore a pull-on chainmail hauberk or scale armour and metal helmet. Those who served in the forward ranks used a thirteen-foot *kontarion* tipped with an eighteen-inch socketed spearhead.

solenarion: A Byzantine short composite bow modified into a dart thrower that utilized a hand-held grooved channel or tube held up against the side of the composite bow. The dart's length was between a normal arrow and the later crossbow bolt. This weapon is identical to the Islamic *majra* or *nawak* and could be fired at great range and velocity.

spangenhelm: An Indo-European open-faced helmet conical in shape and characterized by its composite construction. The *spangenhelm* consisted of a framework formed by a single headband on which were attached six or more *spangens*. This type of helmet was used by Germanic tribes, Viking warriors and Norman soldiers in the medieval period.

spathion: A straight double-edged long sword dating back to the late Roman Empire used by Byzantine infantry and cavalry.

strategos (**plural** *strategoi*): Commanding general of a Byzantine thematic army who often serves as the governor of his military district.

tagmata: (7th–15th centuries CE) The core of the Byzantine army consisting of professional soldiers organized in homogenized cavalry or infantry units. The *tagmata* were equal to the size of the *thema*. These soldiers were the best-trained troops in the empire, serving as Constantinople's garrison and as the chief expeditionary force for the emperor. When the emperor went on campaign, the *tagmata* and local *themae* combined to create a field army.

thema: (7th–15th centuries CE) A Byzantine division commanded by a *strategos*. The *thema* replaced the legion as the premier strategic unit of manoeuvre in Byzantine warfare. The soldiers of a particular frontier province (*theme*) were the legal holders of the land itself, a development that came in the form of imperial land grants within the particular region and were similar to the land grants during the early Roman Empire. Although the soldiers did not work the fields or run farms on a full-time basis, their ownership brought about a personal stake in the defense of their respective *theme*.

tzikourion: A one-handed war axe used by Byzantine infantry and cavalry.

Varangian Guard: (10th–11th centuries CE) Russo-Swedish and Scandinavian mercenaries in the service of the Byzantine emperor. Many of these Vikings returned to Scandinavia to carve out kingdoms.

Zhayedan: (Persian for 'Immortals') An elite band of Sassanian Persian soldiers who served the king as a bodyguard.

Select Bibliography

Medieval Sources

Ammianus Marcellinus, *The Later Roman Empire*, trans. Walter Hamilton (New York: Penguin Books, 1986).

Al-Tabari, *The History of al-Tabari, Vol. III: The Children of Israel*, trans. William Brinner (Albany, NY: State University New York Press, 1991).

Al-Tabari *The History of al-Tabari, Vol. XII: The Battle of al-Qadisiyyah and the Conquest of Syria and Palestine*, trans. Yohanan Friedmann (Albany, NY: State University of New York, 1992).

Attaleiates, *Michaelis Attaleiates Historia*, ed. Immanuel Bekkar (Corpus Scriptorum Historiae Byzantinae, Bonn, 1853).

Bryennios, *Historia*, ed. A. Meineke, Corpus Scriptorum Historiae Byzantinae (Bonn, 1836).

Dennis, George T. *Three Byzantine Military Treatises*, trans. George T. Dennis (Washington DC: Dumbarton Oaks Texts, 2008).

Dennis, George T., *Maurice's Strategikon: Handbook of Byzantine Military Strategy*, trans. George T. Dennis (Philadelphia: University of Pennsylvania Press, 1984).

Dennis, George T., *The Taktika of Leo VI*, trans. George T. Dennis (Washington DC: Dumbarton Oaks Texts, 2010).

Ibn Ishaq, *The Life of Muhammad: A Translation of Ibn Iraq's Life of Muhammad*, trans. Alfred Guillaume (Oxford: Oxford University Press, 1967).

Mango, Cyril and Roger Scott, eds., *The Chronicle of Theophanes the Confessor: Byzantine And Near Eastern History, AD 284–813* (Oxford: Clarendon Press, 2006).

Matthew of Edessa, *Chronicles*, French trans. Eduard Dulaurier (Paris, 1858).

Michael the Syrian, *Chronicles, Volume III*, French trans. J.B. Chabot (Paris, 1905).

Procopius, *History of the Wars*, trans. H.B. Dewing (Cambridge and London: Harvard University Press, 1914).

Talbot, Alice-Mary and Denis F. Sullivan, trans., *The History of Leo the Deacon* (Washington DC: Dumbarton Oaks Texts, 2005).

William of Tyre, *A History of Deeds Done Beyond the Sea*, trans. E.A. Babcock and A.C. Krey (New York: Columbia University, 1943).

Modern Sources

Akram, Ibrahim, *The Sword of Allah: Khalid bin al-Waleed, His Life and Campaigns* (New Delhi: Adam Publishers, 2009).

Asbridge, Thomas, *The First Crusade: A New History* (Oxford: Oxford University Press, 2004).

Ayton, Andrew, 'Arms, Armour and Horses' in *Medieval Warfare: A History*, ed. Maurice Keen (New York and London: Oxford University Press, 1999).

Bachrach, Bernard S., 'Procopius, Agathias and the Frankish Military' in *Speculum* 45 (1970), 435–441.

Barfield, Thomas J., *The Perilous Frontier: Nomadic Empires and China, 221 BC to AD 1757* (Cambridge, MA: Blackwell, 1989).

Blankinship, Khalid Yahya, *The End of the Jihad State: The Reign of Hisham ibn Abd al-Malik and the Collapse of the Umayyads* (Albany, NY: State University New York Press, 1994).

Boyle, J.A. and Stanley Grossman, eds., *The Cambridge History of Iran: The Saljuq and Mongol Periods, Volume 5* (Cambridge: Cambridge University Press, 1968).

Browning, Robert, *Justinian and Theodora* (London: Thames and Hudson, 1987).

Cahen, Claude, '*La campagne de Manzikert d'apres les sources musulmanes,*' *Byzantion,* IX (1934), 613–642.

Chambers, James, *The Devil's Horsemen: The Mongol Invasion of Europe* (New York: Atheneum, 1985).

Chandler, David G., *The Art of Warfare on Land* (New York: Penguin Books, 1974).

Cheynet, Jean-Claude, 'Mantzikert: Un desastre militaire?' *Byzantion* 50 (1980), 410–438.

Contamine, Philippe, *War in the Middle Ages,* trans. Michael Jones (Oxford and New York: Basil Blackwell, 1984).

Cowdrey, H.E.J., 'The Gregorian Papacy, Byzantium and the First Crusade', *Byzantinische Forschungen,* 13 (1988), 145–169.

Davis, Paul K., *100 Decisive Battles from Ancient Times to the Present* (New York: Oxford University Press, 2001).

Dawson, Timothy, *Byzantine Cavalryman, c.900–1204* (Oxford: Osprey, 2009).

Dawson, Timothy, *Byzantine Infantryman: Eastern Roman Empire, c.900–1204* (Oxford: Osprey, 2007).

Delbruck, Hans, *History of the Art of War within the Framework of Political History,* trans. Walter J. Renfroe, Jr, Vol. II: *The Barbarian Invasions.* Vol. III: *Medieval Warfare* (Westport, CT, and London: Greenwood Press, 1982).

DeVries, Kelly, *Medieval Military Technology* (Peterborough, Ontario: Broadview Press, 1992).

Donner, Fred M., *The Early Islamic Conquests* (Princeton: Princeton University Press, 1981).

Farrokh, Kaveh, *Shadows in the Desert: Ancient Persia at War* (Oxford: Osprey, 2009).

Farrokh, Kaveh, *Sassanian Elite Cavalry, 224–642,* (Oxford: Osprey, 2005).

Findley, Carter Vaughn, *The Turks in World History* (Oxford: Oxford University Press, 2005).

Freely, John, *Storm on Horseback: The Seljuk Warriors of Turkey* (London: I.B Tauris, 2008).

Friendly, Alfred, *The Dreadful Day: The Battle of Manzikert* 1071 (London: Hutchinson, 1981).

Fuller, J.F.C., *A Military History of the Western World,* Vol. 1: *From the Earliest Times to the Battle of Lepanto* (New York: Funk and Wagnalls, 1954–1957).

Gabriel, Richard A. and Donald W. Boose, Jr, *The Great Battles of Antiquity: A Strategic Guide to Great Battles that Shaped the Development of War* (Westport, Connecticut: Greenwood Press, 1994).

Gabriel, Richard A. and Donald W. Boose, Jr, *Muhammad: Islam's First Great General* (Norman, OK: University of Oklahoma Press, 2007).

Golden, Peter B., 'Wolves, Dogs and Qipchaq Religion', *Acta Orientalia Academiae Scientiarum Hungaricae* 50, nos. 1–3 (1997), 88–93.

Gore, Terry L., *Neglected Heroes: Leadership and War in the Early Medieval Period* (Westport, CT: Greenwood Press, 1995).

Griffith, Paddy, *The Viking Art of War* (London: Greenhill, 1995).

Grousset, Rene, *The Empire of the Steppes: A History of Central Asia,* trans. Naomi Walford (New Brunswick, NJ: Rutgers University Press, 1970).

Haldon, John, *The Byzantine Wars* (Stroud, Gloucestershire: The History Press, 2008).

Hamdani, A., 'Byzantine-Fatimid Relations Before the Battle of Manzikert', *Byzantine Studies* II/2 (1974), 169–179.

Hanson, Victor D., *Carnage and Culture* (New York: Doubleday, 2001).

Hitti, Philip K., *History of the Arabs* (Hampshire, UK: Palgrave Macmillan, 2002).

Heath, Ian, *Armies of the Dark Ages 600–1066,* 2nd Edition (Worthing, England: Wargames Research Group, 1980).

Hildinger, Erik, *Warriors of the Steppe: A Military History of Central Asia, 500 B.C. to 1700 A.D.* (New York: Sarpedon, 1997).

Hillenbrand, Carole, *Turkish Myth and Muslim Symbol: The Battle of Manzikert* (Edinburgh: University of Edinburgh Press, 2007).

Hyland, Ann, *The Medieval Warhorse from Byzantium to the Crusades* (London: Grange Books, 1994).

Jenkins, Romilly, *Byzantium: The Imperial Centuries A.D. 610–1071* (New York: Random House, 1966).

Jones, A.H.M., *The Later Roman Empire, 284–602,* Volume One (Norman, OK: University of Oklahoma Press, 1964).

Jones, Archer, *The Art of War in the Western World* (Urbana and Chicago: University of Illinois Press, 1987).

Kaegi, Walter E., *Byzantium and the Early Islamic Conquests* (Cambridge: Cambridge University Press, 1992).

Kaegi, Walter E., *Herakleios: Emperor of Byzantium* (Cambridge: Cambridge University Press, 2003).

Karasulas, Antony, *Mounted Archers of the Steppe 600 BC–AD 1300* (Oxford: Osprey, 2004).

Kennedy, Hugh, *The Armies of the Caliphs* (New York: Routledge, 2001).

Kennedy, Hugh, *The Great Arab Conquests* (Philadelphia: Da Capo Press, 2007).

Luttwak, Edward N., *The Grand Strategy of the Byzantine Empire* (Cambridge: The Belknap Press of Harvard University Press, 2009).

Marsden, John, *Harald Hardrada: The Warrior's Way* (Stroud, Gloucestershire: Sutton Publishing Limited, 2007).

Milner-Gulland, Robin, *The Russians: The People of Europe* (London: Wiley-Blackwell, 2000).

Nicolle, David, *The Armies of Islam, 7th–11th Centuries* (London: Osprey, 1982).

Nicolle, David, *The Great Islamic Conquests, AD 632–750* (Oxford: Osprey, 2009).

Nicolle, David, *Medieval Warfare Source Book Volume 2: Christian Europe and Its Neighbours* (London: Arms and Armour, 1996).

Nicolle, David, *Poitiers AD 732* (Oxford: Osprey, 2008).

Nicolle, David, *Romano-Byzantine Armies, 4th–9th Centuries* (London: Osprey, 1992).

Nicolle, David, *Saladin and the Saracens* (London: Osprey, 1986).

Nicolle, David, *Yarmuk 636 AD: The Muslim Conquest of Syria* (London: Osprey, 1994).

Norwich, John, *Byzantium: The Apogee* (New York: Alfred A. Knopf, 2006).

Oman, Charles, *A History of the Art of War in the Middle Ages, Volume One: 378–1278 AD* (New York: Methuen, 1924; reprint, London: Greenhill, 1991).

Ostrogorsky, George, *History of the Byzantine State*, trans. Joan Hussey (New Brunswick, New Jersey: Rutgers University Press, 1969).

Riley-Smith, Jonathan, *The First Crusaders, 1095–1131* (Cambridge: Cambridge University Press, 1997).

Rodinson, Maxime, *Muhammad*, trans. Anne Carter (New York: New Press, 2002).

Rosen, William, *Justinian's Flea: Plague, Empire and the Birth of Europe* (New York: Viking, 2007).

Runciman, Steven, *The Emperor Romanus Lecapenus and His Reign: A Study in Tenth Century Byzantium* (Cambridge: Cambridge University Press, 1963; reprint, 1988).

Runciman, Steven, *A History of the Crusades, Volume I: The First Crusade and the Foundations of the Kingdom of Jerusalem* (Cambridge and New York: Cambridge University Press, 1951).

Scherman, Katherine, *The Birth of France: Warriors, Bishops, and Long-Haired Kings* (New York: Random House, 1987).

Shoufani, Elias, *Al-Riddah and the Muslim Conquest of Arabia* (Toronto: University of Toronto Press, 1973).

Smail, R.C., *Crusading Warfare, 1097–1193*, 2nd Edition (New York: Cambridge University Press, 1995).

Soucek, Svat, *A History of Inner Asia* (Cambridge: Cambridge University, 2000).

Tarassuk, Leonid and Claude Blair, eds., *The Complete Encyclopedia of Arms and Weapons* (New York: Simon and Schuster, 1982).

Treadgold, Warren, *Byzantium and Its Army, 284–1081* (Stanford, CA: Stanford University Press, 1995).

Treadgold, Warren, *Byzantine State and Society* (Stanford: Stanford University Press, 1997).

Treadgold, Warren, *A Concise History of Byzantium* (New York: Palgrave, 2001).

Treadgold, Warren, 'The Struggle for Survival (641–780 AD)' in *The Oxford History of Byzantium*, ed. Cyril Mango (Oxford: Oxford University Press, 2002).

Turnbull, Stephen, *The Walls of Constantinople, AD 324–1453* (Oxford: Osprey, 2004).

Vryonis, Speros, Jr, *The Decline of Medieval Hellenism in Asia Minor and the Process of Islamization from the Eleventh through the Fifteenth Century* (Berkeley and Los Angeles: University of California Press, 1971).

Watt, Montgomery W., *Muhammad at Medina* (London: Oxford University Press, 1956).

Whittow, Mark, *The Making of Byzantium, 600–1025* (Berkeley: University of California Press, 1996).

Zakkar, S., *The Emirate of Aleppo 1004–1094* (Beirut, 1971).

Index